Ephesians

Pentecostal Commentary Series

General Editor

John Christopher Thomas

Deo Publishing

EPHESIANS

Trevor Grizzle

deo
PUBLISHING

BLANDFORD FORUM

Pentecostal Commentary Series

Published and produced by Deo Publishing,
P.O. Box 6284, Blandford Forum, Dorset DT11 1AQ, UK

The Odyssea Greek font used in the publication of this work is available from Linguist's Software, Inc., www.linguistsoftware.com, P.O. Box 580, Edmonds, WA 98020-0580 USA, tel. (425) 775-1130.

Printed by Henry Ling Ltd, at the Dorset Press, Dorchester, DT1 1HD, UK

British Library Cataloguing-in-Publication data
A catalogue record for this book is available from the British Library

ISBN 978-1-905679-19-5

This volume is dedicated to my wife, Maureen,
in whose love I have found life.

Contents

Editor's Preface

The purpose of this commentary series is to provide reasonably priced commentaries written from a distinctively Pentecostal perspective primarily for pastors, lay persons, and Bible students. Therefore, while the works are based upon the best of scholarship, they are written in popular language. The aim is to communicate the meaning of the text, with minimal technical distractions.

In order to explain the need for such an attempt to read the biblical text, it is necessary to understand something of the ethos of Pentecostalism.

Pentecostalism is a relatively recent phenomenon in comparison to its Christian siblings, given that its formal origins go back about a hundred years. By any means of calculation it continues to grow very rapidly in many places around the globe and accounts for a not insignificant percentage of the world's Christians. Current estimates of those who would identify themselves as part of the Pentecostal-Charismatic movements range from 380,000,000 to 600,000,000. According to David Barrett, the global profile of Pentecostalism is as follows:

> Some 29 percent of all members worldwide are white, 71 percent are nonwhite. Members are more urban than rural, more female than male, more children (under eighteen years) than adults, more third-world (66 per cent) than western world (32 per cent), more living in poverty (87 per cent) than affluence (13 per cent), more family-related than individualist.[1]

Yet, despite its demographic significance, Pentecostalism continues to be largely misunderstood by many outside the movement. For example, there are those who '... see Pentecostalism as essentially fundamentalist Christianity with a doctrine of Spirit baptism and gifts added on' and others who view it '... as an experience which fits equally well in any spirituality or theological system – perhaps adding some needed

[1] D. Barrett, 'Statistics, Global', *Dictionary of the Pentecostal and Charismatic Movements* (S.M. Burgess and G.B. McGee, eds.; Grand Rapids: Zondervan, 1988), p. 811.

zest or interest.'² Yet, those who know the tradition well are aware how far from the truth such assessments are. As Donald W. Dayton³ and Steven J. Land⁴ have demonstrated, standing at the theological heart of Pentecostalism is the message of the five-fold gospel: Jesus is Savior, Sanctifier, Holy Spirit Baptizer, Healer, and Coming King. This paradigm not only identifies the theological heart of the tradition, but also immediately reveals the ways in which Pentecostalism as a movement is both similar to and dissimilar from others within Christendom. When the five-fold gospel paradigm is used as the main point of reference Pentecostalism's near kinship to the holiness tradition is obvious, as is the fundamental difference with many of those within the more reformed evangelical tradition. It also reveals the surprising similarities between Pentecostalism and the Roman Catholic and Orthodox traditions.

Therefore, the production of a Pentecostal Commentary Series representative of the tradition's ethos requires more than simply selecting contributors who have had a glossolalic experience. Rather, the process of composition as well as the physical format of the commentary should be in keeping with the ethos and spirituality of the tradition.

In the attempt to insure a writing process representative of the tradition, each contributor has been urged to incorporate the following disciplines in the writing of the commentary on a particular biblical book.

Writers have been encouraged to engage in prayer for this project, both as individuals and as members of a community of believers. Specifically, the guidance of the Holy Spirit has been sought in these times of prayer, for the leadership of the Spirit in interpretation is essential. Specific times of prayer where the body intercedes on the writer's behalf and seeks to hear from the Lord have been encouraged.

Given the Pentecostal commitment to body ministry, where various members of the body have specific calls and responsibilities, writers have been asked to explore ways in which their scholarship might be contextualized within their own local church body and thereby be strengthened by the dynamic interaction between the Holy Spirit, the body of Christ, and the Word of God. Writers were encouraged to covenant with their churches concerning this writing project in order to seek out their spiritual support. Where possible, writers were asked to explore the possibility of leading a group Bible study on the given

---

²Steven J. Land, *Pentecostal Spirituality: A Passion for the Kingdom* (JPTS 1; Sheffield: Sheffield Academic Press, 1993), p. 29.

³Donald W. Dayton, *The Theological Roots of Pentecostalism* (Peabody, MA: Hendrickson, 1991).

⁴Land, *Pentecostal Spirituality*.

biblical book. Ideally, such groups included representatives from each group of the target readership.

Writers were also encouraged to seek out the advice and critique of gifted colleagues who would join with them in this project so as not to work in isolation. This endeavor was conceived as too difficult and far reaching to go alone. Rather it is conceived of as part of the ministry of the body of Christ, for the glory of God.

The commentary attempts to be in keeping with the ethos and spirituality of the tradition in its physical format as well. Specifically, the commentaries seek to reflect the dialogical way in which the tradition tends to approach the biblical text. Thus, each commentary begins with a series of questions designed to lift up corporate and individual issues that are illuminated in the biblical book under examination. This section identifies those key issues that are taken up in the commentary which follows. As a hermeneutical task, this section invites the reader to interpret his/her life context in a confessional-critical manner, revealing the need(s) to be addressed by the text. Such an opening serves to contextualize the commentary in the life of the church from the very beginning and serves to teach the reader how the Bible can legitimately be used in contemporary life.

Flowing out of this initial section, the introduction proper seeks to inform the reader as to the need, process, purpose, time, and place of composition. As a trajectory of the initial section, the introduction proper seeks be a necessity for the reader, and seeks to avoid the strange and irrelevant discussions that introductions often pursue. The introductions normally include topics of special interest to Pentecostals along with the normal introductory matters of authorship, place of composition, destination, audience, date, and theological emphases. A rather detailed discussion of the genre and structure of the book forms the basis of organization for the exposition that follows. In addition, a section devoted to the book's teaching about the Holy Spirit is included in the introduction.

The commentary proper provides a running exposition on the text, provides extended comments on texts of special significance for Pentecostals, and acknowledges and interacts with major options in interpreting individual passages. It also provides periodic opportunities for reflection upon and personal response to the biblical text. The reflection and response components normally occur at the end of a major section of the book. Here, a theme prominent in a specific passage is summarized in the light of the reading offered in the commentary. Next, the readers encounter a series of questions designed to lead them in corporate and personal reflection about this dimension of the text. Finally, the readers are encouraged to respond to the biblical text in specific ways. Such reflection and response is consistent with the tradition's practice of not simply hearing the words of Scripture but responding to them in concrete ways. It is the literary equivalent to the altar call.

In the attempt not to overtax the popular reader footnotes have been used *carefully and sparingly*. However, when additional, more technical discussions are deemed necessary, they are placed in the footnotes. In addition, Greek and Hebrew words are ordinarily found only within parentheses or in the footnotes.

Every attempt has been made to insure that the constituency of the movement are represented in some way among the contributors. It is my hope and prayer that the work of these women and men, from a variety of continents, races, and communities, will aid the Pentecostal community (and other interested individuals and communities) in hearing the biblical text in new and authentic ways.

The General Editor

Author's Preface

I was asked to write this volume on Ephesians during a most difficult and painful time in my life. While grief serves as a fillip to spur some people on to greater achievement, it had the opposite effect on me. The heartrending loss of my first wife of twenty years, Beverly, ostensibly smothered the fires of the mind and drained the wells of literary desire, shifting my interests to more practical concerns of the Christian faith. That delayed the completion of this work but, hopefully, has not diminished its benefit to the reader. Notwithstanding the challenges researching and writing it, I felt the process was a delightful and entrancing adventure into deeper and richer divine secrets whose discovery has deepened my love for the Lord and his word. As a young Christian, and even into more mature spiritual adulthood, Ephesians, probably more than any book of the Bible, had a most profound influence on my spiritual growth. My heart has been warmed by the divine fire that burns at its core and my spirit set aglow with its divine truths. Its message of God's extravagant grace, clothed in unrehearsed, reverent, and passionate prayer has lifted my spirit to a plane of holy rapture, filled my mind with wonder, and tuned my heart to grateful praise. Sermons preached and lectures delivered based upon this work have borne fruit that will ever redound to the glory of God.

Few, if any, meaningful undertakings are brought to completion without the inspiration and assistance of others. This volume is no exception. How can I say thanks enough to my lifelong friend and ministry colleague, George Peart, whose oft piquant words of encouragement came as a cattle prod when I was seemingly paralyzed by inertia? No less can be said of Leonard Lovett who has blazed an intellectual trail in rough weather and through rugged terrain. His suggestions were most helpful. Gerald Ellison's constancy throughout the journey provided light and strength all the way. My brother-in-law, Clifton Clarke, deserves specific mention for the scholarly insights and motivation he provided. I owe a great debt to Thomson Mathew, Dean of the School of Theology and Ministry at Oral Roberts University. He was a refreshing well of motivation, his assistance and love of God's word offering invaluable incentive to go on.

What can I say of my ORU faculty colleagues: James Norwood, Robert Mansfield, Brad Young, William McDonald, Edward Decker,

Charles Snow, Ken Mayton, Larry Hart, James Barber, Raymond Smith, Cheryl Iverson, Tim Ekblad, Lillian Breckenridge, James Breckenridge, and Dan Thimell, who not only provided a fertile environment for academic endeavor, but gently and frequently fanned the embers of enthusiasm with their thoughtful words? They are unsung heroes whose contribution was crucial in the outcome of the battle, but who worked "behind the lines." Special acknowledgment must be given to my students at the School of Theology and Ministry at Oral Roberts University, who served as the sounding board and anvil upon which ideas were battered out, straightened, tested, honed, and refined; and my church, Hope International Ministries, where I taught and preached some of the truths culled from this writing and received valuable critique and spiritual support. Marlene Mankins deserves deep and abundant gratitude for her meticulous editing of the manuscripts.

Heartfelt thanks and deserved recognition are due my children, André, Renée, and Trevor II, of whom I am "humbly proud," for whom I am deeply grateful to God, and in whom I find joy and fulfillment; and my grandchildren, Dominic and Jasmine, whose youthful inquisitiveness and eagerness to learn, and what spark of imagination this project may ignite in the future, have given added lift to go on. But none is due any greater recognition or deeper gratitude than my wife, Maureen. She was fresh air in the swirling, stifling mist and an oasis of encouragement during the sweltering heat of the long desert trek. Her seraphic devotion, amaranthine love, unfaltering encouragement, winsome presence, and inexhaustible patience, at times shouldering much of the load to allow me time to research and write, were decisive in bringing this commentary to completion.

I would be remiss not to express my deep debt of appreciation to my dear friend, John Christopher Thomas, for his invitation to contribute to the Pentecostal Commentary Series. A trailblazing undertaking, the PCS is forging a path through virgin territory. It is hoped that its distinctive approach to interpreting Scripture will enrich the lives of not only adherents of the Pentecostal and Charismatic tradition but also believers in the wider compass of Christendom.

My prayer for you who read this volume is borrowed from Paul's in Ephesians 3:16-19: "I pray that out of his glorious riches he will strengthen you with power through his Spirit in your inner being, so that Christ may dwell in your hearts through faith. And I pray that you, being rooted and established in love, may have power together with all the saints, to grasp how wide and long and high and deep is the love of Christ, and to know this love that surpasses knowledge — that you be filled to the measure of all the fullness of God."

To God be all the glory!

Introduction

What role, if any, does human choice play in divine election and predestination? Are the present actions and ultimate destination of each person predetermined? How does one reconcile the idea of divine sovereignty and human choice and responsibility? What is God's plan for the church in the world? Is it possible to reconcile communities ripped apart by racial, ethnic, and social strife? What does it mean that the church is united in Christ? What is the nature of this unity? Is it mystical and spiritual, or is it visible and practical? How does it relate to the appeal for unity in the priestly prayer of Jesus in John 17? Does unity entail centralized organizational governance and uniformity of beliefs and practices? How does the reality of myriad denominations and church communions represent this unity? How does the local church relate to the universal church? What does it mean that a Christian is in Christ and seated with him in the heavenly realms? In what sense do believers constitute the body of Christ? How do the people of God benefit from the diversity of ministry gifts Christ has bequeathed to the church? What is the personal and communal consequence of the inconsistency between what a Christian believes and how he or she lives? What difference is there between biblical holiness and religious legalism? What attitudes or sins are potentially most damaging to harmony in the local church? How can they be curbed? How does the Holy Spirit aid believers in living Christ-like lives? What are marks of the Spirit-filled life? How should the biblical teaching of the submission of a wife to her husband be understood? What is God's plan for marriage and the family? What does putting on the full armor of God entail? In the relentless warfare with diabolical forces, how can the church and the individual believer experience conquest amid conflict, triumph amid turmoil? Is there hope for the hapless millions mired in the morass of our urban communities now hemorrhaging the last drop of moral value and staggering from the savage blows of escalating violence? Is there hope for the areas of our world caught up in the vortex of grinding poverty and disease, with millions left to a dismal, cruel, and hopeless fate of habitual hunger and homelessness?

The Nature of the Epistle

Regarded by many as Paul's *magnum opus*, Ephesians is no ordinary Epistle. It is not a dispassionate discourse written with the tidy orderliness of a passionless logician or with the detached irrelevance of an ivory-tower theoretician. As in no other Epistle, the apostle appears to teach on his knees[1] – clothing and expounding theology in the unrehearsed and reverent language of passionate prayer. 'The quintessence of Paulinism',[2] a divine fire burns at its core, warming the heart and setting the spirit aglow with divine truth. Its message of God's redemptive display of an extravagant grace lifts the spirit to a plane of holy rapture and fills the mind with wonder and the heart with grateful praise. In Ephesians God's secret plan, his sacred mystery to establish a redeemed community of both Jew and Gentile to express Christ's fullness on earth (1.15-23), unfolds with divine unobtrusiveness.

Ephesians evokes humility and grateful recognition and celebration of God's greatness and goodness in our salvation. God's vision for all humankind, now unfolding in history, spans eternity past (1.4; 3.9) and eternity future (1.10; 3.21). His ultimate aim in saving us, however, is not only for our personal benefit; it is more so 'to the praise of his glorious grace', a truth that throbs throughout the Epistle, but is mentioned specifically in 1.6, 12, 14.

Much unlike the combative tone of Galatians and Colossians and the dour despair of 2 Corinthians, a high note of celebration and resounding praise echoes throughout Ephesians. To borrow a coruscating expression, in this Epistle 'we step into the hush and stillness of the temple'.[3] Ephesians intones 'impassioned contemplation, dominated by prayer and praise'.[4] Springing from a heart overflowing with gratitude for God's amazing grace in both re-creation and reconciliation, such redolent worship invites an antiphonal response from the contempo-

---

[1] Curtis Vaughan, *Ephesians* (Bible Study Commentary; Grand Rapids: Zondervan, 1977), p. 11. E.F. Scott has noted that 'just as Handel composed the "Hallelujah Chorus" on his knees, so Paul wrote this sublime Epistle'. 'Ephesians' (*The Moffatt New Testament Commentary*; London: Hodder and Stoughton, 1930), p. 125.

[2] F.F. Bruce, *The Epistles to the Colossians, to Philemon, and to the Ephesians* (NICNT; Grand Rapids: Eerdmans, 1984), p. 229; *Paul: Apostle of the Free Spirit* (Exeter/Grand Rapids: Eerdmans, 1977), p. 424.

[3] George G. Findlay, *The Epistle to the Ephesians* (The Expositor's Bible, repr., 6; Grand Rapids: Eerdmans, 1950), p. 7.

[4] C.H. Dodd, 'The Message of the Epistles: Ephesians', *Expository Times* 45 (Nov. 1933), p. 63.

rary church gathered in worship and from every heart set free by divine love.

The Value and Contemporary Significance of the Epistle

Recognition of Ephesians' immense value and significance for the Christian life and faith has echoed in fitting tributes over the years. It is regarded as Paul's crowning work[5] and 'the most authoritative and most consummate compendium' [6] of Christian faith. Ephesians largely recapitulates the major themes of Paul's writings, the central basis of his ministry as apostle to the Gentiles, and opens new vistas of thought cradled in the earlier letters.[7] An abridgment of Paul's teaching on Christ-in-his-church, it adds a number of liturgical features taken from the worshiping life of the apostolic communities which Paul knew well.[8]

Though the people and culture Ephesians targets are nearly two thousand years removed from our own, the Epistle speaks with engaging relevance and contemporary applicability to our situation in life. It does not only present a church *coram Deo*, but a church in overalls, a church in the marketplace, a people exposed to biting cold and blistering heat, experiencing life's bane, engaging the world. Perhaps no New Testament writing has greater existential relevance, attracting the attention of both Protestant and Roman Catholic scholars in their attempt to find common ground in addressing the divisive doctrinal and ecumenical issues that plague Christendom.[9] Its ecumenical message offers peace to our world war-torn and windswept by destructive cyclonic forces of polarizing tribal, ethnic, ideological, and religious aspirations. Our fractured society, split by gaping chasms of social and spiritual dislocation, needs to hear its message of reconciliation. Adrift on the intemperate sea of postmodern pessimism and moral relativism in a fragile raft without chart or compass, it needs to hear the message that God offers a nobler way, a new life, an abiding hope. To a Western world bewitched by the tawdry splendor of the promise of Oriental mysticism and the occult to provide hope and satisfy the yawning spiritual hunger of the soul, Ephesians lifts up a living, relevant Christ

---

[5] Dodd, *Ephesians* (The Abingdon Bible Commentary, ed. F.C. Eiselen et al.; Nashville: Abingdon, 1957), pp. 1224-25.

[6] John Mackay, *God's Order: The Ephesian Letter and this Present Time* (New York: Macmillan, 1964), p. 15.

[7] F.F. Bruce, *Colossians, Philemon, Ephesians* (NICNT; Grand Rapids: Eerdmans, 1984), p. 229.

[8] Ralph P. Martin, *Ephesians* (BBC 11; Nashville: Broadman, 1971), p. 126.

[9] Ralph Martin, *New Testament Foundations,* vol. II (Grand Rapids: Eerdmans, 1978), p. 223.

in whose sufficiency humankind's hopes and spiritual needs are fully met.

Ephesians inveighs against the vulgarity of sensuality that masquerades as enlightenment and freedom, and seeks to rescue human dignity from the bathos and banality into which it has plunged. Our contemporary church, torn by denominational and doctrinal strife, must grasp Ephesians' message of the unity of all believers in Christ. Scarred by the crush of the self-centered materialism and insular individualism of popular culture, believers must see the global sweep of God's redemptive activity. By a sovereign act of grace, God has reconciled believing individuals to himself (2.1-10), but he has also reconciled redeemed individuals to each other (2.11-22). The church comprises a third race – men and women reconciled to God through Christ and joined together to create a new society which stands as a 'microcosm of God's ultimate design for a broken and sinful race'.[10] The unity of the church is a mirror reflection of the unity of the Godhead, believers having God as one Father (3.14; 4.6), Christ as one Lord (1.22; 4.5), and the Spirit as the one access to God (2.18; 4.4).

Unity and harmony are tokens of the Spirit's presence in the church (4.1-6). By unity and harmony Paul means neither religious syncretism nor theological universalism, for God has seated Christ 'above all rule and authority, power and dominion, and every title that can be given' (1.21), and 'has placed all things under his feet and appointed him to be head over everything for the church'[11] (1.22). Christ is not a mere *primus inter pares* among the founders of religion in the world. He alone is Lord and Savior of all humankind.

Always in danger of being sucked up into the vortex of an expanding postmodern world with no theological or moral center, and propelled into a swirling, distorting and disorienting fog that offers neither direction nor hope, the church can ill afford to barter the truth claims of the faith 'once for all entrusted to the saints' (Jude 3). It must champion a well-reasoned theological orthodoxy matched by an equally unwavering allegiance to a scrupulously biblical orthopraxy. That salvation transports the believer out of darkness into light, a radical spiritual and moral transformation which demands a life patterned after God and Christ (2; 5.1-8), is an oft-repeated reminder in Ephesians. A Christianity that is incandescent, sparkling, and alive – a faith that burns brightly as a beacon in the present darkness – is what Paul calls the church to offer to the world. But neither truth nor ethics should adulterate or mute the church's message of a God whose boundless

---

[10] Ralph Martin, *Ephesians, Colossians and Philemon* (Interpretation; Atlanta: John Knox, 1991), p. 9.
[11] Except where otherwise indicated, the NIV is the translation used.

love seeks and embraces the loveless, the lonely, the least, and the broken of our world. Recipients of that love, believers today are repeatedly invited to refract and reflect it so that the world might know and be reconciled to God.

Amid fierce spiritual conflict and the cosmic authority of the sovereign Lord, the church stands triumphant. The thought of conquest through a risen and victorious Christ ought, on the one hand, to rid believing Christians of a defeatist mentality that conduces to a crippling inertia, retreat, or a quick hoisting of the white flag of surrender in the battle for souls. Awareness of the inevitability of conflict, on the other hand, is a necessary balance to the rabid Christian triumphalism that has bewitched that brand of Christianity which is seemingly oblivious of the redoubtable and fearsome spiritual forces arrayed against the people of God, makes little of the scandal of the cross, the bitter antagonism the name of Christ provokes, and a church that has increasingly become the target of brutal religious and political persecution around the world. If a triumphant people, believers presently share the joys and freedom of Christ and the glorious hope of an eternal future with him.

If a persecuted people, they are certainly a privileged people – a marvelous truth interwoven into the fabric of Ephesians. Christ has 'blessed us in the heavenly realms with every spiritual blessing in Christ' (1.3). God 'chose us in him before the creation of the world' and 'predestined us to be adopted as his sons' (1.4, 5). We were 'made ... alive with Christ even when we were dead in transgressions ... that in the coming ages [God] might show the incomparable riches of his grace, expressed in his kindness to us in Christ Jesus' (2.5, 7). Once Godless aliens, we are now 'fellow citizens with God's people and members of God's household' (2.19). Attention has been drawn to the very significant images that describe the church in Ephesians, images like body, bride, temple, building, new humanity, family, in Christ, and marriage. For this reason, many conclude that no other New Testament book boasts as high an ecclesiology.[12] In a world in which people are often devalued, depersonalized, and ostracised, Ephesians presents a God who bestows true value, identity, and belonging to his people and a fellowship where these qualities are daily cultivated and promoted.

With its abundant use of the word *all* (50 times) and the word *one* (14 times), Ephesians challenges all cultural myopia and dismisses provincial claims to social, racial, or gender superiority. Christ has broken down all such barriers, and has reconciled and united all believers in

[12] Peter O'Brien, *The Letter to the Ephesians* (PNTC; Grand Rapids: Eerdmans; Cambridge, UK: Apollos, 1999), p. 3.

himself ('in Christ', 'in whom', and similar phrases appear 34 times in the Epistle, mainly in chs. 2 and 4). To homes ripped apart at the foundations and crumbling under the weight of demoralizing and destructive forces Ephesians holds out God's healing remedy.

A clarion call to evangelism reverberates throughout Ephesians. As God's redemptive agent in the world, the church is obliged to proclaim God's saving, eternal purposes to all humankind. Hers is the task to dispense the message of reconciliation and to display God's multifaceted wisdom everywhere (3.9-10) till all have seen and heard of the goodness and greatness of God. But evangelism is effective only as it breathes the pure air of intercession that so pervades the Epistle.

Authorship[13]

That Paul wrote Ephesians, Philippians, Colossians, and Philemon from Rome during his first imprisonment was the traditional view of the church for nearly eighteen centuries. To be sure, questions concerning its destination were raised quite early by fathers of the church and stylistic deviations from others of Paul's Epistles acknowledged in the 16th century. Ephesians' Paulinity went undisputed, however, until the emergence of rational criticism in the late 18th and early 19th centuries.[14] Ever since, arguments have been raised concerning its authorship, origin, destination, and date. Determining the milieu of the Epistle in the development of early Christianity is decisive in the contemporary scholarly debate. Does Ephesians represent a later stage of Christian reflection on the church's Christology and ecclesiology? Is it an abridgment of Paul's life's work and theology? Or, is it a post-Pauline tribute by an ardent follower to enhance the waning influence and fading image of the apostle? Was it written by Paul at all?

---

[13] For a more complete discussion of issues concerning authorship, see C.L. Mitton, *The Epistle to the Ephesians* (Oxford: Clarendon, 1951); Andrew Lincoln, *Ephesians* (WBC 42; Dallas: Word, 1990), pp. xxxvi-LXXiii; Donald Guthrie, *New Testament Introduction* (Downer's Grove: InterVarsity, 1976), pp. 479-516; Rudolf Schnackenburg, *Ephesians* (trans. Helen Heron; Edinburgh: T & T Clark, 1991), pp. 21-37; A. van Roon, *The Authenticity of Ephesians* (NovT Supp, 39; Leiden: Brill, 1974).

[14] O'Brien, *Ephesians*, p. 4. Theodore of Mopsuestia (d. 428) and Jerome (d. 430) had questions about its destination and Erasmus noted stylistic differences with other Epistles of Paul. Edward Evanson was the first to question the authenticity and universal acceptance of the Epistle, in 1792 declaring it as a forgery. W.M. de Witte (1826) and F.C. Baur (1845) and his school would escalate the attack based exclusively on internal grounds.

Early Evidence for Pauline Authorship

Early external evidence for the Pauline authorship of Ephesians is abundant, perhaps going back to 95 CE. The earliest collection of the Pauline Epistles contained Ephesians, and Ephesians is accorded Pauline authorship in the earliest Latin and Syriac versions. It appears among the Pauline Epistles in every Greek manuscript, including the Chester Beatty papyrus ($\mathbf{p}^{46}$), which excludes the Pastoral Epistles. Marcion's *Instrumentum*[15] (c. 140 CE) lists it as from the pen of Paul, but written to the Laodiceans. Irenaeus, the Muratorian Canon (c. 180 CE), Clement of Alexandria, Origen, and Tertullian all endorsed it as Pauline. After careful study, Eusebius included it among 'the fourteen (letters) of Paul,' at the same time pointing out the disputed nature of the letter to the Hebrews.[16] This weight of early external evidence should summon greater confidence[17] in the authorial integrity of any letter from antiquity that bears the imprimatur of the early church 'unless there is very strong evidence to the contrary'.[18] This plea should not be dismissed cavalierly, because it becomes 'highly significant' when applied to Ephesians, whose authenticity bears early and consistent attestation to its apostolic authorship.[19]

The Current Debate about Authorship

Popular scholarly opinion today is divided on the authorship of Ephesians, with the majority of scholars voting against Paulinity.[20] In favor of Paulinity is Paul's personal authorial claim (1.1; 3.1; cf. 4.1). In addition, Ephesians' occasion (6.21-22) is identical with that of Colossians (4.7-9) and Philemon (1, 10, 23-24), letters with which it shares a common bearer, chronology, and provenance. One anti-Pauline view urges that while the alleged author calls himself Paul, claims apostolic authority, and describes himself as suffering for Christ, he gives no details of his suffering or imprisonment, has no specific knowledge of

---

[15] So listed in his *apostolikon* also. See Tertullian, *Against Marcion*, 5.17.

[16] *Ecclesiastical History*, III 4, 5.

[17] William Klein urges that 'We ought to be cautious about abandoning [such] collective wisdom'. See *Ephesians* (The Expositor's Bible Commentary, 12; Grand Rapids: Zondervan, 2006), p. 29.

[18] O'Brien, *Ephesians*, p. 4. O'Brien observes that in the third century Paulinity was regularly ascribed to the Epistle by persons both of the orthodox and heretical camps. In n. 9 he says, 'The onus of proof lies with those who deny the claim of authenticity' (*Ephesians*, p. 4).

[19] O'Brien, *Ephesians*, pp. 45, 46.

[20] Raymond Brown estimates that 70 to 80% of contemporary critical scholarship rejects Pauline authorship of Ephesians. *An Introduction to the New Testament* (ABRL; New York: Doubleday, 1997), p. 629.

the addressees, and gives no personal greetings.[21] The reason for the
impersonal tone of Ephesians may lie in the probability that it was a
circular letter addressed to mainly Gentile churches in southwestern
Asia.[22] Direct personal allusions can hardly be expected in such a document.[23] Further, stylistic anomaly may be influenced by the nature of
the Epistle. Unlike a pastoral letter written to address specific doctrinal
or practical concerns in a local church, Ephesians is 'an exalted prose-
poem on the theme "Christ-in-his-church"' and bears the influence of
a 'liturgical, rhetorical, and catechetical strain'.[24] Finally, the *berakah* or
eulogy (1.3-14) recalls comparable poems in Phil. 2.5-11 and Col.
1.15-20.

Proponents of Pauline authorship contend that Ephesians' theology,
structure, literary style, and language betray the hand and mind of Paul.
The Epistle's claim and the church's long historical attestation to its
Paulinity are so solid that anti-Pauline theories face a huge challenge to
prove otherwise.[25]

Opponents embrace one of two options. The first is that, during his
lifetime, Paul employed the services of a secretary who was given great
editorial liberty. While partially answering linguistic and stylistic questions, this theory does not, however, settle theological issues often
raised against Pauline authorship. The second option is the deutero-
Pauline hypothesis, which argues that a later ardent and gifted disciple
of the apostle[26] either composed Ephesians as a quilt sewn from the
variegated materials of Paul's Epistles, or wrote the Epistle in Paul's
name long after his death. A modified version of this theory accepts the
Epistle's teaching as Pauline, but its collection and publication as the
work of a trusted and gifted disciple-colleague and amanuensis depu-
tized by the apostle. Of the 44 words that appear only in Ephesians and
not in others of Paul's Epistles, 25 are found in Luke-Acts. Based upon
this linguistic and other stylistic connections, it is concluded that Luke

---

[21] Lincoln, *Ephesians* (Word Biblical Commentary 42; Dallas: Word, 1990), pp. lx-lxi.
See also Schnackenburg, *Ephesians*, pp. 32-37.

[22] O'Brien, *Ephesians,* pp. 86-87; Martin, *Ephesians, Colossians and Philemon*, p. 6.

[23] Notwithstanding its impersonal nature, Ephesians does mention Paul's commendation of Tychicus, who accompanied Paul from Greece to Jerusalem at the conclusion of
his Ephesian ministry (Acts 19.21; 20.2-4), to the letter's readers (6.21-22), and provides
specific information that helps to situate its composition historically by comparing the
letter with Acts and other Pauline writings (Acts 19.10-20, 26; Eph. 2.11; 3.1; 4.17; Acts
28.20, 30-31; Eph. 3.1, 13; 4.1; 6.20).

[24] Martin, *Ephesians, Colossians and Philemon*, p. 6.

[25] Donald Guthrie, *New Testament Introduction* (Downer's Grove: InterVarsity Press,
1976), p. 482.

[26] Onesimus, Tychicus, and Luke have been suggested as this Pauline enthusiast.

gave the document its final shape and published it under Paul's auspices, either during his final imprisonment or after his death.[27]

Arguments against the Paulinity of Ephesians rest almost solely on internal grounds. Only a brief and basic statement of the major issues and scholarly discussions that abound will be given here.

The arguments may be classified under five headings: linguistic, stylistic, literary, historical, and doctrinal.[28] Ephesians contains forty words used only once in the New Testament and fifty-one found nowhere else in the undisputed Pauline letters (e.g. 'devil' instead of 'Satan' and 'in the heavenly realms', in place of the adjective used elsewhere),[29] many of which are, however, encountered in later post-apostolic literature. Additionally, Ephesians has the Jew–Gentile controversy settled (2.14), which favors a date after the destruction of the temple in 70 CE. Theologically, Paul not only diminishes the death of Jesus, he fills common words with different meaning (e.g. church, mystery, stewardship, fullness).

Proponents of Pauline authorship dismiss these claims, urging that the statistics of words is not decisive evidence since other New Testament writings betray similar numerical comparisons. Romans and 1 and 2 Corinthians, respectively, for example, contain a hundred words that are unique in the Pauline corpus; Philippians includes about fifty such words and Galatians more than thirty.[30] The dissimilarities between Romans and Galatians are said to be nearly insurmountable in some ways, and the method used to demonstrate the un-Paulinity of Ephesians, if applied to Romans, could easily prove the implausibility of Paul's having written Romans.[31] Many of the uncommon terms in Ephesians relate to the topics addressed. Verbal parallels in post-apostolic literature may indicate the church fathers' linguistic debt to Paul, rather than the other way round. Linguistic and theological arguments cast Paul in an unnecessary and unreasonable mold. Change of theme, purpose, and circumstances often demand a change of language. Given a different readership and different circumstances, it is neither unrealistic nor unreasonable to think of Paul 're-expressing, developing and modifying his own thoughts'.[32]

[27] Martin, *New Testament Foundations*, pp. 224, 230-32.
[28] C. Leslie Mitton, *Ephesians* (New Century Bible; Greenwood, SC: Attic Press, 1976), pp. 4-6.
[29] Lincoln, *Ephesians*, p. lxv. Cf. A. Skevington Wood, *Ephesians* (The Expositor's Bible Commentary, 11; Grand Rapids: Zondervan, 1978), p. 5.
[30] Markus Barth, *Ephesians* (The Anchor Bible 34; Garden City, NY: Doubleday, 1974), p. 4. See also O'Brien, *Ephesians*, pp. 5-6.
[31] Gordon Fee, *God's Empowering Presence* (Peabody, MA: Hendrickson, 1994), p. 660, n. 6.
[32] Clinton Arnold, *Dictionary of Paul and His Letters*, ed. G.F. Hawthorne, R.P. Martin, and D.G. Reid (Downers Grove, IL and Leicester, England: InterVarsity, 1993), p. 243.

Its more cumbersome style, slower than any of Paul's other writings and lacking in vigor and brevity, is another argument advanced against the traditional view of the Epistle's authorship. Added to the stylistic aberration are its unusually long sentences (e.g. 1.3-14; 1.15-23; 2.1-10; 3.1-9) and poetic and liturgical tone. In response, advocates appeal to Paul's literary versatility and a change in historical circumstances. Any antagonist to Pauline authorship must consider whether an imitator could have produced a work 'at once so authentic and yet so original'. If he matched Paul in spiritual faculty and facility, 'it is strange that the primitive church knew nothing of him'.[33] It is with great difficulty that one could even imagine someone so completely assimilating another person's thoughts 'as to reproduce him in this way'.[34]

Challenges to Paul's authorship are also based upon historical grounds. Ephesians is mute on the Jewish-Gentile controversy. Such silence, it is argued, hints that the issue no longer existed. Objectors say that problem could not have been resolved in Paul's lifetime. They similarly contend that the universal church Paul portrays is a second-century, post-Pauline development.

The very term holy apostles (3.5), antagonists further urge, reflects a post-apostolic date when the church bestowed special reverence upon the apostles. But holy here (often translated saints), which Paul uses in his letters to describe all believers, means nothing more than set apart for God. Pseudepigraphy constitutes the final historical point at issue. The practice was so common in the post-apostolic period that opponents say that someone writing Ephesians in Paul's name would not have created a problem regarding its canonicity.[35] This argument lacks foundation. Not only has no single book of the New Testament been proven to be pseudepigraphical, but the early church rejected all such known writings. A book's proven historical genuineness and authority were criteria for its inclusion in the canon. No biblical writing achieved canonical status when adopted into the canon; it was accepted as genuine before becoming canonized. Authorial anonymity was viewed more favorably than pseudonymity when a document was

[33] Skevington Wood, *Ephesians*, p. 7.

[34] Fee, *God's Empowering Presence*, p. 659. See also n. 5. In his recent massive, encyclopedic and detailed commentary on Ephesians Harold Hoehner, after an exhaustive examination of opposing views presents perhaps the stoutest known scholarly defense of Pauline authorship. See his *Ephesians: An Exegetical Commentary* (Grand Rapids: Baker Academic, 2002), pp. 2-60. He similarly zealously and cogently argues for an Ephesian destination of the letter, concluding that 'both the external and internal evidence favor the inclusion of *en Epheso* in 1.1 (p 148).

[35] Bruce Metzger remarks, 'There is scarcely an illustrious personality in Greek literature or history from Themistocles down to Alexander, who was not credited with more or less extensive correspondence'. 'Literary Forgeries and Canonical Pseudepigrapha', *Journal of Biblical Literature* 91, p. 10.

considered for canonization. If asked whether a document can be both pseudonymous and canonical, the answer is: it can be 'one or the other, but not both'.[36]

Doctrinal or theological divergences and changes in outlook are the final argument marshaled against Pauline authorship. The apparent waning of eschatological emphasis, a highly developed doctrine of ministry, the near-metaphysical description of the church as the body of Christ, and the Epistle's predisposition toward a moralizing ethic are factors, it is argued, that support a post-Pauline authorship. Furthermore, opponents of Pauline authorship assert that Ephesians contains an early catholicism which presents the church as unified and universalized, and a church looking upward to the heavenly realms where an inheritance awaits believers. Such a church is a development later than Paul.

To the charge of a catholicized church, Pauline supporters reply with evidence of similar emphasis in other letters of Paul (Col. 1.18; 2.19; 3.15), some of which are earlier than Ephesians (1 Cor. 12.12-31; Rom. 12.5). Furthermore, while a vast gulf separates the local church from the global church which the author accentuates, it does not strain the imagination to see Paul universalizing concepts represented in the local body.[37] What is more, the ecclesiastical unity of which Paul speaks is spiritual rather than organizational. As regards the matter of a fading *parousia*, it is clear that Paul places a greater emphasis upon the Lord's return in his earliest letters (1 and 2 Thessalonians) and less in his later Epistles. Yet, on several occasions Ephesians refers to the end of all things (1.10, 13-14, 18; 4.30; 5.5-6, 27). Paul's emphasis on a realized soteriology and eschatology was probably necessary to strengthen his readers against the danger of inimical powers.[38] Finally, to a lesser or greater degree, ethics is present in all of Paul's Epistles, Paul customarily following the doctrinal section of each with an ethical appeal that theology affects how the believer lives.

Literary Relationship between Ephesians and Colossians

The literary relationship between Ephesians and Colossians bears directly upon the question of authorship. Objections to Pauline author-

---

[36] O'Brien, *Ephesians*, p. 45. See his discussion on pseudonymity on pp. 37-45.

[37] William W. Klein, *Ephesians* (The Expositor's Bible Commentary, 12; Grand Rapids: Zondervan, 2006), p. 25. Klein has shown that by the time Romans was written Paul had developed the concept of the 'totality of believers' in Christ. For him to take another step and conceptualize the church as 'a total and cosmic reality existing in the heavenly realms "in Christ" does not strain credulity' (*Ephesians*, p. 26).

[38] Clinton Arnold, *Ephesians: Power and Magic* (Cambridge: Cambridge University Press, 1989), pp. 145-57.

ship center upon the verbal and conceptual affinities Ephesians shares with Luke–Acts, the Gospel of John, 1 Peter, Hebrews and, in particular, Colossians. No two New Testament Epistles bear a closer literary resemblance than Ephesians and Colossians. This is the most decisive factor against Pauline authorship of the former. Approximately one-fourth of the vocabulary and one-third of Ephesians' content are paralleled in Colossians.[39] Ephesians 6.21-22 and Col. 4.7-8; Eph. 3.2 and Col. 1.25, to mention a few examples, reflect verbatim agreement. These and other factors led some to conclude quite early in the twentieth century that Ephesians is a catholicized version of Colossians.[40] A significant number of scholars today concur. No matter what one's position on the Epistle's authorship one cannot dismiss these resemblances as merely coincidental. But how may such similarities be explained? And what of the differences? Do these concerns inevitably demand the conclusion of non-Pauline or pseudonymous authorship? In response to the above literary conclusions, advocates of Pauline authorship contend that parallels between Ephesians and other Pauline Epistles argue more in favor of Paul than the reverse. For a forger to imitate Paul so closely would constitute 'a psychological impossibility'.[41] Such a person must have matched, if not outclassed, Paul mentally and spiritually. 'Of such a second Paul early Christian history has no knowledge'.[42]   Until a compelling reason emerges to justify a forger's motive and ultimate goal in impersonating Paul in Ephesians, the lack of credibility of the non-Pauline argument will keep it unappealing and unattractive.[43] All the questions concerning Pauline authorship of Ephesians may never be fully resolved to the satisfaction of all. There is 'no consensus of expert opinion', because 'argument answers argument without clear outcome'.[44] Reputable scholars on opposite sides of the issue will continue to advance cogent arguments for their position. In

[39] Arthur G. Patzia, *Ephesians, Colossians, Philemon* (NIBC; Peabody: Hendrickson, 1990), p. 124. Lincoln states that 34% of the words in Colossians show up in Ephesians and 26.5% of the words in Ephesians echo in Colossians. Such striking resemblances carry through to the overall structure, thematic material, and sequence of the letters (*Ephesians*, p. xlviii). O'Brien argues that such 'statistical parallels' do not strike a decisive blow against Pauline authorship, so most advocates 'place more weight on the similar overall structure and sequence of the two letters with their same thematic material' (p. 9).

[40] J. Moffatt, *An Introduction to the Literature of the New Testament* (Edinburgh: T&T Clark, 1911), p. 393.

[41] F.W. Farrar, *The Life and Work of St. Paul* (London, Paris & New York: Cassell, 1884), p. 634.

[42] F.F. Bruce, *The Epistle to the Ephesians* (London: Pickering & Inglis, 1961), pp. 11-12.

[43] Klyne Snodgrass, *Ephesians* (NIV Application Commentary; Grand Rapids: Zondervan, 1996), p. 22.

[44] J.H. Houlden, *Paul's Letters from Prison* (Westminster Pelican Commentaries; Philadelphia: Westminster, 1977), p. 236.

the debate serious thought must be given to the idea whether it is more probable that an impersonator in the first century created a writing 'ninety or ninety-five percent in accordance with Paul's style or that Paul himself wrote a letter diverging five or ten percent from his usual style'?[45]

The debate about the authorship of Ephesians may never be settled. No question may ever be answered to everyone's satisfaction. Evidence and arguments adduced against Pauline authorship thus far are, however, inadequate. What cannot be denied in the discussion is the canonical authenticity of the Epistle. Ephesians is in the canon because its message is God-breathed and is useful for teaching and training in righteousness (2 Tim. 3.16).

Occasion and Purpose

The purpose and authorship of Ephesians are inseparably bound. Traditionally classified among the Prison Epistles of Paul (3.1; 4.1; 6.20), Ephesians was probably composed and dispatched at about the same time as Colossians since Tychicus was the bearer of both Epistles (Col. 4.7-8; Eph. 6.21-22). Most of Paul's Epistles were written on a specific occasion to meet a specific need. Ephesians is no exception. However, no unanimity exists in determining its occasion and purpose. Some have conjectured that it was a baptismal homily or a sermon for renewing baptismal vows. Intimation of a baptismal tradition in 4.22-24 cannot be extrapolated as the overall purpose of the Epistle. Unlike Colossians in which heresy is unmasked and refuted, the irenic and non-combative tone of the Epistle suggests the presence of no particular false teaching, controversy, or crisis.[46]

Many scholars who subscribe to the theory of a Gnostic background marshal support from what they regard as Gnostic words[47] the author uses. Ephesians' use of similar language and concepts found in Colossians may adumbrate the presence of the same local concerns in Ephesus, although no longer demanding the same urgent attention and action.[48] The close connection between Ephesians and Colossians directly impinges upon the purpose of the former,[49] although Paul's tone

---

[45] H.J. Cadbury, *The Dilemma of Ephesians*, p. 101.

[46] Schnackenburg and Kümmel perceive a crisis of leadership and a spiritual crisis as reasons for the writing of Ephesians. See Rudolph Schnackenburg, *Ephesians: A Commentary* (Edinburgh: T. & T. Clark, 1991), pp. 34-35 and Georg Kümmel, *Introduction to the New Testament* (trans. Howard Clark Kee; Nashville: Abingdon, 1975), p. 364.

[47] Words such as *knowledge, mystery, fullness, perfection, revelation, heavenly union, principalities and powers, new man,* etc. are conscripted in the service of these scholars' argument.

[48] Lincoln, *Ephesians*, p. lxxxii.

[49] *New Testament Introduction*, p. 515.

betrays no alarm.[50] Both churches facing similar dangers, coupled with
the mention of Tychicus the bearer in parallel passages in both Epistles
(Eph. 6.21-22; Col. 4.7-9), his association with Asia Minor and Ephe-
sus (Acts 20.4; 2 Tim 4.12), and the close geographical proximity both
Epistles' destinations share – all are factors impinging on the purpose of
Ephesians.

A number of scholars have stressed that the Epistle's purpose and interpretation are inseparably and indispensably connected to an understanding of its cultural environment, the religious ethos of first-century
Ephesus, and the complicated relationship between Christianity and
Judaism during this period. It is argued that during Paul's absence of
seven years from Ephesus, five of which he spent in prison, the mainly
Gentile house churches he founded and the Jewish ones which were
loosely tethered to him and existed before his arrival in the city, 'went
in various theological and social directions.'[51] This may explain Paul's
resounding appeal for and emphasis on unity throughout the Epistle. In
addition, the Ephesian believers were in constant conflict with the
broader Greco-Roman environment, with its imperial cult, worship of
Artemis, and fascination with magic. Though Ephesians gives no hint
of looming apostasy, the temptation to assimilate to the pagan culture
was a real one the discouraged Christians (3.13) faced. The situation
elicited Paul's reminder to them of God's power and grace, their role
as the church in God's plan of cosmic unification in Christ, and their
ethical responsibility as the people of God.[52] The believers' ethical responsibility, 'identity formation', reminding the believers of the marvelous work Christ had done in them, how they ought to live as
Christians, and the importance of their maintaining unity is viewed by
some scholars as the Epistle's main purpose.[53]

Contrary to the theory that Ephesians was expressly written to combat speculative Judaism or Judaistic Gnosticism, there is no indication
that the Colossian heresy had infected the assemblies in and around
Ephesus. It may be conceded, however, that Ephesians would serve as
a shield against the onset of such a virulent incipient heresy.[54] Believers

[50] Snodgrass and Klein share a modified version of this view, urging that the key to
unlocking Ephesians' purpose lies in Colossians. See Klyne Snodgrass, *Ephesians* (NAC;
Grand Rapids: Zondervan), p. 23; W. Klein, 'Ephesians', p. 36.
[51] Frank Thielman, *Ephesians* (Baker Exegetical Commentary on the New Testament;
Grand Rapids: Baker, 2010), p. 28.
[52] Thielman, *Ephesians*, p. 28.
[53] Snodgrass, *Ephesians*, p. 23; Klein, *Ephesians*, p. 36.
[54] John Eadie regards Ephesians as 'prophylactic more than corrective in nature'. See
Commentary on the Epistle of Paul to the Ephesians (Grand Rapids: Zondervan, 1979), p. li.
F.C. Baur, Petr Pokorny, Hans Conzelmann, Hans Schlier, and Ernst Käsemann represent a school of scholars who view Ephesians as an antiheretical tract in which Paul

armed with the truths the Epistle contained would not then be swayed by the speculative and philosophical teachings plaguing the Colossian church.

Attempts to link Ephesians with the Dead Sea Scrolls and the Qumran community, with hopes of showing the Epistle's dependence upon Qumran literature, consume the time and energy of another group of scholars. The speculative argument, erected upon Jülicher's, that Ephesians was written as an introduction to the Pauline corpus, compiled about 90 CE by one of Paul's ardent devotees (probably Onesimus, former slave and later bishop of Ephesus),[55] has progressively lost appeal over the years. The theory that Eph. 6.10-20 reveals a church facing persecution under Domitian (96 CE) and, therefore, needing encouragement, is highly ingenious. Even a cursory reading of the context rules out such a possibility. A spiritual battle is what the passage describes. While Ephesians contains hymnic, liturgical, catechetical, baptismal, and eucharistic elements, the Epistle's purpose cannot be confined to any or a combination of all of those elements. Rather, they are used to serve a broader goal.

Ephesians' emphasis on unity has led to the conclusion that in the wake of Jewish-Gentile tension Paul's aim was to secure unity among the believers.[56] Or his purpose may well have been to instruct Gentile converts in essentials of their new-found faith.[57] While addressing no specific problem or need, in keeping with its encyclical, ecumenical, and impersonal character, Ephesians, written to a largely Gentile church, does, however, reflect a twofold strategy. In the first half of the Epistle (1.3–3.21), which is an extended benediction and prayer, Paul seeks to broaden the spiritual horizons of the believers to the dimensions of the eternal purpose and grace of God and the true nature of the church, of which they are a part. The second half (4.1-6.20) exhorts erstwhile pagans to a greater conformity to Christian ideals, challenging them to the highest levels of personal and social morality.

adopts and adapts the language of the Gnostics to counter Gnosticism which was threatening the church.

[55] Edgar J. Goodspeed, *The Meaning of Ephesians*, p. 225.

[56] Margaret MacDonald argues that no Jewish-Gentile conflict existed in the Ephesian church. At best, what is hinted at in 2.11-22 is nothing more than a general reference to the live realities of burgeoning Gentile majority and a dwindling Jewish minority in the community. *Colossians and Ephesians* (Sacra Pagina Series; Collegeville, MN: Liturgical Press, 2000), p.19.

[57] D.A. Carson, Douglas J. Moo, and Leon Morris, *An Introduction to the New Testament* (Grand Rapids: Zondervan, 1992), pp. 311-12.

Place of Composition

The product of his fertile mind and soaring spirit during captivity (3.1; 4.1; 6.20-21), Ephesians commands a place among the Prison or Captivity Epistles[58] of Paul. While few would debate the significance of the Epistle, the question as to the place of Paul's imprisonment remains a live issue in scholarship today. Three possible places have been suggested: Rome, Ephesus,[59] and Caesarea.[60]

Luke concludes Acts with Paul under house arrest in Rome for two years (28.30), during which time the apostle freely proclaimed the gospel (28.16-17, 23, 31). The freedom accorded Paul doubtless afforded him the time and peace to write. Personal references in other Prison Epistles favor a Roman imprisonment (Phil. 1.13; 4.22). So does the presence of Luke (Col. 4.14; cf. Acts 28.14-16) and Aristarchus (Col. 4.10; cf. Acts 27.2). Both men had accompanied Paul to Rome. Paul's conscious awareness that he might receive capital punishment accords well with Rome (Phil. 1.19-26; 2.17, 23). With the Enlightenment came the first challenge to the church's belief that Paul wrote Ephesians from Rome.

Though Acts records no imprisonment of Paul in Ephesus, some scholars feel this is at least hinted at in the Corinthian correspondences. In 1 Cor. 15.32 Paul says he has 'fought wild beasts in Ephesus'. He speaks of deliverance from a 'sentence of death', and 'a deadly peril' in 2 Cor. 1.9-10. These verses may mean nothing more than escape from some life-threatening opposition or hardship (cf. Acts 20.29). Paul does refer to being subject to 'beatings, imprisonments and riots' (2 Cor. 6.5), and to being 'in prison more frequently' (2 Cor. 11.23). Interestingly, Paul's imprisonment at Philippi is the first recorded in Acts (16.19-40). If it be granted that Acts does not provide an exhaustive catalogue of Paul's experiences, one must answer whether these imprisonments which Paul mentions would have allowed him sufficient time to write the correspondence which constitutes the Captivity Epistles.

In further support of an Ephesian imprisonment, it is argued that Ephesus was the nearest city to which the runaway slave Onesimus could abscond on foot, and the shortest route from Colosse (Col. 4.12; Phlm. 23) and Philippi (Phil. 2.25-30) to visit Paul. Ephesus also provided a natural hub around which Paul's helpers would gather (Col.

---

[58] Colossians, Philemon, and Philippians complete this group.

[59] H. Lisco, A. Deissmann, W. Michaelis, and G.S. Duncan lead a group of scholars that champion an Ephesian captivity of Paul.

[60] Heinrich G. Paulus, Ernst H. Lohmeyer, Heinrich A. Meyer, and Van Roon are proponents of the Caesarean captivity theory.

4.10-11) and from which correspondence could be more easily distributed to the cities in the Lycus Valley.

A Caesarean origin of Ephesians finds some strong advocates. For two years Paul was confined in Herod's palace at Caesarea Maritima (Acts 24.23), a pawn of Felix the Roman governor. Afforded the privilege of entertaining visitors, Paul, it is believed, had the time and freedom to write. It is highly debatable, however, whether Paul would have been able to prosecute at this venue the ministry he describes in Phil. 1.14-20. What is more, Paul's hope of a release, reflected in his request to Philemon for lodging (Phlm. 22), argues against Caesarea, where any hope of release hinged on paying Felix a bribe – something Paul refused to do (Acts 24.26). Paul expressed no hope of release under Festus, Felix's successor. Rather, he appealed his case to Caesar – hence his subsequent journey to Rome.

Advocates of a Caesarean imprisonment further assert that Caesarea, which was some five hundred miles away, would have been a more attractive option for the runaway slave Onesimus since it was farther away than Ephesus, but not as far away as Rome. The unanswered question is whether Caesarea would have afforded the safety and security a runaway slave needed. The traditional theory of a Roman imprisonment has been highly attractive among scholars historically, its authoritative persuasiveness being undergirded by the history of the church, external and internal evidence, and a well-reasoned and consistent logic.

Destination

Determining a specific destination for Ephesians is a legitimate problem noted even in some modern Bible translations (NEB, NIV, RSV, GNB). Questions in this regard largely stem from the omission of the words at Ephesus (1:1) from the earliest and presumably the most reliable Greek manuscripts. They do not appear in the second-century Chester Beatty papyrus ($\mathbf{p}^{46}$) or in the fourth-century Vaticanus (B) and Sinaiticus (ℵ) codices. Marcion in the middle of the second century considered Ephesians to have been addressed to the Laodiceans. Neither Origen in the third century nor Basil in the fourth indicated any knowledge of the words at Ephesus in the salutation.

That Paul spent about three years of missionary service at Ephesus is clearly attested by Luke (Acts 20.31). In his final meeting with the Ephesian elders deep, mutual affection is shared (Acts 20.17-38). Yet, the apostle writes Ephesians as though a stranger to the believers, circumstances, and events related to the church (1.15; 2.2-3; 4.21). While he greets a large number of believers at Rome (Rom. 16.1-16), a church he never founded or visited, the absence of personal greetings and reminiscences in Ephesians, and the remote distance from which he speaks to the recipients, present an awkwardness.

How does one reconcile the conflicting theories concerning the Epistle's destination? The following explanations have been offered. The first argues for an Ephesian destination. Based upon the long tradition of the Christian church, it holds that Paul addressed the Epistle directly to the Ephesians, but intentionally cast it in a form suitable to neighboring churches. The Ephesian destination has in its favor the wide geographical distribution of Greek manuscripts that include 'in Ephesus'. Furthermore, not only is no other city mentioned in manuscripts of this Epistle, but the prescript 'To the Ephesians' appears in every manuscript.

Adolf von Harnack championed the theory that Laodicea was the original destination of Ephesians. Because of the unfavorable publicity Laodicea received in Revelation (3.14-22), the name was erased and that of Ephesus put in its place. No manuscript with a Laodicean destination has been found, however. Conversely, Paul's admonition that the Colossian letter be read in the Laodicean church and the Laodicean letter in turn be read in the Colossian church (Col. 4.16), has been construed by some to mean that Ephesians is the so-called letter from Laodicea.

The encyclical theory, first proposed by Theodore Beza at the end of the sixteenth century and popularized by Archbishop James Ussher in the seventeenth, holds that Ephesians was a circular letter intended for the various churches in Proconsul Asia of which Ephesus was the chief. It was the fact of Ephesus' eminence among the cities in Asia that caused its name to become attached to the letter. This view, though highly conjectural, has a lot to commend it.[61] A circular theory without a specific address of any kind may be supported by the general address, 'to the saints who are faithful in Christ Jesus' (1.1). It is not beyond possibility that Paul's original, or a copy of it, found its way to Ephesus and that, subsequently, the letter became identified with the city. 'In Ephesus' was probably inserted during the process of manuscript copying,[62] and all subsequent copies in all likelihood derived from it. To take the idea further and suggest that a blank space was left in v. 1 for Tychicus, its bearer, to add his own comments (see 6.21) or for each church to fill in its own name, detracts from the merit of the argument since the very preposition *at/in* is omitted from the original salutation.

---

[61] MacDonald contends there is nothing in the Epistle to suggest it was meant for more than one church community (*Colossians and Ephesians*, p. 17).

[62] Klein, *Ephesians*, p. 35.

Scrupulous examination has led to the conclusion that in view of the fact that 'in Ephesus' has overwhelming external evidence supportive of its inclusion, internal evidence should be given a less determinative role.[63] What is more, Ephesus is the name that appears in all the extant manuscripts with a city inserted.[64] While this traditional view of an Ephesian destination of the Epistle has a long history of ardent supporters and well-reasoned arguments have been advanced in its defense, we must conclude that it is not entirely conclusive – nor is any other theory.

Date

If written from confinement in Ephesus, the Epistle may be dated between 54 and 57 CE; if Caesarea Maritima, 59-61 CE. Based upon firm patristic evidence, the traditional view holds that the Prison Epistles likely share a common date during the first imprisonment of Paul in Rome – probably between 62 and 64 CE – and a common bearer. Upon returning Onesimus to his master, Paul entrusted to his care a personal letter to his master Philemon, and a letter to the church at Colosse to the care of his coworker Tychicus (Col. 4.7-9). Opponents of Pauline authorship date the Epistle anywhere from 70 CE, if 2.14 is taken as a reference to the literal destruction of the Temple, to 170 CE, based upon alleged linguistic and historical considerations. Some date Ephesians about 90 CE, the supposed date for the collection of the Pauline corpus. Since Clement of Rome cites it, it must be dated earlier than 95 CE, which rules out a second-century date. It is reasonable to assume that Paul wrote the Epistle early during his confinement, probably 61 or 62 CE while under guard in rental quarters (Acts 28.30), based on the fact that Ephesians does not allude to his release from prison, as do Philippians (1.19-26) and Philemon (v. 22) – captivity Epistles written during the same period. The traditional view has much to commend it.

Scholars may never agree on all the 'critical' internal and external matters of Ephesians. That should not, however, diminish the value, significance, and authority of the Epistle. Ephesians' uniqueness or elusiveness may well mirror 'Paul's vision for a universal and unified church consisting of Jewish and Gentile believers'.[65]

---

[63] Hoehner, *Ephesians*, p. 146.
[64] Hoehner, *Ephesians*, pp. 147-48.
[65] Arthur G. Patzia, *Ephesians, Colossians, Philemon* (NIBC; Peabody, MA: Hendrickson, 2004), p. 141.

The Literary Structure of Ephesians

Like other letters of Paul, Ephesians divides into two distinct, though not unrelated, halves – chs. 1–3 and 4–6. Setting forth truths related to God's redemptive plan that spans eternity past, the present, and eternity future, the first half is commonly viewed as the doctrinal or theological section, and the second the practical or ethical. A eulogy praising God for lavishing on his people the riches of redemption accomplished in Christ (vv. 3-14), comprising a lengthy benediction and prayer extolling the achievement of God's eternal purposes in Christ introduces chs. 1–3. The intricate interweaving of prayer, worship, and doctrine in chs. 1–3 instructs us that good theologizing is done in an attitude of prayer with God's glory as its chief goal. In addition to serving as a celebratory thanksgiving, the introduction cradles many of the key ideas Paul will later enlarge upon in the body of the letter.

In chs. 1–3, Paul presents the divine plan of salvation as the cooperative activity of the triune God. God, the 'Father of our Lord Jesus Christ' (1.3), is the fountain, source, and goal of every spiritual blessing (1.6, 12, 14); the Son the sphere and mediator of such blessing (1.3, 4, 9-11); and the Spirit the seal of promised blessings (1.13, 14). For the double alienation the Gentiles have experienced (from God and from Israel) God has expressed salvation in a twofold way: first, in resurrecting them from spiritual death to new life in Christ (2.1-10) and, secondly, reconciling a formerly estranged people to a new family whose father is God and making them a holy temple in which he lives (2.11-22). The contents of ch. 3 reveal striking parallels with ch. 1 (cf. 3.2-13 and 1.3-14; 3.14-21 and 1.15-23).

The practical half of Ephesians (chs. 4–6) transitions from doctrine to duty, from exposition to exhortation. While doctrine carries some implicit ethical demand and ethics some instruction, it is instructive that only one imperative appears thus far in the letter (remember, 2.11). In the five major parts of the ethical section (paraenesis), however, Paul uses the term 'walk' or 'live' (NIV) five times (4.1, 17; 5.2, 8,15), the first four of which are commands. Christian living has biblical teaching as its foundation. Behavior is informed by one's belief. The two are inseparable. Paul's burden in this section is preservation of the unity of the church and the winsome and wise living of the Christians before a hostile pagan world.

The Church at Ephesus

Ephesians is unique among Paul's letters. It is addressed to no specific church, nor are its recipients acquainted with the apostle personally (1.13, 15, 16). Christianity probably reached Ephesus ahead of Paul.

His second missionary journey completed, Paul left Greece bound for Syria and ultimately Jerusalem. He made a brief stopover at Ephesus, where he left Priscilla and Aquila, who had accompanied him from Corinth (Acts 18.18-21). Before Paul returned, the eloquent Alexandrian Jew, Apollos, visited Ephesus and taught boldly and accurately about Jesus in the synagogue. Inviting him to their home after this, Priscilla and Aquila 'explained to him the way of God more adequately' (18.26). When Apollos decided to move on to Achaia, the Ephesian believers 'encouraged him and wrote to the disciples [Christians] there to welcome him' (18.27). Upon Paul's return to Ephesus, 'he found some disciples and asked them, 'Did you receive the Holy Spirit when you believed'? (19.1, 2).

By whom and when was the gospel first brought to Ephesus? It might be the fruit of Paul's labor over a three-year period, probably 54-57 CE (Acts 20.31), but no unequivocal answer can be given. There is no evidence that it was the effort of the Asian Jews present at Pentecost (Acts 2.9). What can at least be said with some degree of certainty is that Paul consolidated the work, organized the church, and expanded its outreach during the three years he spent there (Acts 20.31).[66]

In keeping with his usual missionary strategy, Paul began his ministry at Ephesus in the synagogue. Fierce opposition compelled him to discontinue and to engage in a two-year ministry centered in the lecture hall of Tyrannus (19.8-10), a philosopher or rhetorician about whom very little is known. Vital years these! The hall of Tyrannus became a nerve center for discipleship training, and Ephesus a spiritual beacon that radiated beyond the city limits into the far-flung reaches of the province (19.10). The worship of Artemis suffered debilitating setbacks (19.26), and the magical arts devastating reversals during this time (19.18-19). Driven from the city by violent opposition, Paul did not return to Ephesus again until after his release from his first Roman imprisonment (1 Tim. 1.3).

For a long time, the Ephesian church served as mother and leader to the other churches in the province of Asia, and would later play a significant role in early ecclesiastical history. Regrettably, Paul's worst fears of wolves savaging the church after his departure (Acts 20.29-31) came true, confirmed by Jesus' scathing indictment of the church some thirty years later. 'Remember the height from which you have fallen! Repent and do the things you did at first. If you do not repent, I will come to you and remove your lampstand from its place' (Rev. 2.5).

[66] Acts 19.10 says two years – actually two years and three months when the three months of synagogue ministry are added (19.8). The Jews reckoned any part of a year as a full year, hence three years (20.31).

Jesus' words apparently fell upon deaf ears. The lampstand was removed, and spiritual darkness blanketed the city.

Outline of the Epistle

The following outline will help conceptualize the structure and flow of Paul's thought throughout the Epistle.

I.   Salutation (1.1-2)

II.   The Church's Doctrine (1.3–3.21)

    A.   Salvation: God's Plan of the Ages (1.3-23)
    B.   Salvation: Humankind's Privilege in Christ (2.1-10)
    C.   The Church: A New Inclusive Community (2.11-22)
    D.   The Church: A Mystery Disclosed (3.1-13)
    E.   Paul's Prayer for the Church (3.14-19)
    F.   Doxology (3.20-21)

III.   The Church's Duty: Live Worthily of God's Call (4.1–6.24)

    A.   The Church: A Community Called to Divine Purpose (4.1-16)
    B.   The Church: A Community that Practices Purity (4.17-24)
    C.   The Church: A Community that Promotes Integrity (4.25-29)
    D.   The Church: A Community that Propagates Forgiveness (4.30-32)
    E.   The Church: A Spirit-filled Community (5.1–6.9)
    F.   The Church: A Community at War (6.10-20)
    G.   Closing Greetings (6.21-24)

Significant Themes

Of its 2,429 words, Ephesians contains 40 *hapax legomena* (unique instances of words) found nowhere else in the New Testament. No single problem dominates the Epistle. No heresy commands its central focus. The term *one* occurring fourteen times,[67] especially in chs. 2 and 4, strikes a dominant note of unity that reverberates throughout much of the Epistle. A reconciled and united universal church of Jews and Gentiles in Christ, both a miracle and marvel of divine grace alone, recurs with unwearying regularity. The indispensable basis for unity, love, in

---

[67] Eph. 2.14, 15, 16, 18; 4.4, 5, 6, 7, 16; 5.33. The term 'unity' (ἑνότης), used only in this Epistle, appears in 4.3, 13.

both its verb and noun forms appears twenty times, eleven[68] of which describe the believers' love for each other. But Paul's notion of oneness reaches beyond the church to encompass all creation (1.10, 22, 23). No one can read Ephesians without noticing its unique ecclesiology. Where 1 Corinthians emphasizes the indivisibility of the body and Colossians accentuates Christ's headship over the church, Ephesians stresses the church as the Body of Christ, but a body inseparable from, interdependent with, and inextricably united to its head. The picture of the universal nature and scope of the church in Ephesians is inescapable.

Fittingly in support of this theme, the idea of God as Father is found eight times in Ephesians, more than in Paul's other letters, and Christ the agent to whom reference is made thirty-four times with the phrase 'in Christ', or 'in whom'. The word *all* appears no fewer than fifty times, suggestive of diversity in unity and unity amidst diversity. Purity is an inescapable theme, especially in the ethical section. Echoes of Christ's triumph over evil powers on behalf of the church and believers' present position of victory fill the Epistle. The overarching theme of the Ephesians is God's eternal redemptive purpose and the role of Christ and the church as his Body in it.[69]

Significant Words

'Heavenly realms' (ἐπουράνιος) appears five times in Ephesians (1.3, 20; 2.6; 3.10; 6.12) and nowhere else in the writings of Paul. Particularly evident in Ephesians, and in keeping with the theme of unity in the Epistle, is the use of the preposition 'with' (σύν) with a number of compound words denoting the believers' union with Christ and joint and equal sharing of Jews and Gentiles in the benefits of salvation. 'Unity,' ἑνότης, used nowhere else in the NT, occurs in 4.3 and 4.13.

English Term	Greek Term	Location
Made (us) alive with (Christ)	συζωοποιέω	2.5
Raised (us) up with (Christ)	συνεγείρω	2.6
Seated (us) with (him)	συνκαθίζω	2.6
Joined together	συναρμολογέω	2.21; 4.16
Being built together	συνοικοδομέω	2.22
Joint heirs	συγκληρονόμος	3.6
Joint members of the body	σύσσωμος	3.6
Joint partners	συμμέτοχος	3.6
Held together	συμβιβάζω	4.16

---

[68] This is quite instructive considering that the verb form, which occurs ten times in this Epistle (nine in the practical section), is found only thirty-four times in all (both the capital and disputed) of Paul's writings.

[69] Some scholars see unity as the primary theme.

The Holy Spirit

Ephesians is an Epistle of the Spirit.[70] Direct mention of 'Spirit' is made no fewer than twelve times, each chapter bearing vital testimony to the Holy Spirit's variegated ministry. His divinity is clearly affirmed in 4.30, Paul warning not to 'grieve the Holy Spirit of God, with whom you were sealed for the day of redemption'. Consonant with the rest of the New Testament, Paul views the coming of the Spirit as the sign of the last days of which Joel prophesied. 'In the last days, God says, I will pour out my Spirit on all people. Your sons and daughters will prophesy...' (Acts 2.16-21; cf. Joel 2.28-32). The last days constitute the present era. Inaugurated by the death and resurrection of Christ, it is the age of the Holy Spirit characterized by universal and singular activity of the Spirit in salvation, miracles, and signs and wonders.

The Spirit's role is central in the three concerns that govern the letter – God's redeeming and reconciling Jew and Gentile, Christ's defeat of evil powers on behalf of the church, and that God's people maintain the unity of the Spirit. Paul introduces the first of these in 1.11-14 and expands upon it in 2.11-22 and 3.1-13. Believers' present involvement in Christ's triumph over malevolent forces by the Holy Spirit is a theme diffused throughout the Epistle. Finally, the redeemed and reconciled people of God, who have become one through a common experience of the Spirit, maintain that unity by the way they conduct their lives corporately in both their public (worship) and domestic relationship (4.1–5.20; 5.21–6.9).

In fulfillment of the prophecy of Jeremiah, the Spirit now writes God's law 'not on tablets of stone but on tablets of human hearts' (2 Cor. 3.3), and makes God's servants competent ministers of the gospel. Giving life, righteousness, and freedom is his work (2 Cor. 3.6-18).

Part of the Spirit's function is to impart both life and light to the believer and the community of faith. As both 'seal' and 'guarantee' of God's promises to the church, 'the promised Holy Spirit' (1.13, NIV) insures and assures that we are God's possession, and guarantees the future resurrection and glorious inheritance of the people of God (1.14; cf. 4.30 and Rom. 8.9-28). This truth, along with the Spirit's baptism of believers into the body of Christ (4.4-5; cf. 1 Cor. 12.13), is Paul's distinctive contribution to the work of the Holy Spirit that beams through Ephesians.

It is the Holy Spirit who enlightens to divine truth (1.17-18; 3.5), and makes access to God possible (2.18). He it is who empowers Christian living (3.16), and has baptized us into one corporate body

---

[70] Of the fourteen occurrences of Spirit/spirit in Ephesians only two refer to the human spirit. Gordon Fee believes the Pauline nature of Ephesians' theology is most evident in its 'Spirit materials'. *God's Empowering Presence*, p.660.

(4.4-5). Christian worship and witness are inspired by the Spirit (5.18-20). Effective use of the sword of the Spirit – the word of God – is possible only through him (6.17). The Spirit it is who makes praying effectual (6.18). Finally, revealing the person and message of Jesus and enabling believers to be like Jesus is the abiding work of the third person of the Trinity.

Believers are exhorted to be 'filled with the Spirit' (5.18). 'Filled' translates the Greek present tense, which indicates a habitual experience of being under the control of the Spirit. Spirit-fullness yields both liturgical and ethical results, inspiring worship (5.18-20), and enabling victorious Christ-like living (5.21-33). The Spirit glorifies the Father through the Son (5.20). Holy by nature, he also makes people holy.

Ephesians 1

I. Salutation (1.1-2)

As in every age, letter-writing in the Greco-Roman world conformed to a standard form – the prescript identifying the writer and readers, followed by a greeting and wish or prayer for health. Paul adopts and adapts this method in all his letters, but elevates it to a higher level by christianizing it, filling common, customary greetings with Christian content and describing both writer and readers from the perspective of their relationship to God. His salutation rises above the usual wish for good health to a sacerdotal entreaty for the recipients' personal experience of God's favor and *shalom*. Ephesians is no exception in this regard. More than a letter to meet the present needs of a local church, however, Ephesians at many points has the air of a sermon, the holy hush of a prayer, and the surging climax of a doxology.

In all thirteen of his Epistles Paul identifies himself by his Roman name. *Paulus* is the Latin counterpart of the Hebrew שָׁאוּל, Saul, associated with the verb 'to ask'. Adopted by the apostle early in his first missionary journey (Acts 13.6-12), perhaps as a mark of identification with his Gentile readers, the name means 'little'. The second-century apocryphal work, *The Acts of Paul and Thecla*, describes Paul as a short man. Sicilians were fond of the name. As a Roman citizen Paul would have had three names (praenomen, nomen, and cognomen, similar to our first, middle, and last name in the West), but chose not to use them all – perhaps in deference to the many lower-class Gentiles whom he served.

In all of his Epistles, except Philippians, 1 and 2 Thessalonians and Philemon, he begins his letters by mentioning his apostleship. By doing this he establishes his authority and apostolic credentials, elicits respect for, and legitimates his message and ministry. Probably an erstwhile member of the Sanhedrin (Acts 9.1, 2; 22.4, 5; 26.10-12), he is now, however, an apostle[1] of Christ, an authorized agent and representative of Jesus Christ. The word 'apostle' designates a representative, a commissioned messenger, an envoy. It approximates the Latin *mitto* (send) from which the word 'missionary' derives, and conveys the idea of the

---

[1] The term is not restricted to the Twelve and Paul, but is used also of Barnabas, Apollos, and Timothy (Acts 14.14; 1 Cor. 4.6, 9; Phil. 2.25; 1 Thess. 2.6; 1 Cor. 15.7). While the office of the original Twelve and Paul is irreplaceable the function continues with some modern missionaries and church leaders.

Hebrew שליח – which signifies one sent with the master's authority and in the master's name, and equipped with his power to carry out his assignment. The modern concept of power of attorney approximates the meaning. In modern Hebrew *shaliach* is the term for an ambassador.

Paul is a person under royal orders from heaven. He is no loose cannon, no maverick. He is called, commissioned, and authorized by divine appointment to represent Christ in the gospel (Gal. 1.1, 11-12). An apostle 'by the will of God', he is not his own; he belongs to another and answers to another – namely Jesus Christ, from whom he has received grace and apostleship (Rom 1.5; Gal. 1.1). To him is given responsibility; from him accountability is expected.

The saints in Ephesus[2] are the addressees of the Epistle and are further described as 'faithful in Christ'. 'Saint' translates ἅγιος, 'holy'. One of Paul's commonest descriptions of believers (Rom. 1.1; 1 Cor. 1.1, 2; 2 Cor. 1.1; Phil. 1.1), the designation harks back to the Old Testament where Israel is described as God's holy people (Exod. 19.6) and appointed to serve him, but is now applied to an international community composed of former pagans and Jews, transformed by the miracle of divine grace to become the Israel of God (Gal. 6.16).

To be holy is to be separated from defilement and dedicated to the purposes of God. As God's people, saints are a holy people – though not a perfect people. It is instructive that Paul uses the plural 'saints'. God's people are saints not in isolation, but in fellowship. Sainthood is both a present reality and a future goal, both being and becoming for all believers. 'No man is ... a believer who is not also a saint; and, on the other hand, no man is a saint who is not a believer'.[3] Not only are Christians saints, they are also faithful. Related to the verb πιστεύω, the adjective πιστός, which is rendered 'faithful', carries the ideas of trustworthiness and dependability.

Of the 529 occurrences of the word 'Christ' in the New Testament, 379 are found in Paul's writings. It appears forty-six times in Ephesians and, along with its equivalents, no fewer than fifteen times in the first fourteen verses of ch. 1. 'Christ' (χριστός) derives from the verb χρίω, whose Hebrew counterpart (משח) means 'to anoint/smear' (with oil), and was used for the anointing of individuals chosen by God (such as kings, priests, and prophets) to perform special tasks. The title 'Christ' in both Greek and Hebrew means 'the Anointed One'. Jesus was God's anointed and empowered representative sent to earth on a redemptive mission.

---

[2] For the views regarding the recipients and destination of the letter, see the introduction.

[3] John Calvin, *The Epistles of Paul and the Apostles to the Galatians, Ephesians, Philippians and Colossians,* trans. T.H.L. Parker (Grand Rapids: Eerdmans, 1974), p. 123.

The term 'in Christ' ('in whom' or 'in him') occurs 11 times, and refers to the believer's vital union with and incorporation into Christ – 'as branches are to the vine and members to the body'.[4] Believers are situated in various geographical locations but spiritually united in Christ. More than any other of Paul's writings, Ephesians centers upon the believer's union with Christ, referenced thirty-six times in the Epistle. The phrase 'points to the closest of unions with the Savior. Christians are people whose entire lives are bound up with Christ'.[5] All of God's accomplishments for his people, and from which he derives praise, have been achieved in and through Christ.[6]

Borrowing the customary Greek and Hebrew secular greetings, 'grace' and 'peace' (v. 2), Paul fills them with Christian and theological content. Of the 155 times it is found in the New Testament, 'grace' appears 100 times in Paul's writings, twelve of which are in Ephesians. 'Peace' occurs in the Epistle seven times. Grace and joy are closely related in Greek (χάρις and χαρά respectively), intimating that the elemental notion in grace is 'that which causes joy'.[7] Grace is God's free saving initiative, his unearned favor, undeserved mercy bestowed on undeserving sinners. It expresses the reason for and manner of God's initiative toward lost humankind (Eph. 2.5, 7, 8). For the writers of the New Testament, peace was not merely the absence of conflict. The Hebrew *shalom* that lies behind εἰρήνη, peace, expresses well-being, wholeness, reconciliation, and prosperity – all flowing from a right relationship with God.

Christ is God's grace embodied (Tit. 2.11). He is also 'our peace' (Eph. 2.14), who has 'made peace' through the cross (2.15) and came and 'preached peace' (2.17). Grace and peace find their source in 'God our Father and the Lord Jesus Christ'. 'God' adumbrates the majesty, awesomeness, transcendence, and power of this deity. 'Father' intimates his nearness, his tenderness, his accessibility.

II. The Church's Doctrine (1.3–3.21)

A. Salvation: God's Plan of the Ages (1.3-23)
Verses 3-23. This section gives a broad sweep of the redemptive work of the triune God from eternity to eternity. God's plan for human redemption, conceived in eternity (vv. 3-5, 9, 11), includes all that

---

[4] John R.W. Stott, *The Message of Ephesians* (Leicester, UK/ Downer's Grove, IL: InterVarsity, 1979), p. 22.

[5] Leon Morris, *Expository Reflections on the Letter to the Ephesians* (Grand Rapids: Baker Books, 1994), pp. 11-12.

[6] Peter O'Brien, *The Letter to the* Ephesians (Pillar New Testament Commentary; Grand Rapids, MI: Eerdmans / Cambridge, UK: Apollos, 1999), 90.

[7] Morris, *Expository Reflections on the Letter to the Ephesians*, p. 12.

exists in heaven and earth and has the glory of God as its aim. This plan is achieved in history in Christ (vv. 6-8, 11-14), who is the mediator of all of God's blessings, and will be consummated in Christ when history ends (v. 10). The Spirit is both seal and pledge, authenticating and validating the Christian experience and guaranteeing that God's promises to his people will be realized (vv. 13-14).

In Greek twelve verses of 202 words (3-14) forming an extended *berakah* (eulogy, doxology; cf. 2 Cor. 1.3-4; 1 Pet. 1.3-5) are squeezed into a single sentence to give voice to a heart overflowing with adoration, gratitude, and joyous praise to God for every spiritual blessing he has bestowed upon his people in Christ (v. 3). Unfettered, unpunctuated, uninterrupted, Paul's words cascade from his lips in one continuous torrent. *Berakoth* (eulogies) of this nature are reminiscent of the cult and Israel's worship (1 Kgs 8.15, 56), later with the more elaborate liturgy of the Psalter (e.g. Ps. 41.13; 72.19-20), and rabbinic Judaism (cf. The Eighteen Benedictions). Ephesians 1.3-14 contains many of the concepts upon which Paul will later elaborate in the Epistle, but more importantly it throbs with Paul's heartfelt desire that the praise that rises in his spirit to God for his gracious purposes in Christ may spill over to the Asian believers and that they in turn would glorify God in like manner.

This effusive benediction – a 'rhapsodic adoration' – begins with the term 'blessed' (εὐλογητός, = Heb. ברוח, v. 3). It is a word applied only to God and found nowhere in classical Greek. For persons who are deemed blessed the participle εὐλογημένος is employed. The difference in meanings is not contrived. God is by nature blessed, and is worthy to be praised for who he is and what he does. Humans bless (εὐλογέω) him by praising him, and are blessed when they receive the good gifts (εὐλογία) he bestows. Paul calls the divine benefactor 'God and Father' (v. 3), presenting a perfect picture of his transcendence and nearness, his greatness and goodness, his power and love. A balance every healthy theology will maintain!

1. Salvation Anticipated – the Father (1.3-6)

This God and Father, here depicted as the conceiver of salvation, 'has blessed us in the heavenly realms with every spiritual blessing in Christ'. 'Heavenly realms' (ἐπουρανίοις) appears five times in Ephesians (1.3, 20; 2.6; 3.10; 6.12) and nowhere else in Paul's writings. The term refers to a place of victory where the exalted Christ, seated (1.20) and believers seated with him (2.6), pours out spiritual blessing (1.3); the sphere where malevolent powers rule (3.10; 6.12). Since it is a place of spiritual conflict for believers (6.12), it cannot refer to heaven or any physical spatial realm. Nor can the adjective, which functions here as a noun, refer to people (as in 1 Cor. 15.48). 'Heavenly realms' or 'heavenly places' rather than 'heavenly beings' is the best translation of the Greek, and depicts a realm of spiritual conquest and conflict (cf. Job 1.6-12; Dan. 10.13, 20).

But to what does it refer precisely? Some regard the term as designating 'the unseen world of spiritual reality'[8] relating to the events of salvation seen from Paul's eschatological perspective. Thus in keeping with the Jewish two-age structure, heaven 'is seen from the perspective of the age to come, which has now been inaugurated'.[9] The heavenly realms are not merely a future that bursts upon us beyond life's veil; it is a sphere of conquest in which believers presently experience Christ's victory and blessings and also simultaneously engage in spiritual conflict.

God is the origin and source of every blessing that comes to his people (v. 3). He has blessed us (v. 3), he chose us, (v. 4) predestined us (v. 5), and 'begraced us' (v. 6). The doctrine of election cradled here has its background in the Old Testament, beginning with God's gracious choice of Abraham whom he blessed to be a blessing to all the peoples of the earth (Gen. 12.1-3). From among the nations he chose Israel to be his prized possession (Deut. 7.6-8; 14.2) – a privilege that is now shared by Christians.

Paul delineates the reality ('God has blessed us'), site ('in the heavenly realms'), scope and nature ('with every spiritual blessing'), and the sphere ('in Christ') of God's blessings to his people (v. 3). This encapsulates every blessing of salvation 'from eternal election to eternal glory'.[10] God has withheld nothing from his children. He has provided and placed everything at their disposal.

It is unlikely that by 'spiritual' Paul here means the gift of the Spirit himself (Acts 19.1-7), the gifts of the Spirit (1 Cor. 12), or simply the opposite of material. (In the OT God's blessings to Israel were primarily material.) Ephesians is a book of the Spirit, and salvation is a Trinitarian work in which the Spirit participates. In eternity God made the believer his choice. Through the cross, Jesus put that decision into effect in history, and through the conviction of the Holy Spirit it becomes an individual and personal experience. Reflective of the nature of Ephesians, 'spiritual' (πνευματική) refers to 'Spirit blessings, blessings that pertain to the Spirit' through whom 'God appropriates to the believing

---

[8] Stott, *The Message of Ephesians*, p. 35.

[9] O'Brien, *Ephesians*, p. 97; Witherington does not see much difference between 'in the heavens' and 'in the heavenlies', the latter reflective of 'a piece of Asiatic epideictic rhetoric' which is more impressive (*Captivity Epistles*, p. 232).

[10] Bruce, *Colossians, Philemon, Ephesians*, p. 254.

community the "blessings" that flow from the redemptive work of Christ'.[11] What Ephesians clearly teaches, but is echoed elsewhere in Scripture, is that the blessings the Father purposed are provided in the Son and procured through the Spirit. Spiritual blessings bequeathed upon the saints are 'Spirit-communicated'.[12] Paul describes some of these blessings in 1.4-14. Under the old covenant, God's promised blessings to compliant Israel were primarily material (Deut. 28.1-14). His blessings under the new covenant are distinctively spiritual, though not exclusively so (Phil. 4.19).

All of God's benefits come through Christ the head to his children who are his body. The phrase 'in Christ,' together with its related cognates, depicts Christ as the sphere, agency, and means by which God's blessings come to us. Christians share a most intimate union with Christ. As the body draws life from the head, so the believer draws life from Christ. Whatever happens to the head also happens to the body (Acts 9.4-5). Paul later adopted and developed the head-body metaphor and made it basic to his ecclesiology and Christology (1 Cor. 12.12, 27; Eph. 1.22-23). Believers share all the experiences of Christ their head.

Resembling elements of synagogue liturgy and practice and probably Christian tradition, 1.3-14 with its Trinitarian structure may have been a source for the Apostles' and Nicene creeds. Reference to the Trinity testifies to the importance of human salvation and the divine investment in it: the Father electing (vv. 4-6), the Son saving (vv. 7-12), and the Spirit sealing (vv. 13-14), each stanza ending with the catchphrase 'to the praise of his glory' (vv. 6, 12, 14). It is because of the Father's selecting (vv. 4-6), the Son's sacrifice (vv. 7-12), and the Spirit's sealing (vv. 7-12) that believers are blessed.[13] The entire context of 1.3-14 clearly underscores the primacy of God's role in salvation, his absolute autonomy and unfettered freedom in his purpose, decisions, and actions being repeatedly emphasized throughout.

In vv. 4 and 5 Paul introduces two truths that are both crucial to and controversial in God's saving program – election and predestination. He states in v. 4 that 'God chose us in him [Christ] before the creation of the world'.[14] 'Chose' translates ἐξελέξατο, derived from the

---

[11] Fee, *God's Empowering Presence*, pp. 666, 667. See also Charles Hodge, *A Commentary on the Epistle to the Ephesians* (Thornapple Commentaries; Grand Rapids: Baker, 1980), p. 28.

[12] Ruth Paxon, *The Wealth, Walk and Warfare of the Christian* (Westwood, NJ: Revell, 1939), p. 26.

[13] John F. Walvoord and Roy B. Zuck, eds., *The Bible Knowledge Commentary* (2nd ed., Colorado Springs: Victor, 2000), p. 616.

[14] Creation/foundation of the world translates καταβολὴ κόσμου, a common expression in Second Temple Judaism and early Christianity. Denoting God's creative work in

root ἐκλέγομαι, which refers to God's gracious initiative in eternity in saving those who would believe in Christ. This term belongs to a word family which has the basic meaning of 'to gather' and by extension 'to say, speak'. The middle voice (ἐκλέγομαι) connotes choosing or picking out,[15] and in the NT primarily refers to people, although it is sometimes used of things (Lk. 10.42; 14.7). The middle voice when used in the NT stresses 'the relation of the person chosen to the special purpose of him who chooses',[16] in the Eph. 2.4 depicting God as the primary actor in the choice. The term often alludes to selection for a position of service, and is used of Jesus' twelve disciples (Lk. 6.13; cf. Mk 3.13-14), Jesus himself as the Elect One (Lk. 9.35), and the church as his elect people (1 Pet. 1.1; 2.9).

'Predestine' (v. 5) renders προορίζω, which means to define, determine or mark out something or someone beforehand. The participial form used here (προορίσας), modifying the verb 'chose' (ἐξελέξατο), is best taken as modal and expresses the way God's election is exhibited. Closely related to election and far from being a cold-hearted determinism, it means that God's loving choice was in his eternal purpose. The doctrine of election originated neither with Augustine of Hippo nor Calvin of Geneva. It courses through the whole Bible, pulsing steadily in the writings of Paul like blood through a vein. God's choice of Abraham whom he blessed to be a blessing to all the peoples of the earth (Gen. 12.1-3; cf. Deut. 7.6-8; 14.2) set in motion a strategy of redemptive commerce with earth. God chose Isaac over Ishmael and Jacob over Esau. Without any merit on its part, he elected Israel from among the nations to be his prized possession to accomplish his eternal designs.

Election in the NT knows neither personal nor national boundaries. A choice God made in eternity based upon his own love and free decision, it does not abrogate human will. A pre-temporal election of individual humans is here ruled out; rather election and destining are corporate. Just as Israel was God's elect nation and anyone in Israel was part of God's elect people, so God has chosen Christ and all who are in him based on their response to the gospel.[17] Scripture teaches, without discussion or resolution of the mystery, both the place of God's sover-

---

the beginning (Gen. 1.1), it derives from the laying of stones in a foundation or the depositing of a seed in the ground, and thus the point from which historical dates can be calculated. See the *NIV Theological Dictionary of New Testament Words*, ed. Verlyn Verbrugge (Grand Rapids: Zondervan, 2000), pp. 653-54; Thielman, *Ephesians*, p. 48.

[15] Joseph H. Thayer, *A Greek-English Lexicon of the New Testament* (Grand Rapids: Zondervan, 1974), p. 196.

[16] Brooke Foss Westcott, *Saint Paul's Epistle to the Ephesians* (Minneapolis: Klock & Klock, 1978), p. 8.

[17] Witherington, *Captivity Epistles*, pp. 234-35.

eign choice and human freedom and responsibility (Jn 6.37; 15.16; Rom. 8.29; 2 Thess. 2.13; 2 Tim. 1.9; 1 Pet. 1.2). An adequate biblical theology will maintain this balance, over-emphasizing neither to the diminution of the other. Both truths should be equally received, valued, and proclaimed. Scripture nowhere teaches that God has predestined some people to heaven and others to hell (double predestination). Predestination applies only to the people of God, and does not of necessity presume the rejection and condemnation of the lost (reprobation).

For Paul, election implies a goal and purpose: 'to be holy and blameless in his sight' (v. 4). With this great privilege comes a great responsibility. Far from giving a false sense of smug complacency to sin, far from encouraging moral laxity, election places an ethical demand upon the Christian.

God's goal and purpose in election is not merely to restore what Adam lost or to repair the damage sin caused, but to fashion a new humanity that bears the perfect resemblance of Christ (Rom. 8.29-30). His 'predestinating love' is 'commended more by those who lead holy and Christ-like lives' than by those who engage in 'logic-chopping'.[18] It is not without significance that the 'holy and blameless' couplet recurs elsewhere in Paul (Eph. 5.27; Col. 1.22) in the context of the *parousia* – the second coming of Christ. Paul is here teaching a truth that echoes in Heb. 12.14, 'without holiness no one will see the Lord'.

As the purpose of election is to live a holy and blameless life so the goal of predestination is adoption (or sonship) and 'the praise of his glorious grace' (v. 6). Paul's concept of the adoption of individuals into God's family (see also Rom. 8.23; 9.4; Gal. 4.5) is borrowed from the Roman world. The OT or Hebrew culture reflects no such custom. Under Roman law, the adoptee severed all relations with his natural father. Now surrendered to the absolute control of the new father for life, he possessed the family name and full rights and privileges of a natural born son to assume property ownership and continue the family line.

Paul's implication and application is that God has adopted sons of disobedience and children of wrath (Eph. 2.2-3) into his family, bestowing upon them all rights and privileges of natural sons, including immediate inheritance rights. Adoption is both a present reality and a future goal. Presently, believers are full adult members and heirs in God's family (Gal. 3.25-26; 4.1; Rom. 8.14-17), and can immediately claim their spiritual inheritance. The resurrection of their bodies and transformation into glorified bodies is future (Rom. 8.23-24). This will be the final stage of adoption. Then the full realization of the inheritance will be experienced.

[18] F.F. Bruce, *The Epistle to the Ephesians* (London: Pickering & Inglis, 1961), p. 28.

The phrase 'in accordance with his pleasure and will' (κατὰ τὴν εὐ-δοκίαν τοῦ θελήματος αὐτοῦ, 1.5) should not be glossed over. It informs us that adoption into God's family was not a hard unwilling act on the part of the Father. Rather, such loving decision was based upon his benevolent will.

Important as going to heaven is, salvation is not merely to provide an escape hatch out of hell. Redeemed souls must live 'to the praise of his glorious grace' (v. 6). 'Praise' implies commendation and applause, 'glorious' means magnificent and celebrated, and 'grace' bespeaks the generosity of the benefactor and the unworthiness of the beneficiary. The ultimate purpose of God's beneficent action in election is the display of his excellence and undeserved favor to lost sinners. This acclaim is not only the manifest beauty and inherent splendor the deed announces but also the rapturous and thankful laudation it evokes from those who have experienced the joyous freedom grace begets.

As God chose Israel to live to his praise (Isa. 43.21), so Christians who are chosen and blessed must honor God with their lives and bring him glory (Mt. 5.45). In acknowledgment of God's act of national and personal deliverance the psalmist summons the whole earth in fitting tribute to 'sing the glory of his [God's] name' and to 'make his praise glorious' (Ps. 66.2). The redeemed of Christ who have experienced his love and grace in an infinitely greater dimension can do no less. Such praise cannot but trip from the lips of those whose hearts are filled with gratitude and be loudly announced by lives transformed by divine grace. Giving praise to God for his marvelous grace is not restricted to the here and now. Paul tells us later that like trophies on display in heaven the saints will forever 'show the incomparable riches of his grace, expressed in his kindness to us in Christ Jesus' (Eph. 2.7).

The phrase 'in love' at the end of verse 4 may correctly be taken either with what precedes or what follows in v. 5. If the former, it means believers are 'holy and blameless before God in love' – a life of moral excellence in which love consists of being part of the goal of election (AV, RV, NEB); if the latter, 'in love God predestined us' – it states God's foreordaining attitude in eternity (RSV, NASB, NIV). Scholarly opinion is divided as to which Paul intends. Both are theologically correct, though the syntax is ambiguous.

2. Salvation Accomplished – the Son (1.7-12)

In vv. 1-6 God's redemptive plan and design is set forth. Much like he did with ancient Israel, by a complete act of grace he has now chosen and lavishly blessed a new people to be uniquely his own. Human salvation, one of God's blessings to believers, is inextricably wrapped up with Christ, his Beloved. Paul says that God has blessed us with every spiritual blessing 'in Christ' (v. 3) and chosen us 'in him' (v. 4). Election to holiness and sonship with its attendant blessings is a part of God's great plan accomplished in Jesus (vv. 4-5). In v. 7 Paul continues his benediction of praise and thanksgiving to God for his extravagant blessings, this time for his rescue from spiritual bondage and restoration to fellowship with him. This gracious act of God Paul calls redemption.

Redemption (v. 7) is one of God's blessings his children presently enjoy. ἀπολύτρωσις means release by paying a price. Biblical redemption has its roots in the OT, and resonates with the undertones of covenant and commerce. The idea of purchasing or buying back someone or something is involved in both cases. Lands and persons could become the property of another by the paying of a price (Lev. 15.25-27, 47-49; Num. 18.15). For example, through covenant Boaz redeemed the land belonging to Naomi's husband and earned the right to marry Ruth (Ruth 4.1-12). Slaves in Egypt and later in Babylon, the people of Israel were redeemed by God and became his own possession (Exod. 15.13; Deut 7.8; Isa. 48.20; 52.9).

Redemption in the Greco-Roman world was associated with the purchase of the freedom of slaves by paying a ransom. Seven of the ten occurrences of the term in the NT are in Paul's letters, three of which appear in Ephesians (1:7, 14; 4.30), and nearly always carry the basic meaning of release on the payment of a price. Hence Jesus said he had come to 'give his life as a ransom for many' (Mt. 20.28), and Paul reminded the Corinthians that they had been 'bought at a price' (1 Cor. 1.20). With the statement 'we have redemption through his [Christ's] blood' (Eph. 1:7) by implication and application, Paul shows the costliness of human redemption (cf. 1 Pet. 1.18-19). It is because Jesus died, thus paying the price of sin, that we are redeemed.

In v. 7 Paul equates the forgiveness of sins with redemption (see also Col. 1:14). Forgiveness translates ἀφεσις, which literally means a 'letting go', 'dismissal', or 'carrying away', bringing to mind what happened on the Jewish Day of Atonement. After killing one of two goats specially selected, the high priest sprinkled its blood on the mercy seat. Placing his hands upon the live scapegoat, he confessed the sins of Israel over it and sent it away into the wilderness (Lev. 16:15-22). Seeing Christ prefigured in this custom, John declared Jesus to be 'the Lamb of God, who takes away the sin of the world' (Jn 1.29).

The term for forgiveness (ἀφεσις) was commonly used in the contexts of the release of captives, and release from punishment and financial obligation (see Lev. 25.10; Isa. 58.6; Jer. 34.8). Jesus used it to describe in part his mission in the world – 'to proclaim freedom for the prisoners' (Lk. 4.18). Through his death on the cross he has permanently released sin's prisoners who have received him as Savior, canceled sin's indictment, removed the guilt of our past, and turned aside sin's punishment. God's forgiveness to undeserving sinners is 'in accordance with the riches of [his] grace that he lavished on us' (v. 7). God does not bless his children merely 'out of' (ἐκ) his abundant wealth; he does so 'in accordance with' (κατά) his wealth — his great riches providing the measure and standard by which he gives. This gracious unstinting generosity demonstrates superabundance of unearned and undeserved love, 'inexhaustible in God and freely accessible through Christ'.[19] It truly surpasses knowledge and understanding!

Wisdom and understanding (σοφία and φρόνησις, v. 8) lie behind God's abundant grace and forgiveness. The interpretive challenge here is whether wisdom and understanding refer to a part of God's gift lavished upon Christians to impart enlightenment on what he has done (AV, ASV, NEB, NIV), or how God has revealed the mystery of his will (RSV, NASB). Both ideas are possible. God has given believers insight into what he has done and also wisdom how to live in the world. But, how God has dealt with sin and what God has done in our salvation reflects his own wisdom.

Wisdom and understanding were two of the Spirit's attributes with which the coming Messiah would be endowed, equipping him to execute his messianic mission wisely and judiciously. 'The Spirit of the LORD will rest on him — the Spirit of wisdom and of understanding, the Spirit of counsel and of power, the Spirit of knowledge and of the fear of the LORD' (Isa. 11.2). Messiah, therefore, 'will not judge by what he sees with his eyes, or decide by what he hears with his ears; but with righteousness he will judge the needy, with justice he will give decisions' (vv. 3, 4). Spirit does not refer merely to a disposition, but to the Holy Spirit. Believers have received the same Spirit of wisdom and understanding. Elsewhere Paul mentions the Holy Spirit's role in imparting discernment (1 Cor. 2.7-10).

God does not intend to keep his people in the dark about his saving purposes. He has revealed to them 'the mystery of his will' (v. 9) — what he willed in eternity concerning their salvation. The word 'mystery' (μυστήριον) is used twenty-seven times in the NT, twenty times by Paul, six of which occur in Ephesians (1.9; 3.3, 4, 9; 5.32; 6.19). In the ancient world, 'mystery' was associated with the mystery cults to whose initiates alone certain truths were revealed and who were bound by oath to keep the secrets of their society. Mystery today is generally understood to mean that which is puzzling or baffling — a conundrum. Paul has neither of these ideas in mind. For him 'mystery' is a truth or

---

[19] Charles Hodge, *An Exposition of Ephesians* (Wilmington, DE: Sovereign Grace, 1972), p. 16.

reality, obscure or hidden or both, which the human mind could neither fathom nor discover but which has been revealed by the Spirit and has now become an 'open secret'.

Verse 10. The future aspect of God's plan – that of restoring universal unity – Paul calls 'a summing up' of all things in Christ 'when the times will have reached their fulfillment'. The expression derives from ἀνακεφαλαιόω, a cognate of κεφάλαιον, meaning 'main point' or 'summary', and was used for the adding up of columns, the summing up of speeches, or the conclusion of letters in ancient Greek. Its only other NT usage is in Rom. 13.9 where Paul says all the commandments of the second table of the Law 'are summed up in this one rule: "Love your neighbor as yourself"'. The summing up of all things in Christ means that all things become a coherent totality in him. Subsequently, Paul will explain what is entailed in God's 'summing up' or unifying the whole cosmos in Christ. Included in this act is the bringing together of the conflicting and discordant elements in the heavens – powers inimical to God's purposes (1.20-22) – and on earth, a formerly alienated and fractured people – Jews and Gentiles (2.1-10, 11-22).

But this term also carries the meanings of restoration and headship, the latter fitting well the context of Ephesians 1 where Christ's headship (κεφαλή) is stated (v. 22), a lordship under which all things are brought together in unity and harmony. The NIV adopts this view, which holds out the hope that the discord, dislocation, and fragmentation presently in the world will one day find unity and bond, reunification and harmony, under Christ's sway (see Phil. 2.10-11; Col. 1. 20). Christ's work encompasses 'all things in heaven and on earth'. This must include the church triumphant in heaven and the church militant on earth. But Paul seems to have a lot more in mind. 'All things' generally denotes the whole universe, and used here with 'heaven' and 'earth' it means the rebellious evil powers and discordant elements in both the material and spiritual realms. Inseparably connected, these worlds will share 'cosmic renewal' and 'that liberation of the groaning creation'.[20] Universal reconciliation or reunification here has nothing to do with universal salvation of rebellious human beings and angels. Salvation is limited to Adam's descendants who have put their trust in Christ.

All this, Paul says, will take place 'when the times will have reached their fulfillment' (1.10). Literally translated, the Greek says, 'in the dispensation of the fullness of the times'. 'Dispensation' (οἰκονομία), which appears three times in Ephesians (1.10; 3.2, 9, KJV) of the six times Paul uses it, can also be rendered 'administration' or 'stewardship', and principally referred to the management of a household or

[20] Stott, *The Message of Ephesians*, p. 44.

the responsibility of one who managed it (1 Cor. 4.1-2; 9.17; 1 Pet. 4.10). Here it is Christ's management, administration or stewardship of all things and the universe that is in view. It is translated 'to be put into effect' in the NIV which views 'fullness of times' – 'a sequence of periods of time under God's direction'[21]– as the eschatological endpoint and goal of God's purpose for all his creation. Just as Jesus came when God's time had reached its completion (Gal. 4.4), so in his providence God will bring about the consummation when the time is ripe. The universal reunification or summing up of all things in the fullness of times need not be taken as an exclusively future event. In the context of Ephesians where the exalted Christ already exercises lordship over the church and evil powers (1.21; 2.2), and where an 'already-not yet' eschatology is present, it is reasonable to see what is expected at the end as already in progress – observably demonstrated in the uniting of Jews and Gentiles in Christ.

Verse 11. Not only has God purposed a uniting of all things in Christ, but presently believers are God's heritage in him. The passive verb ἐκληρώθημεν, which describes what God has done on behalf of his people, comes from κληρόω, which means 'to appoint or choose by lot' or 'to obtain a lot'. In the OT it is used with reference to the division of the Promised Land by lot or allotment (Num. 26.55, 56). The struggle of the interpreter/translator lies in determining whether believers have been chosen as something or called to receive something. Several versions translate the verb, 'we have obtained an inheritance' (AV, NKJV, NASB, NRSV) or with some slight variation but the same meaning, i.e. believers receive a share of what God has (NEB, JB, NJB). Those translators who view believers as God's inheritance, render it, 'we were made a heritage' (ASV, RV) or 'we were also chosen' (NIV).

In Col. 1.12 Paul thanks God who has qualified believers 'to share in the inheritance [κληρός] of the saints'. Seeing believers as God's heritage in the Ephesian passage more closely parallels other NT passages which present the believer's inheritance as being among the saints (Acts 20.32; 26.18). Colossians' point of view need not, however, be seen as being at odds with that in Ephesians. God's qualifying believers for a certain destiny is the point being made in Colossians; in Ephesians 'they have been allotted a destiny or appointed by God'.[22] Because of the term's associations with God's choice of Israel as his own possession (Deut. 9.26, 29; 32.9; cf. Deut. 4.20; 7.6), and since God's purpose in appointing the church, expressed in v. 12 as 'for the praise of his glory', coincides with Israel's purpose and echoes the language of her destiny (Isa. 43.7, 21; 48.9-11), translations that show the church as God's

---

[21] Lincoln, *Ephesians*, p. 32.
[22] Lincoln, *Ephesians*, p. 36.

heritage are to be preferred. Ultimately, God works his purposes for his ultimate glorification – and that is his goal for his people. God's people exist for God's praise and God's glory.

'We, who were the first to hope in Christ' (Eph. 1.12) most likely refers to Paul and his fellow Jewish believers, contrasted with the Gentiles (you) in v. 13. This view is consistent with the historical preaching of the gospel (Acts 11.19; Rom. 1.16). Concerned as Ephesians is with unity and Jewish Christian and Gentile relations, views that overlook this desire of Paul are less tenable.

3. Salvation Applied – The Spirit (1.13-14)

The Father's plan in eternity was to elect a people, adopt them into his family, and make them his own treasured possession. Included in God's plan were the Gentiles, a people despised and detested by the Jews. What God has planned, the Son has accomplished by his death on the cross, and the Spirit has made a reality. His attention turned particularly toward the Gentiles in these verses, Paul mentions three things that relate to their salvation: hearing the gospel, believing it, and being sealed by the Spirit.

Verse 13. 'And you also' clearly refers to the Gentiles. In Christ and through his mediation they are included in God's great plan and purpose for his people. They are part of God's heritage. They, too, are the recipients of his lavish generosity. This is clearly Paul's point as he transitions from vv. 11-12. Like the Jews (Acts 11.19; Rom. 1.16), the Gentile Christians had heard the message of the gospel, received and believed it, and were incorporated into the new people of God.

The message the Ephesians heard Paul calls the 'word of truth' (v. 13), which means it consists in truth in its essence and substance (Col. 1.5). When faith is placed in Christ through the preached word, God comes in and seals the believing person with the Holy Spirit (Eph. 1.13). The Spirit's role in salvation in the context is not without significance. First, he is called the Spirit of promise because both the prophets (e.g. Ezek. 36.26-27; Joel 2.28-32) and Jesus (Lk. 24.49; Jn 14.16, 17; Acts 1.8) promised his advent, and because he is the one who guarantees the fulfillment of God's promises (Gal. 3.14), especially as it has to do with the Gentiles' inclusion in the body of Christ. Joel, writing probably about 900 years before Pentecost, announced God's promise, 'I will pour out my Spirit on all people' (2.28). Jesus restated the promise in Lk. 24.49, 'I am going to send you what my Father has promised'.

In interpreting the phenomenon of Pentecost to his audience, Peter declared that Jesus 'Exalted to the right hand of God, ... has received from the Father the promised Holy Spirit and has poured out what you now see and hear' (Acts 2.33). Second, the Spirit is described as seal and down payment or pledge (cf. 2 Cor. 1.21-22). A seal was affixed to certain documents to show their authenticity (*4 Ezra* 6.5; Rev. 7.1-8; 9:4) or the completion of a transaction. It sometimes indicated security or protection from destruction (Ezek. 9.4-6) or tampering (Mt. 27.62-66). By giving the Gentiles the Holy Spirit, God declared his ownership of them (1 Cor. 6.19-20) and attested to the genuineness of the believers' experience (Rom. 8. 9).

An experience subsequent to conversion, water baptism, or confirmation need not be read into the metaphor of Spirit-sealing. It is the principal proof that one belongs to the new people of God, and in this context ushers these Gentile believers into the inheritance of the new covenant and assures their final destiny.[23] The Spirit's function in uniting the disparate racial, ethnic, and cultural groups in the early church cannot be easily overlooked. At Pentecost the Spirit fell upon the Jews, authenticating their experience as the new people of God (Acts 2). Acts 8 records the Samaritan Pentecost, Peter and John being given visible proof that the hated and ostracised Samaritans had also received the Holy Spirit, validating their experience.

What is often called the Ephesian Pentecost occurs in Acts 19. On arriving at Ephesus, Paul found twelve disciples who had received John's baptism of repentance. 'Did you receive the Holy Spirit when you believed?' Paul asked them (v. 2). 'No, we have not even heard that there is a Holy Spirit', was their reply. Paul asked them to believe in Jesus, and baptized them in Jesus' name. Paul laid his hands on them, 'the Holy Spirit came on them, and they spoke in tongues and prophesied' (v. 6). In all four incidents the Holy Spirit became the legitimating and discriminating sign that marks God's people as his special possession.

In addition to being God's seal upon believers, the Holy Spirit is also God's *arrabōn* (ἀρραβών) 'guaranteeing our inheritance until the redemption of those who are God's possession' (1.13). *Arrabōn* is a Semitic loan word which occurs six times in the scriptures, three in the OT (Gen. 38.17, 18, 20), and three in the NT (2 Cor. 1:22; 5:5; Eph. 1.14). It carries the idea of pledge in the OT, but became a commercial term in Hellenistic Greek, and is variously translated as 'pledge' (NEB, NRSV), 'earnest' (AV, ASV, RV), 'first installment', 'down payment', 'guarantee' (GNB) or 'deposit' (NIV). The original refers to 'a payment

---

[23] Fee, *God's Empowering Presence*, p. 670.

which obligates the contracting party to make further payments'.[24] In modern Greek *arrabōna* means an engagement ring – which is the promise and pledge of the consummation of a special relationship.

'Until/for the redemption of the possession' is a literal translation of v. 14b. 'Redemption' connotes release from sin's bondage through Christ's death (v. 7). 'Possession' renders περιποίησις, which means 'preservation' and 'possession/acquisition' in both classical and biblical Greek (2 Chron. 14.13; Hag. 2.9; Mal. 3.17). Both ideas are also present in the NT, Paul using it for the believer's acquisition of salvation and glory (1 Thess. 5.9; 2 Thess. 2. 14), Peter as a description of believers as God's possession (1 Pet. 2:9), and the writer of Hebrews as the preservation of the soul (Heb. 10.39). Interpreters are not unanimous about how it should be understood. In an interpretive translation the NIV translates it 'until the redemption of those who are God's possession'. The NEB, as do a number of other translations (cf. ASV, NASB, RV), renders it 'until God has redeemed what is his own', and the RSV 'until we acquire possession of it'. At issue is whether believers will be God's possession or taking possession of the promised inheritance.

Believers presently share in God's inheritance for them – but only partially. They await a future day of full possession (Eph. 4.30; 1 Thess. 5.9; 2 Thess. 2.14). The notion that God's people are his possession appears to fit the context better, finding support in the OT which describes Israel as God's special possession among the nations (Exod. 19.5, 6; Deut. 14.2; 26.18-19; Mal 3.17; Isa. 43.21) and the NT which denotes believers as 'a chosen people, a royal priesthood, a holy nation, a people belonging to God' (1 Pet. 2.9). As Israel was chosen to be a holy nation and royal priesthood 'that they may proclaim [God's] praise' (Isa. 43.21) so Paul says the church was elected 'to the praise of [God's] glory' (Eph. 1.14).

God's people exist now to bring praise and honor to God. Three times Paul tells the Ephesians that all that God has done is 'for the praise of his glory' (1.6, 12, 14). The Father has elected, adopted, and accepted us 'to the praise of his glory' (v. 6). The Son has redeemed, forgiven, and made us God's heritage 'to the praise of his glory' (v. 12). The Spirit has sealed believers and become the down payment that guarantees their future blessing 'to the praise of his glory' (v. 14). When redemption is complete, throughout the ages the saints will magnify his praise for his gracious and glorious salvation.

---

[24] BAGD, 'ἀρραβών', 109.

4. Salvation Acknowledged: Paul's Thanksgiving and Prayer for Enlightenment (1.15-19)

Having blessed God for what he has done for the Ephesian believers (1.3-14), Paul now gives thanks for them and assures them of the constancy of his prayer for them (vv. 15-16). His prayer contains a petition for enlightenment about the great wealth they possess (vv. 17-18) and the great power at work in them (v. 19), a power demonstrated in the resurrection and exaltation of Christ (vv. 20-23). Because Jesus is supreme head over all things for the church, no opposition can ultimately prevail over his people. The prayer is one both of praise and petition, intercession and instruction.

Verses 15-16. 'For this reason' (v. 15) may point back to v. 14 or to the whole doxology (vv. 3-14), especially as it applies to Gentiles who now share positional equality with the Jews. What the divine Trinity has done provides the inspiration for Paul's prayer; that people may know experientially all the benefits mentioned in the doxology is its intent. Intercession for spiritual understanding that believers may know what they possess, not material things they lack, is a special feature of Paul's prison prayers (Eph. 1.15-23; 3.14-21; Phil. 1.9-11; Col. 1.9-12), and forms the content of his prayer here. What Paul exhorts us to do is both to make our praise of God unceasing that in Christ all spiritual blessings are ours and equally to pray incessantly that we may know the fullness of what he has given us.[25]

Paul had no doubt received information about the spiritual progress of the Ephesians from not only Tychicus and Epaphras, but also others. Though not unaware of the believers' flaws, as with nearly all the churches to which he wrote (e.g. Rom. 1.8-10; 1 Cor. 1.4-5; Phil. 1.3-4), Paul finds something for which to give God thanks and makes it the reason for praise. In the case of the Ephesians, he has learned of their firm faith that is anchored in the Lord Jesus and their fervent love for all the saints (v. 15). These two acid tests of genuine Christianity prompt his unfailing and unwearying intercession (v. 16) and reveal that he exemplifies that which he enjoins the saints to do – pray continually (1 Thess. 5.17; cf. Eph. 6.18; Rom. 12.12; Col. 4.2). The magnet that attracts people to God also draws people together. Genuine faith always focuses on Christ and emanates in love to others. Firm faith and fervent love are necessary Christian virtues, but they are not the sum and circumference of the Christian life. Paul, therefore, moves from praising God for the Ephesians to petitioning God that he might grant them enlightenment concerning their possession and position in Christ (vv. 17-19). The burden of the prayer is that the believers will

---

[25] Stott, *Ephesians*, p. 52.

have an enlarged understanding of the faith, that they will grow and develop in it more and more.

Verses 17-19. Paul directs his prayer to 'the glorious Father' (v. 17) – the God characterized by glory, to whom all glory is due, and whose divine splendor, radiance, and power fill the earth (Num. 24.11; Pss. 29.3; 24.7-10; 1 Cor. 2.8). His petition is that this God will impart the 'Spirit of wisdom and revelation'.

Spiritual things are spiritually discerned (1 Cor. 2.9-15) – hence Paul's prayer for wisdom and revelation (v. 17). 'Spirit' translates πνεῦμα, and may refer to a spiritual disposition or endowment (1 Cor. 4.21; 2 Cor. 4.13; Gal. 6.1), but this understanding seems less likely in the context. Such a notion becomes nonsensical when 'disposition' is combined with 'revelation'. Of the fourteen times *pneuma* occurs in Ephesians, all but two (2.2; 4:23) refer to the Holy Spirit. The centrality of the Spirit's role here in Paul's prayer should not be overlooked. Its goal is for God to grant them the Spirit, represented here in the symbols wisdom and revelation. To take no notice of the Spirit, the font of both the revelation and empowering, is to 'miss Paul's prayer by too much'.[26] Believers thus enabled, the Spirit subsequently will afford the wisdom to understand what he also unveils to them about God and his ways.[27] A further reception of the Spirit is not Paul's intent – experiencing these gifts resident in the Spirit is.

In Eph. 1.13 Paul refers to the Spirit as the divine seal that guarantees the believer's inheritance. In 3.5 he presents him as the revealer of divine insight to the other apostles. Elsewhere the Spirit is referred to as the revealer of truth (1 Cor. 2.9-15; Col. 1.9; Jn 14.26; 16.13). 'Spirit of wisdom' is used frequently in the OT, for example, to describe the inspiration given to the makers of Aaron's garments (Exod. 28.3), the craftsman Bezalel (Exod. 31.3), Joshua (Deut. 34.9), and in combination with 'understanding' to describe Israel's coming Messiah (Isa. 11.2). Spiritual discernment comes from the Holy Spirit who is called 'the Spirit of wisdom and of understanding, the Spirit of counsel and of power, the Spirit of knowledge and of the fear of the Lord' (Isa. 11.2).

'Wisdom' has its roots in ancient Greek literature and the OT, and entails practical knowledge, principles, and outstanding skills. In 1 Corinthians it is one of the gifts of the Spirit (12.8). Here it refers to the ability to make correct decisions, to know God's will (Col. 1.9) and to live in a way that pleases the Lord (Col. 1.10). Wisdom also means

---

[26] Fee, *God's Empowering Presence*, pp. 674, 675.
[27] Fee, *God's Empowering Presence*, p. 676.

sound, practical speech and advice that give sure direction to one's life and decisions (Prov. 1.1-5).

That God would impart to them spiritual revelation – divine unveiling of what was hidden or mysterious – is the second component of Paul's prayer for the Ephesians. Revelation is of two kinds – both the work of the Spirit. The first is what the Reformers called *Testimonium Spiritus Externus* – the outward witness of the Spirit that imparted inspiration to the biblical authors; the second the *Testimonium Spiritus Internus* – the inner witness of the Spirit in the Word *and* in the reader giving illumination and understanding. The latter is what Paul calls enlightenment of the eyes of the heart (v. 18), that is, a turning on of the light in the inner self. In Scripture, 'heart' (Heb. לֵב) refers to the seat of thought, will, emotion, and moral decision-making – the total inner person.

The ultimate goal of the Spirit's work of granting wisdom and illumination is that 'you may know him [God] better' (Eph. 1.17). Clearer and fuller knowledge (ἐπίγνωσις) of God's truth is for greater understanding of and deeper commitment to God. Personal knowledge of God himself provides the context to know truths about what he has prepared for believers both in the present and future life (vv. 18, 19). Paul mentions three truths that the Spirit will illuminate to them: the hope of God's call (18b), the wealth of God's glorious inheritance (18c), and his incomparably great power in us (vv. 19-23). The writer of Hebrews calls hope 'an anchor for the soul' (6.19). Christians are a people of hope (Rom. 8.24). Anchored in a faithful and all-powerful God, Christian hope speaks of confident expectation – guaranteed, absolute certainty that God will do what he has promised.

This hope is related to one's call (v. 18), and spans time and eternity. It is retrospective, looking back to the commencement of faith (Rom. 1.6; 1 Cor. 1.9); progressive, dealing with the cultivation of faith (Rom. 1.7; 1 Cor. 1.2; Gal. 5.1, 13; Eph. 4.1-6); and prospective, anticipating the consummation of faith (Phil. 3.14; 1 Thess. 2.12). The goal of God's call is both immediate and ultimate, temporal and eternal.

That believers may know 'his glorious inheritance in the saints' (v. 18) is the second part of Paul's prayer. Either the inheritance God receives or the inheritance he grants could be in view here, i.e. God's inheritance or that which belongs to his children. As a person's wealth may redound to his or her praise, so God's people who are his possession will bring him ultimate praise (Eph. 1.11-12, 14; 1 Jn 3.2). Believers themselves will receive a heavenly inheritance from the Father (Col. 1.12; Acts 20.32), one which Peter calls 'an inheritance that can never perish, spoil or fade – kept in heaven for you' (1 Pet. 1.4). God's full possession of his people and his people's full possession of his riches will coincide in the future.

The final request of Paul is that believers may know God's surpassing power at work in them and for them (vv. 19-23). Paul prays a similar prayer in 3.14-19. There he petitions that the saints may be empowered in the inner being by the Holy Spirit so as to grasp the dimensions of God's love and that they be filled with all the fullness of God. Both prayers must be examined together.

Our problem as Christians is not only ignorance, but also impotence. Knowledge without power ridicules our inability. Whatever God promises, he provides the power to bring it about. It takes God's power to experience God's provisions and to achieve his purpose. If it be granted that Paul's prayer up to this point has focused more upon the past and the future, here the spotlight is clearly on the present.

Like no other NT Epistle, Ephesians employs an array of words for power, four in v. 19 alone. Before presenting the nature and facets of this power, Paul speaks of it not merely as great, but as exceedingly or incomparably great (v. 19). The phrase used to denote its size and scope (ὑπερβάλλον μέγεθος) is literally translated 'surpassing or excelling greatness'. The magnitude (μέγεθος) of God's power exceeds (ὑπερβάλλον) all bounds or measurement. The apostle then stacks up four terms to express the vastness, surpassing greatness, and 'all-crushing omnipotence'[28] of this power, the first of which, δύναμις, depicts God's potential ability to act or accomplish his will. The second, ἐνέργεια, from which the English word 'energy' derives, is used in the NT only of superhuman ability,[29] whether divine (Eph. 3.7; 4.16; Col. 1.29; 2.12) or satanic (2 Thess. 2.9). This term denotes inherent, efficient and energizing strength. Power to overcome obstacles, power demonstrated in action as might, mastery, or dominion is represented by the third term, κράτος. The last term, ἰσχύς, speaks of power that is possessed 'like the strength of human beings'.[30] Paul's aim in the display of this assortment of terms to describe God's power is more than to illustrate subtle nuances of meaning among them or than merely to strain the limits of human language and understanding of the greatness of God's power. His intent is simply that we might know (v. 18) that this vast and immeasurable power is 'for us who believe'.

Only enlightened spiritual eyes can begin to grasp the immensity and awesome majesty of this power. It takes divine insight and wisdom

[28] R.C.H. Lenski, *St. Paul's Epistles to the Galatians, Ephesians and Philippians* (Minneapolis: Augsburg, 1961), p. 399.

[29] W. Robertson Nicoll, ed., *The Expositor's Greek Testament*, vol. III (Grand Rapids: Eerdmans, 1974), p. 276.

[30] Hoehner, *Ephesians*, p. 270.

to know how to harness and utilize it. But the intent of the Spirit's illumination is not that Christians cease using their minds. Faith and reason are never in conflict. While faith goes beyond reason, reason is the foundation upon which faith rests. 'Knowledge is the ladder by which faith climbs higher, the springboard from which faith leaps. . .' Thus knowledge and faith are interdependent. 'Faith cannot grow without a firm basis of knowledge; knowledge is sterile if it does not bring forth faith.'[31]

The accumulation of power terms doubtless has some overlap, and like pieces of weapon in the divine panoply, illustrates the magnitude and awesome power God has made available to all who believe. This life-giving power, which is nothing short of that which raised Jesus from the dead and elevated him to a position of great authority, honor, and power (vv. 21-22), God is now exercising in us, through us, and on our behalf. A mind-boggling thought!

For Christians, Christ's resurrection and ascension are two most decisive and unrepeatable historical moments, displaying God's transcendent power as sovereign ruler over life and death, bringing about 'a new dimension of human experience'.[32] Because of the resurrection and exaltation, Jesus is both Savior and sovereign Lord (Acts 2.25-36). The Resurrection proclaims 'He lives – and that forever'; the Exaltation announces 'He reigns – and that forever'. Christ's resurrection is determinative for Christians. It is both the bedrock of their present faith and the hinge upon which their future resurrection swings (1 Cor. 15.12-22). But Christ's exaltation also has implications for the church. As triumphant and victorious Lord, Christ bestows gifts upon the church (Eph. 4.7-10).

United to Christ their head, believers share a vital union with him in death, resurrection, and exaltation (Rom. 6.3-6; Col. 2.20; 3.1). Any power shortage on our part cannot be blamed on a lack of divine provision. Any defeat on our part cannot be attributed to a lack of resources. Paul says that God's incomparable power is 'for us' – without discrimination – who believe. Our problem is not with availability; it is more with appropriation and application.

5. Christ's Exaltation and its Results (1.20-23)

God not only raised Christ from the dead; he also seated him at his right hand. The imagery, drawn from Ps. 110.1 and reflected in Heb. 1.13, symbolizes the bestowal of highest honor, privilege, and power (1 Kgs 2.19; Mt. 26.64; Heb. 1.3-4, 13). The posture of sitting is one

---

[31] Stott, *The Message of Ephesians*, p. 67.
[32] Stott, *The Message of Ephesians*, p. 59.

of rest, intimating the completion of the work of salvation (Heb. 10.12-13). Except for Acts 7.55, where he stands to welcome home his brave and battle-scarred soldier, in heaven Jesus is always seen seated.

Verse 21 indicates the unrivaled, universal, and unending authority of Christ. God has exalted Jesus far above all. Far above all principalities and powers; far above all spiritual and human intelligences and dignitaries in this age and the one to come! Jesus bows to no one; but every authority – earthly or heavenly; every enemy – human or spiritual – no matter what title they possess; all must bow to him and declare his absolute supremacy as Lord (Phil. 2.6-11). Christ is in control of the powers in the universe, having won a decisive and celebrated victory over them on the cross (Col. 2.15) and at the resurrection (Eph. 1.20-22).

Paul, quoting Ps. 8.6, states that 'God placed all things under his [Christ's] feet' (1.22). 'All' includes everything in creation. The idea of placing something or someone under one's feet depicts not only conquest but a complete and humiliating victory over an enemy, and was drawn from ancient custom in which the winner of a duel placed his foot upon the neck of his defeated opponent (Josh. 10.24; cf. 2 Sam. 23.39). Such dominion was first given to Adam (Gen. 1.26-30), who failed in Eden. Christ's universal authority far exceeds that of the first Adam, not merely restoring what Adam lost in the Garden but providing immeasurably more.

The picture here in Paul's mind is of Christ, the last Adam, who succeeded where the first Adam failed, and now has everything under his absolute control – friend and foe, angels and men (cf. 1 Pet. 3.22). Christ's dominion is only a partial reality, however, because in light of the ongoing warfare against his people (Eph. 6.12) not until he returns will he exercise the full authority he presently possesses (1 Cor. 15. 24-28; Heb. 2.5-9; 10.12-13).

In 1.22b-23 Paul unpacks the implications of Christ's double triumph of resurrection from the dead (v. 20) and present enthronement (v. 21) for the church (v. 22). Christ's universal headship is expressed in the words, God 'appointed him to be head over everything for the church' (v. 22) – things in heaven, on earth, and under the earth (Phil. 2. 9-11). A more literal, and better, translation is that God 'gave him as head over everything', the verb calling attention to God's gracious action toward the church. 'Head' is used in a variety of ways in the scriptures. Metaphorically, it sometimes means 'source', 'leader' or 'ruler' (Deut. 28.13; Judg. 10.18; 11.11), 'guide', and 'authority over'. Amid the conflicting positions, interpretive arguments and counter-arguments represented by different scholars, it seems apparent that context is determinative for meaning. In the context of words like 'under', 'over', and 'feet', head can hardly mean source or origin.

It is a dizzying thought that God has given Christ, who is supreme head and imperial Lord of the universe, as gift 'to' the church and 'for the church' — 'for the benefit of believers'.[33] This indicates that Christ presides over and directs it (Eph. 4.15; Col. 1.18; 2:19), and that nothing else equally attracts his attention and receives his affection. It further suggests that Christ is graciously disposed toward his people and is working on their behalf.

How Paul's concluding thought, 'the fullness of him who fills everything in every way' (1.23), is to be understood has tested the competence of many an interpreter. The *crux interpretum* is determining the reference of the word 'fullness' ($\pi\lambda\acute{\eta}\rho\omega\mu\alpha$). Scholars offer three major explanations, each ably defended by renowned advocates. The first regards Christ as the fullness of God, and God as the one who fills Christ and everything else (cf. Col. 1.19; 2.9). This view founders upon two obstacles: nowhere in the NT is Christ ever referred to as the fullness of God, and both Ephesians and Colossians identify Christ, not God, as the one who fills everything (Eph. 4.10; Col. 1.16-17). The next two approaches perceive the church as both the body and fullness of God. At issue is whether 'fullness' carries an active or a passive meaning. If active, it means 'that which fills' — the contents. If passive, it indicates 'that which is filled' — the container.

Interpreters who adopt the active meaning regard the church as that which fills or completes Christ. This explanation has the head–body imagery in vv. 22, 23 as support. Just as a head cannot exist without a body, so Christ cannot exist — is incomplete — without the church. By this, Paul appears to mean that 'in some mysterious sense the church is that without which the Christ is not complete, but with which He is or will be complete'.[34] The indissoluble union of Christ and the church is portrayed in the bride/groom imagery. As bridegroom Christ is incomplete without his bride. Stated *inter alia*, 'as vine he cannot be thought of without the branches; as shepherd he is not seen without his sheep; and so also as head he finds his full expression in his body, the church'.[35]

This view falters at two points. First, it can be found nowhere in the NT that the church completes Christ; rather, it is Christ who completes the church (cf. Eph. 3.19; 4.10, 13; Col. 2.9-10). Appeal cannot be made to Col. 1.24 since the verse refers to a quota of sufferings for Christ that Paul had to undergo for the sake of the church. Secondly,

---

[33] Lincoln, *Ephesians*, p. 67. The Greek dative case can be translated 'to' or 'for'.

[34] J. Armitage Robinson, *Commentary on Ephesians* (Grand Rapids: Kregel, 1979), pp. 42, 43. See also p. 45.

[35] William Hendriksen, *Exposition of Ephesians* (Grand Rapids: Baker, 1967), 104.

the position sets up an awkward redundancy – the church completing Christ who is being filled in every way.

Far less problematic is the third alternative, which acknowledges Christ who, as fullness, fills the church and as its head directs it.[36] As the temple of God, the church is indwelt and filled by the presence of Christ (2.21-22). But this same Christ also fills everything, the earthly and heavenly realms, entirely and with all his fullness.

Reflection and Response (Part 1)

Reflection
Christ's lordship and its implications for the church is a major theme of 1.1-23. The chapter covers the whole scope of the saving work of the triune God from eternity to eternity. Redemption, conceived in eternity (vv. 3-5, 9, 11), is its central focus, and includes all that exists in heaven and earth. God's glory is the aim of this redemption. But God's redemptive purpose is opposed by hostile human and superhuman forces, which God vanquishes in the resurrection and exaltation of Christ. The chapter concludes with all things placed under the feet of Jesus, indicating his absolute lordship.

For Christians, Christ's resurrection and exaltation are two decisive and determinative historical moments that announce that he is both Savior and sovereign Lord (Acts 2.25-36). His resurrection declares that he lives; his exaltation proclaims that he reigns forever. Paul observes that God has seated him at his right hand 'far above all rule and authority, power and authority', and 'placed all things under his feet and appointed him to be head over everything for the church' (Eph. 1.21, 22). This clearly indicates Christ's celebrated victory, unrivaled authority, and universal dominion. It is a staggering, yet humbling, thought that God has given him who is supreme Lord of the universe, of spiritual and human intelligences in this age and the one to come, as gift *to* and *for* the church – for the profit and benefit of believers (v. 22). Simply put, the church participates in Christ's victory. Christ's supreme lordship and its implications for the church will be the topic of the reflection that follows. The ensuing questions are raised to encourage and facilitate reflection on this vital subject.

In general, what is the attitude of fellow Christians about Christ's lordship in the world and the church? What are some of the beliefs and understandings about Christ's lordship amongst Christian communions you know? How precisely is belief in Christ's lordship reflected in the lives and conduct of the believers with whom you associate? What evidence do you see that substantiates your conclusion? How well does

---

[36] Stott, *The Message of Ephesians*, p. 65.

the evidence correspond with the scriptural expectation of people who submit to Christ's rulership? What are some of the theological and moral implications of Christ's lordship for believers and the Christian community?

In an effort to stimulate reflection of a personal nature, the following additional questions are asked. What is your own perspective and attitude about the lordship of Christ? How does it noticeably influence your life and behavior? What difference does it make to your Christian walk? How are your relationships guided and governed by your commitment to Christ's lordship over your life? How effective is your testimony before your friends based upon how you express Christ's sovereignty in your life?

Response

The reflection section has focused on Christ's lordship and its implications, and has raised questions that solicit your personal response.

1. Employing the questions introduced in the reflection as a compass or template, state how you understand the lordship of Christ in the world and the church.

2. Identify how Christ's lordship impinges upon your life, conduct, and relationships.

3. With the assistance of a mature and trusted Christian friend explore attitudes and areas of your life that have not yet come under the rulership of Christ.

4. Through times of personal prayer, reading of Scripture, and corporate worship invite the Holy Spirit to transform you and help you to submit your will, affections, and desires to the lordship of Christ.

Ephesians 2

B. Salvation: Humankind's Privilege in Christ (2.1-10)

In ch. 1 Paul set forth the believer's possession in Christ, and with a heart overflowing with thanksgiving burst into unrestrained prayer and praise to God for his lavish generosity. Though the redolent language of prayer and praise that laces through 1.3-23 no longer echoes in ch. 2, praise still gushes from a heart filled with gratitude, now for the believer's position in Christ. In 1.3-23 such praise forms two sentences in Greek, in 2.1-10 also two sentences in Greek, vv. 1-7 and 8-10. A threefold division emerges in 2.1-10: (a) humankind's past plight outside of Christ (vv. 1-3), (b) humankind's present privilege through God's great love and mercy (vv. 4-6), and (c) the nature and purpose of salvation (vv. 8-10).

Ephesians 2.1-10 connects directly with Paul's prayer in 1.15-23, in which the apostle prays that the spiritual eyes of the Ephesian believers might be illumined by the Spirit in order to understand the implications of their call (v. 18a), the great wealth they possess (v. 18b) and the great power at work in them (v.19), a power demonstrated in the resurrection and exaltation of Christ (vv. 20-23). Previously sinners but now saints by divine grace, in a mystical sense believers have experienced that same awesome power of God that raised and exalted Christ. With Christ, God has raised them from the dead, made them alive, and seated them in the heavenly realms (2.5, 6). In addition, believers share Christ's destiny in the coming ages (2.7).

An adverbial clause that begins the new section completes the main thought in 2.5 with the verb 'he made [us] alive with' (συνεζωοποίησεν). A principal feature of the chapter is its twofold contrast between the pre-Christian plight of believers and their present privilege in Christ. In 2.1-10 'Paul first plumbs the depths of pessimism about man, and then rises to the heights of optimism about God', painting a contrasting picture 'between what man is by nature and what he can become by grace'.[1] As in Romans (1.18-3:20), before revealing the transforming power of grace, Paul shows the absolute hopelessness of humankind without Christ.

A three-verse synopsis of Rom. 5.12-14, Eph. 2.1-3 paints in the darkest hues humanity's hopeless plight and predicament without Christ – dead, decadent, enslaved, doomed – all victims to the evil

---

[1] Stott, *The Message of Ephesians*, p. 69.

present in secular society (world, v. 2), Satan (the ruler of the kingdom of the air, v. 2), and self (sinful nature, v. 3). Paul's language here is no figure of speech. Nor is it describing some wild, uncivilized tribe in the deepest and darkest jungles of our world. No, Paul portrays all of humankind – the leaders of our world: the sophisticates and intellectuals who form the upper classes of our communities, the rich and famous, our sports idols, our movie stars of Hollywood and business tycoons of Madison Avenue. But Paul is also talking about the poor, the nincompoops, the unknowns of our world!

Verses 1-3. 'As for you' (v. 1), the NIV rendition of the Greek conjunction and pronoun (καὶ ὑμᾶς), blurs the continuity between 2.1-10 and 1.20-23. The more literal translation, 'and you', preserves the intended connection showing that the mighty power that raised Jesus from death to life is the same power that raised the believing Gentiles from spiritual death to spiritual life. If 'you' refers to Gentiles, 'we' (v. 3) points to the Jews with all the rest of humankind. Without exception, all shared the same hopeless predicament but also the same hopeful prospect.

Paul describes the human condition as one of death, 'transgressions and sins' (see Col. 2.13) being its cause and consequence, the reason for the transgressors' predicament and the realm in which they once lived (v. 1). It may be that there is a distinction between a 'transgression' (παράπτωμα) and a 'sin' (ἁμαρτία), the former indicating a false step or deviation from the path and the latter a missing of the divine mark or standard. If this is correct, then 'Before God we are both rebels and failures'.[2] In Greek philosophy and literature 'dead' was sometimes used figuratively of moral or spiritual inadequacy; in Scripture it additionally refers to the physical separation of the spirit from the body (Jas 2.26), or metaphorically for separation or estrangement from some source of life (e.g. Isa. 59.2). Speaking to Adam regarding the tree of the knowledge of good and evil in Eden, God said, 'when you eat of it you will surely die' (Gen. 2.17). Adam's disobedience resulted not in physical death, but in cessation of fellowship with God and his being put out of the garden. Similar figurative understandings of death are reflected in Mt. 8.22, Lk. 9.60, the parable of the lost son in Lk. 15.24, 32, and Jn 5.24, 25.

Death is not the same as a disability or dysfunction. The mention of death conjures up a picture of hopeless despair. A dead person is not merely in a deep sleep or comatose. Death speaks of finality, irrevocability. Sin resulted in spiritual death, and sinners can do nothing to save

[2] Stott, *The Message of Ephesians*, p.71.

themselves. God must act on their behalf. He must resurrect them by giving them spiritual life. That he has done in Jesus Christ.

A life of sin characterized the world in which Paul's readers used to live. 'Live' (v. 2) translates a Greek word that literally means 'walk' (περιπατέω). Occurring 95 times in the NT and 8 times in Ephesians, it is often used metaphorically to describe the path and direction in which one goes and one's way of life or conduct. Paul further describes the conduct of the pre-Christian Ephesians as in step with 'the ways of this world and of the ruler of the kingdom of the air' (v. 2). Ways of this world is more literally rendered 'age/era of this world' (τὸν αἰῶνα τοῦ κόσμου τούτου). Though a nuance of the notion of the spirit of the age or worldview cannot be ruled out, the Jewish contrast between this current evil age (עולם הזה), which parades 'a powerful mode of existence characterized by rebellion against God',[3] and the perfect and glorious age to come (עולם הבה) is most likely intended (see 1.21, 2.7 and 3.9, 11).

'World' (κόσμος) carries a broad range of meanings in the NT, encompassing the created order, people, and a diabolically organized system that opposes God and his kingdom purposes. It is the satanically inspired world order (see Jn 15.18, 23; 18.36; 1 Cor. 3.19) that Paul addresses here in 2.2, identifying its leader as 'the ruler of the kingdom of the air' – a personage referred to later as the devil (4.27; 6.11) and evil one (6.16). 'Ruler' designates someone who is 'the first' – 'prince' – and here shows Satan's central and supreme place and function over his evil operatives. He is commander-in-chief of the cosmic evil hordes who reside in the air – the unseen realm, an abode characterized by moral and spiritual darkness (Lk. 22.53; Eph. 6.12; Col. 1.13).

The one who rules the domain of the air (Satan) also rules the spirit that inspires unbelievers whose very nature is to disobey and rebel against God (2.2). 'Spirit' may refer to Satan himself, but more likely to a malevolent principle or disposition working in non-Christians.

What Paul says of the Gentiles, he also says of 'all of us' (v. 3) – including the Jews with whom he takes his stand. Though cognizant of degrees of badness in humanity and that common depravity manifests itself differently among various groups, Paul's conclusion elsewhere is: 'There is no one righteous, not even one. . . for all have sinned and fall short of God's glory' (Rom. 3.10, 23). All are under the common curse and need the common cure – Jesus. The NIV rendition 'cravings of our sinful nature' (Eph. 2.3) is more literally translated 'strong desires/passions of the flesh'.

'Flesh' (σάρξ) in this context, as opposed to its regular meanings of humankind's frailty and the human body, speaks of that element in

[3] Thielman, *Ephesians*, p. 123.

human nature that defies and resists God's claims and fulfillment of his purposes in one's life and in the world. Commonly called 'self-centered human nature,'[4] it is that egocentric aspect of human nature which 'has been corrupted at the source', and epitomized by 'appetites and propensities which, if unchecked, produce 'the works of the flesh' that Paul catalogues in Gal. 5.19-20.[5] The unredeemed are driven not only by the dictates of the physical instinct, impulses and appetites of the flesh, but also by sinful 'thoughts' (v. 3), i.e. an unregenerate mindset and outlook. One's mindset is a mirror of one's fundamental nature. None can claim immunity to sin's contagion, for sin dominates the total self. None have been able to tame the wild, raging and destructive fires of the sinful heart. None have been able to rise above the dark horizons of a dissolute mind. A keen intellect does not in itself generate pure and noble thoughts; high pedigree provides no protection against the downward pull of sin. Outward actions may at times mask the savagery of the monster that lives inside, but sooner or later it breaks out of its cage and reveals its true colors.

Sinful thoughts, resulting in inward turmoil, outward rebellion, and hostility toward God and ultimate eternal death are the fruit of a 'mind of the flesh' – a sinful mind (Rom. 8.6, 7). A mind controlled by the Holy Spirit is the only remedy for a mind controlled by the flesh (Rom. 8.6). Not only does such a mind experience divine life and peace; imbued by the Spirit, it aims at pleasing God and glorifying Christ.

Like the pre-Christian Gentiles, Jews 'were by nature objects of wrath' (v. 3). The Greek renders it: 'were by nature children of wrath'. By nature means naturally endowed, and states the means and cause for becoming the children of wrath; it was by birth and because of being descendants of Adam (Gal. 2.15; cf. Rom. 2.27). As the Hebrew idiom 'son of death' means to be worthy of death (2 Sam. 12.5; cf. Mt. 23.15), so 'children of wrath', similar to 'sons of disobedience', is a Hebraism and means deserving of wrath.

God's wrath is neither peevish outburst nor vengeful action against sin. Nor is it the law of cause and effect running its course. It is, rather, God's settled holy disposition and opposition toward evil. Divine wrath should not be seen in radical contrast to divine love, however. Wrath is love's scream at those who will not listen to God's acts of grace and gentle wooings. God's wrath is governed by his love. God does not show favoritism. His wrath is trained upon both Gentiles and Jews who follow the sinful cravings of the flesh.

---

[4] Stott, *The Message of Ephesians*, p. 74.
[5] Bruce, *Colossians, Philemon, Ephesians*, pp. 283-84.

Verse 4. 'But because of his great love for us ...' Sin is not the last word in the drama of redemption. Death is not the final chapter in the history of the human race. Where sin abounded, grace 'superabounded'. Where sin brought death, grace brought eternal life (Rom. 5.15-20). Grace is greater than sin. That little conjunction 'but' cradles the contrast between human despair and divine goodwill, humankind's ruin and God's redemption, humanity's past predicament without Christ and its present privilege in Christ. It is the polestar, the bright signpost that appears in the night sky to point lost mariners in the direction of home. 'But' occurs a number of times in the NT to show divine interventions on human's behalf. Peter is chained to two guards in a maximum security prison, 'but' the church earnestly prays to God and a miraculous deliverance happens (Acts 12.5-11). As the world stands before the divine tribunal, shuddering helplessly and hopelessly at the eternal night to which it has been sentenced, Paul offers hope with the words, 'But now a righteousness from God ... has been made known' (Rom. 3.21; cf. Gal. 4.4-5).

'But' (δέ) demarcates the passing of the dark night of sin and its consequence and the presence of the dawn of a new day of hope. It draws a line between two periods: the period before Christ and the period after Christ, reminding us that in the dark ground of every midnight of despair lie the seeds of the dawn. Yet 'but' packs no punch on its own. The Greek says, 'but God' (Eph. 2.4), introducing God as the central actor in the divine drama of redemption. He is the source and subject of salvation. God it is who has brought hope and a new future for humankind, transforming human objects of wrath into objects of divine love.

Salvation was solely God's initiative. Paul states the reason and motivation for God's gracious action – his love and great mercy. Love is his unselfish and benevolent disposition that sees something infinitely precious in the worst of sinners. The little adjective 'great' that describes God's love should not be dismissed as insignificant. It indicates the immensity, enormity, and profundity of the divine frame of mind toward us. Human salvation ultimately cost God his only Son. That is the past event Paul alludes to in the verb 'loved' (ἠγάπησεν) – 'His great love with which he loved[6] us' (NKJV, v. 4). In the death of Christ, God gave himself. He had no one better to give, nothing greater to offer. If grace is God's giving us what we do not deserve (salvation), mercy is his not giving us what we do deserve (death). Mercy, which is the fountain head of God's action, is 'his overflowing active

---

[6] Paul does not use the present tense 'loves'. The Greek verb is an aorist indicative which in the context likely adumbrates Christ's death on the cross

compassion[7] toward helpless, hopeless, unworthy, and undeserving
sinners. It is not without significance that Paul says that God is 'rich in
mercy'. 'Rich' speaks of God's lavish and abundant compassion, his
vast reservoir and display of pity toward undeserving sinners. 'Mercy'
regularly translates the Hebrew חסד or רחם and its Greek counterpart
ἔλεός. The first (*chesed*) speaks of kindness or lovingkindness, and is
consistently rendered 'steadfast love' by the RSV. The second (*raham*)
relates to the 'womb' or 'bowels' from which deep sympathy or compassion flows. Steeped in the language of covenant relationship between God and Israel, the terms denote both the visceral feelings of
affection and the ensuing undeserved outward display of kindness (e.g.
pardon, forgiveness, deliverance) of Yahweh toward his people. 'Lovingkindness' combines both the profound emotion and gracious action
associated with the terms while 'steadfast love' (Ps. 145.8) describes
God's unshakable covenant fidelity and willingness to forgive even
when Israel proved unfaithful to its side of the bargain. Micah, along
with others of the prophets, declares that God 'delights in mercy'
(7.18).

God's love and mercy were most profoundly demonstrated at the
cross (Jn 3.16; 15. 13; Rom. 5.6-11). That event is clearly what Paul
has in mind here in Eph. 2.4. No greater love, no greater mercy could
be shown than that manifested at Calvary. At Calvary God gave himself. He had nothing better, nothing greater to give than himself. 'Demand what thou wilt, O God, but grant what thou demandest', says
St. Augustine. The sacrifice God demanded for sin he himself provided. He died the death sin demanded. Love and mercy – to which Paul
will add grace (v. 5) and kindness (v. 7) – marvelous qualities that reveal the heart of God.

As though lost in the wonder of God's great love and abundant
mercy, the thought of human sinfulness and spiritual doom still being
weighed against the incomprehensible divine generosity, not until v. 5
does Paul for the first time reveal the end result, the accomplishment of
such benevolent liberality. 'God has made us alive with Christ even
when we were dead.' We were dead, Paul declares (2.1). There are
only two options for a dead person: burial or resurrection. Burial naturally follows death,[8] forever shutting the door to hope and accepting an

---

[7] Lincoln, *Ephesians*, p. 100.

[8] In his Romans commentary, Stott debunks the popular misunderstanding that to be
dead to sin means to become insensitive, insensible, or immune to it (*Ephesians*, pp. 169-
72). Since Christ himself died to sin once for all (6.10), though he was sinless, and since
Paul urges believers to 'put to death the misdeeds of the body' (8.13), Stott argues rather
that death to sin must be interpreted legally, not physically. Death is the law's penalty for
sin, and since Christ paid sin's penalty for believers in full when he died, the law has no
claim on the Christian. In his words, 'to die to sin and to die to the law are identical.

awful finality. Resurrection is the other alternative, but one that only God can bring about. Spiritual resurrection, not spiritual burial, is God's solution for spiritual death. Restoration to life – that is God's way! God's last word is life, not death.

This restoration to new life, this resurrection, is shared. It is co-resurrection – with Christ.[9] Paul is here speaking neither of a physical resurrection nor a future one. He here addresses our positional resurrection with Christ. What Christ experienced physically, believers presently share spiritually in identification, association, and participation in him. What God did for Christ he also did for believers. As head of the church, Christ identifies with his people. Hence, believers share in his sufferings (Rom. 8.17; Phil. 1.29), his crucifixion, death, burial, and resurrection (Rom. 6.3-10; Col. 2.12-13; 3.1). In addition, we are seated with him in the heavenly realms (Eph. 2.6; Col. 3.3), and shall appear with him in glory (Col. 3.4). Believers share solidarity with Christ. Their life, hope, and destiny are bound up with him.

These are spiritual realities and not mere mystical musings or unattainable ideals and aspirations. They, however, boggle the mind of even the greatest of saints, plead for clarification, and prompt Paul's prayer 'that the God of our Lord Jesus Christ, the glorious Father, may give you the Spirit of wisdom and revelation. . . that the eyes of your heart may be enlightened' (Eph. 1.17, 18). How may we the people of God tap into and unpack their implications for everyday living? How can we bring them out of the spiritual realm, put overhauls on them, and put them to work? I must confess that here I see veiled mysteries, hidden wonders, unexplored trails in the lush tropical landscape of his love and grace. Yet, if but dimly, I see them as realities to which I am invited; if but faintly, I hear them as sounds from the distant and transcendent world, beckoning me as God did John, to 'come hither' and to come higher.

This much even our dim eyes can see: to be raised and seated with Christ in the heavenly realms means our new life should be one of triumph, not one of despairing defeat. From that high and elevated position we experience an enlarged vision of our world. Such an exalted position gives one heaven's perspective, God's point of view, on things. To be in this privileged position means we gain a sense of enhanced values. Satan, sin, and society no longer have a claim on our lives or dictate how we live. Our moral qualities and moral judgments

Both signify that through participation in the death of Christ the law's curse or condemnation on sin has been taken away' (*Romans*, InterVarsity, 1994, p. 194). See also C.E.B Cranfield, *Romans: A Shorter Commentary* (Grand Rapids: Eerdmans, 1985), p. 150.

[9] Charles Hodge has noted that in the NT the Greek verb ζωοποιεῖν (to make alive) nearly always refers to the impartation of life by Christ. See his *Epistle to the Ephesians* (Grand Rapids: Eerdmans, 1966), p. 112.

reflect the majesty of the Father whose children we are. What is more, we no longer live for ourselves, but seeing the needs of earth more clearly from this lofty position, we are driven with a flaming passion to make a transforming difference by the power of God given to us.

Far from embracing a triumphalism that denies the presence of conflict and struggle, the Christian's life of victory is tempered by the reality of life lived in the tension of the 'already' and 'not yet'. Further, the very cross by which the Christian lives symbolizes pain and triggers conflict. We live in victory, yet knowing that no victory is complete in this life. We live joyfully, yet knowing that our joy is incomplete. With the Apostle, we live in hope unseen. We celebrate a D-Day victory, assured that the decisive victory won by Christ in the cross and resurrection guarantees a V-Day final triumph.

Paul concludes v. 5 with what is termed a 'parenthetical outburst',[10] an exclamation repeated in v. 8: 'by grace'. This disruption in the flow of the Apostle's thought shows 'the astonishment Paul has that God should save people out of their living death'.[11] The placement of 'grace' at the beginning of the clause in the Greek text is for emphasis, highlighting the fact that salvation is indeed by grace – nothing else, nothing more! Occurring 155 times in the NT, 'grace' is used by Paul 100 times, 12 of which are in Ephesians. It denotes absolutely free, unearned or unmerited favor, the sheer goodness and generous kindness of God. Grace is God's pure and holy love embracing the unholy and unlovely. The perfect tense connects the past and the present, the Greek perfect construction 'you are/have been saved' (ἐστε σεσῳσμένοι) denoting an action that occurred in the past but which carries ongoing result or effect in the present.[12] The passive voice indicates that salvation is God's action, which involves not only deliverance from bondage and rescue from wrath and death, but God's positive act of imparting life to us, raising us up, seating us with Christ, and transferring us into the new kingdom with its myriad blessings.[13] Both the AV and NEB capture the spirit of the intensive perfect in their translation: 'you are saved', a present experience from a past action of God.

Sin's effects on the human race are far-reaching. Humankind is fractured, fragmented, estranged, severed from the source of life. Just as there are many words to describe humankind in its fallen state, so there are several to describe what God has done in salvation to reverse the

---

[10] Hoehner, *Ephesians*, p. 331.

[11] Snodgrass, *Ephesians*, p. 103.

[12] Paul sees salvation as a past event (Rom. 8:24), a present experience (1 Cor. 1.18, 21; 15.2), and a future anticipation (1 Cor. 3.15; Eph. 1.10, 14; 4.30).

[13] O'Brien, *Ephesians*, p. 169.

curse and its impact. To the condemned God provides justification – right status and standing; to the captive he offers redemption. For the guilty he provides pardon and remission, for the estranged reconciliation. Sin's kingdom does not extend beyond the reach of God's salvation but is overshadowed by it. 'God's response to the sinners' plight is one of mercy, the motive for his compassion is his love for them, and the basis for his action is his grace'.[14]

The believers' union, identification, and participation with Christ receive particular emphasis in 2.6, where Paul says they are 'raised with' and 'seated with' him (cf. Rom. 6.3-8; Col. 2.11-12, 20; 3.1-3). We share spiritually what Jesus experienced physically. He died physically and was raised physically (1.20). We died spiritually and are raised spiritually. This shared experience indicates that when God acted on behalf of Christ he also acted on behalf of his children. Paul does not here paint a picture of the believer's future with Christ; he rather presents what is now a reality, which means that 'transferred from the old dominion to the new reign of Christ'[15] we share the victory and triumph of Christ and can take our stand against the malevolent forces that war against us (6.11-12). Without exception, all Christians are 'made one with the glorified Christ so that His position is their position; his possessions their possession; His privileges their privileges; His power their power; His plentitude their plentitude'.[16]

Verses 7-10. Why has God lavished his mercy and love on lost sinners? Why has he transformed them into saints, raising, exalting, and seating them with Christ Jesus? Paul gives the answer, the reason and God's goal in verse 7: 'in order that in the coming ages he might show the incomparable riches of his grace, expressed in his kindness to us in Christ Jesus'. God's ultimate purpose in our salvation reaches beyond our personal redemption, beyond our present privilege of sharing corporate solidarity with Christ, beyond time. Already in 1.6 Paul has stated that God's goal in our salvation is 'to the praise of his glorious grace'. Here in 2.7 a similar idea is expressed, but expanded. God's eventual goal and purpose in our salvation is that we might display and demonstrate his matchless and measureless grace throughout the coming ages.[17] This is the believer's glorious future prospect. Only in the

---

[14] Hoehner, *Ephesians* , p. 331.
[15] O'Brien, *Ephesians*, p. 171.
[16] Ruth Paxon, *The Wealth, Walk and Warfare*, pp. 222, 223.
[17] The practical mind of the Hebrew, unlike the Greek's, does not view eternity in terms of timelessness but as 'one age supervening on another like successive waves of the sea, as far into the future as thought can reach'. F.F. Bruce, *Colossians, Philemon, Ephesians*, p. 288.

succeeding ages of eternity will the reality of what God has done in those who believe be fully recognized for what it is.

The adjective 'incomparable' (ὑπερβάλλον), which describes God's extravagant grace shown to us (2.7), is used exclusively by Paul in the NT. In Eph. 1.19 he employs it to speak of the power that God exerted in raising and exalting Christ, and in 3.19 to indicate the surpassing greatness of Christ's love. God's extravagant generosity, his incomparable and inexpressible display of grace in saving the lost has as its goal the redeemed becoming his 'eternal exhibit' throughout eternity. The redeemed are and will be throughout eternity the principal objective evidence and proof of God's grace and kindness. It baffles the mind and renders the lips speechless at such an inscrutable and munificent parade of undeserved honor that throughout time and the countless years of eternity the church, 'this society of pardoned rebels', which God designed to be 'the masterpiece of his goodness', will 'provide the pattern' after which the future reconciled universe will be modeled.[18]

The topic of salvation by grace which Paul introduced in 2.5, the display of which will redound to God's praise throughout eternity (2.7), is picked up and explained in 2.8-10. 'For it is by grace you have been saved, through faith – and this not from yourselves, it is the gift of God' (v. 8). 'For' maintains the stress on God's incomparable wealth of grace that inundates believers (vv. 4-7). As in 2.5 Paul again states that grace is the objective ground or cause for human salvation, now adding that faith is the subjective means[19] by which it is appropriated (see Rom. 3.22-26; Gal. 2.16; Eph. 1.13; Phil. 3.9). Grace and faith exclude the possibility of works, standing in stark contrast to human endeavor or merit.

What is this faith (πίστις) that is so crucial to salvation (Hab. 2:4; Rom. 1.17; 4.5; Gal. 3.11)? Its Hebrew counterpart, אמונה, often rendered 'trust' and closely related to a cognate noun, אמת, regularly translated 'faithfulness' or 'truth', denotes the subjective confidence placed in someone or something and the objective basis for such confidence, and is frequently rendered trust, reliability, fidelity, and faithfulness (Deut. 32.20; Jer. 5.1, 3). The NT Greek (πίστις) reflects the influence of the Hebrew, and means faith, trust, reliance, proof, confidence. Principally, the *'mn* word family deals with 'that on which one may rely or the act of relying on something believed reliable. Both sides of the coin are present – relying on something or someone believed relia-ble'.[20] A covenant word, faith, then, is not mental assent; nor is it mere

---

[18] Bruce, *Colossians, Philemon, Ephesians*, p. 288.

[19] We find rather unconvincing the argument that 'faith' here refers to Christ's faithfulness or obedience.

[20] Snodgrass, *Ephesians*, pp. 104, 105.

belief. It is trust and reliance, belief acted on. To be sure, it is human action, but a particular kind of action. It is 'a response which allows salvation to become operative,' a posture which 'receives what has already been accomplished by God in Christ'.[21]

Self-achievement, self-sufficiency, showing that we have earned what we have and have worked hard to accomplish and attain our level of success in life – that is the stuff of which human nature is made. Not so with salvation! In an attempt to exclude human effort from salvation altogether, Paul goes on to add, 'and this is not from yourselves, it is the gift of God' (v. 8). 'Gift' (δῶρον) refers neither to grace nor faith, but the whole concept and process of salvation. The Greek states it quite emphatically: 'God's gift it is.' The word order in Greek further heightens the emphasis upon the divine origin of the gift which is salvation, and contrasting 'God' and 'yourselves' – the divine source of the gift and inability of human effort to achieve it. Irrespective of what some Christians believe, and contrary to what many religions practice, salvation by works finds no place in Paul's teaching. Biblical Christianity avers that salvation is all God's free gift. No good works one does, no matter how noble, can earn it.

Verse 9 further elaborates on salvation as a gratuitous gift from God, a truth Paul teaches in Romans (3.20, 28; 4.1-5) and Galatians (2.16). If we could earn our own salvation, we would have occasion to boast (Rom. 4.2). Since, however, salvation is free of charge, it stands to reason that no one can boast of earning it. Nor can one claim that his or her goodness merited it. In Paul's mind, the gospel of grace slams the door shut in the face of boasting (Rom. 3.27; 4.2; 1 Cor. 1.29). The only boasting the gospel allows is in God (Rom. 5.11) or in the cross of Christ (Gal. 6.14). Therefore, 'We shall not be able to strut round heaven like peacocks. Heaven will be filled with the exploits of Christ and the praises of God.'[22]

Verse 10. 'For we are God's workmanship'. 'For' gives further reason why salvation excludes the possibility of boasting: believers are God's creation. They have nothing to do with bringing about the new life they now possess. Once dead (2.1), they are now alive in Christ. In the Greek, 'God's' (literally, αὐτοῦ, his) is the first word in the sentence, indicating a strong emphasis upon his being the source of this new life; therefore 'there could be no human works prior to that creation to which it could be attributed'.[23] The divine origin of salvation is borne out further in the verse by the participle 'created' (κτισθέντες) which,

---

[21] Lincoln, *Ephesians*, p. 111.
[22] Stott, *Ephesians*, p. 83.
[23] Lincoln, *Ephesians*, p. 113.

viewed as a divine or theological passive, may be translated: God created[24] you.

Paul calls God's new creation God's 'workmanship' (2.10), a term which refers to a product or something that is made. Christians are the 'product' of God's creative genius. 'Workmanship' is the equivalent of the Greek ποίημα, from which our word 'poem' derives. Farfetched though it may seem to us, we Christians are God's poem – the lofty, elegant and rhythmical language that adorns God's thought. A poem, the crafted work of a poet, captures only one essential nuance of the Greek, however – symmetry and beauty. In classical Greek, this term (unlike ἔργον or πρᾶγμα) alluded to any work of a skilled artisan. A person's deed, a decorative vase, a creative painting, a symphony, a car, poetry – all could be called *poiema*.

Though used in a variety of ways in the OT, in its two occurrences in the NT it refers to the material creation (Rom. 1.20) and the new spiritual creation in Christ (Eph. 2.10) – both the skillfully crafted work of God. God's appraisal of the Genesis creation was: 'very good' (Gen. 1.31) – a masterwork. Many Bible interpreters believe the word in the Ephesians passage appropriately describes 'a work of art and see a reference to God's masterpiece'.[25] Believers are God's work of art, his masterpiece, his workmanship evidenced by the good works they perform.[26] Can it be said that in the new spiritual creation (2 Cor. 5.17) God outdid himself? Nothing he created before it can compare with it in beauty and splendor.

Art galleries and art museums around the world exhibit the works of many great artists. Who of us does not marvel at the magnificence and alluring beauty they display? Though possessing none of their skills and creative imagination, I cannot escape the bewitching spell the artistic luminaries cast on me each time I pay them a visit. Apart from the amazing brilliance each parades, whether it is the creation of an immortal legend or that of a relatively unknown modern debutant, there are two commonalities all the works share: each reflects the creative skill of its creator, and only the very best bears the signature of the artist – never the rejects.

God's masterpiece, his new creation – the church – bears his signature and displays his genius. And like any great work of art, it is presently on display – and will be throughout eternity! Paul informs us that

---

[24] The passive form in Greek is more precisely translated 'having been created/you were created', with God as the performer of the action. Hoehner has noted that the Greek κτίζω ('create') is 'used in the NT only of God's acts of creation in both the physical ... and spiritual realms' (p. 347).

[25] Leon Morris, *Expository Reflections on the Letter to the Ephesians* (Grand Rapids: Baker Books, 1994), p. 57.

[26] Bruce, *The Epistle to the Ephesians*, p. 52.

one of the purposes and functions of the church which God has sovereignly designed is 'to do good works' (Eph. 2.10; cf. 2 Cor. 5.10; 1 Thess. 5.15; 1 Tim. 2.10). When God chose us in eternity (Eph. 1.4), he also prepared us to enter upon and conduct a life of good works. Where once we were dead in transgressions and sins (2.1) and followed the course of the world (2.2), we are now called to live a life of goodness based upon the values of the new life we have received.

God is concerned with not only imparting new life to us, but also with how we live. The new life he put in must be lived out in a new lifestyle. While not a condition for salvation, good works are a natural consequence of it. They are the fruit of God's grace working in our hearts (1 Cor. 15.10; Phil. 2.13). Grace establishes the ground of salvation, good works its goal. Good works are practical human expressions of the goodness, graciousness, and greatness of God. They are also demonstrations of the believer's gratitude to him for his marvelous and inexpressible gift of salvation.

Not only is the church currently on display; it will throughout the endless years of eternity 'show the incomparable riches of his grace' (Eph. 2.7). One obvious uniqueness of God's new handiwork is that it was 'created in Christ Jesus' (v. 10), that is, through God's action in Christ. Paul elsewhere declares categorically, 'Therefore, if anyone is in Christ, he is a new creation; the old has gone, the new has come!' (2 Cor. 5.17) and, 'Neither circumcision nor uncircumcision means anything; what counts is a new creation' (Gal. 6.15).

When God created the heavens and the earth, he displayed his awesome power; but when he created the church, he demonstrated his amazing love. The first creation is a mute and unresponsive recipient of its Creator's liberality; the latter an intelligent and volitional respondent to his profligate beneficence. The first God threw out into space from the hollow of his hand; the latter he created in Christ, wooing and winning it by divine love. Of the world God can say, I have made you. Only of the church can he say, I have redeemed you. It takes more to redeem than to create. Redemption cost God dearly. Redemption is greater than creation. Redemption entails more than the renewal of the disintegration, discord, and ruptures of the fall. It means a lot more than the reinstitution of Eden's innocence and pristine beauty. It is 'the creation of a new humanity and a new world, which has previously existed only in the mind and purpose of God'.[27] The redeemed alone, the blood-bought church alone, is worthy to be given to God's Son in marriage.

---

[27] Maxie D. Dunnam, *Galatians, Ephesians, Philippians, Colossians, Philemon* (The Communicator's Commentary; Waco, TX: Word Books, 1982), p. 170.

C. The Church: A New Inclusive Community (2.11-22)

'The wall is gone! The wall is gone!' Unforgettable words! Joyous words! Liberating and immortal words that rang out in frenzied crescendo, filling the German sky with hopeful expectation on the evening of November 9, 1989, as the Berlin Wall began to crash to the ground. Twenty-six miles of concrete stacked some ten feet high, for nearly three decades it had stood as a scowling, defiant sentinel, dividing Germany into two and keeping its people apart by terror, hatred, repression, and fear. On one fateful night, in a matter of hours and against all odds, the erstwhile bastion of evil was definitively breached, quickly to fall entirely, clearing the way for a new and free Germany.

That is exactly what Christ did at the cross 2,000 years ago. Through his death, the dividing wall that separated humankind from God and Jew from Gentile has been torn down. The wall is gone! The wall is gone! is the message that reverberates in Eph. 2.11-22. The sad reality of the fall and the flood is that the unity of humankind which God declared at the creation has given way to estrangement and alienation at every level of human existence. No country or community in the world escapes the disfiguring and fracturing blight of some level of racial, economic, national, class, and gender barriers. Our world, nation, and communities are war-torn, ethnically fractured, ideologically polarized. Disparities, divisions, inequality, and injustice meet us everywhere. What is God's remedy for this problem? Ephesians provides the answer in the reconciling work of Christ.

A 'double alienation', or rather its substitution by reconciliation, serves as the theme of Ephesians 2.[1] The first half of the chapter deals with alienation from God (vv. 1-10), the second the alienation of humans from each other (vv. 11-22). That God would one day 'bring all things in heaven and on earth together under one head, even Christ' (1.10) climaxes the eulogistic prayer of Paul in 1.3-14. This vision of universal unification and reconciliation of all things under the headship and lordship of Christ constitutes part of the revealed 'mystery of his [God's] will' (1.9), fundamental to which is the uniting of Jews and Gentiles in the church (Eph. 3.5-6).[2]

The union of redeemed and reconciled Jews and Gentiles in the church is what Paul discusses in 2.11-22. Before declaring the unity that Christ has brought about between the Jews and Gentiles, Paul discusses the vast gulf and great disparities that separated them. The

---

[1] Stott, *The Message of Ephesians*, p. 90.

[2] Snodgrass has noted, 'Ephesians gives more attention to and makes loftier statements about the church than any other letter, despite the fact that the word *ekklesia* occurs only three times outside the husband-wife analogy in chapter 5' (*Ephesians*, p. 124).

magnitude of the problem that existed between Jew and Gentile is like nothing the modern world has known. The seemingly impassable rift has been described as 'worse than the Hindu caste' system. No room existed for social intercourse. For the devout Jew, to touch a Gentile was polluting, to eat non-kosher food repulsive, and to engage in Gentile religion sacrilegious.[3] What led to this tragic situation was that Israel not only distorted the doctrine of election into one of narcissistic nationalism, but 'became filled with racial pride and hatred, despised Gentiles as "dogs," and developed traditions which kept them apart'.[4]

Early Christians faced an intractable predicament: Given a global mandate, Christianity had the dilemma of being the offspring of Judaism. Unfortunately, the Jews were engaged in 'a double hatred – the world hated them and they hated the world. No nation was more bitterly hated than the Jews.... No nation ever hated other nations as the Jews did.'[5] It is these inveterate enemies that Christ has reconciled, this huge chasm that he has bridged, this seemingly insurmountable barrier that he has destroyed through his death (Eph. 2.14-16).

As to the structure of Paul's thought, Eph. 2.11-22, which continues a formal 'formerly ... now' schema (vv. 11-13, 19) begun in 2.1-10, divides into three parts. Verses 11-13 contrast the Gentiles' pitiful pre-Christian plight with the privileged position of Israel and their present state of favor in Christ. Paul's aim in often referring to their past is not to stir guilt but, rather, to stimulate gratitude for what God has done for them. Explanation of the means whereby the Gentiles have been brought into favor and the divine purpose behind it is given in 2.14-18 (cf. Col. 1.21-23). It is by his cross-death that Christ has reversed the plight of the Gentiles. Through that death both Gentiles and Jews 'have access to the Father by one Spirit' (2.18). Verses 19-22 state the consequences of Christ's reconciling work through which Gentiles experience a new and equal status as members of God's new community, members of a new family, and a dwelling for the Spirit of the living God.

Verses 11-13. 'Therefore, remember that formerly you who are Gentiles by birth ...' (v. 11). The conjunction 'therefore' in Greek, linking what is now taken up in vv. 11-13 with 2.1-10 and directly back to 1.15-23, can also be translated 'for this reason', and provides the basis upon which the Gentiles should now evaluate and appreciate their new

---

[3] J.M. Stifler, *An Introduction to the Study of the Acts of the Apostles* (New York: Fleming & Revell, 1892), pp. 81, 82.

[4] Stott, *The Spirit, the Church, and the World: the Message of Acts* (Downers Grove: InterVarsity, 1990), p. 185.

[5] William Barclay, *The Mind of St. Paul* (New York: Harper & Row, 1975), pp. 9, 10.

status and privileges as Christians compared to their pre-Christian state
of depravity and death from which God has rescued them. Gentile
Christians are twice exhorted to remember (vv. 11, 12, NIV), not because they have actually forgotten their former situation, but because a
conscious awareness and evaluation of their unenviable past will arouse
a greater love and gratitude for their unparalleled present position in
Christ.

Like the Greeks who scorned those who were not members of their
cities, disparagingly calling them pagans (ἔθνη), so the Jews despised
other nations regarding them as heathen, pagans (Heb. גוֹיִם). In addition, although circumcision was not an exclusive practice of the Jews,[6]
it was for them more than a rite of passage; it was the physical sign of
covenant with God (Gen. 17.9-14) and membership with his people.[7]
Its absence among the Gentiles betrayed their estrangement from the
God of Israel and marked them as ceremonially unclean. Elsewhere
Paul speaks of the relative insignificance of circumcision, Christ establishing a different way for people to relate to God. 'Circumcision is
nothing and uncircumcision is nothing. Keeping God's commands is
what counts' (1 Cor. 7.19). 'For in Christ Jesus neither circumcision
nor uncircumcision has any value. The only thing that counts is faith
expressing itself through love' (Gal. 5.6; cf. Rom. 3.30). To Paul Jews
had no advantage over the Gentiles by the simple act of circumcision
since it was a human activity performed by persons who, like the Gentiles, lived 'in the flesh'. What ultimately mattered was the circumcision which resulted in 'the putting off of the sinful nature, not with a
circumcision done by the hands of men but with the circumcision
done by Christ' (Col. 2.11).

Some non-Christians often display a strutting arrogance based upon
their accomplishments and achievements, and look disparagingly at
others less fortunate. Christians live by a different ethic. Yet, we must
ever be on guard against spiritual pride that may cause us to wear
God's special gifts and favors as merit badges or decorative pieces to
make us look better than others. Paradoxically, the assets we possess
can become strangling liabilities. In Romans, Paul declares the privileged custodians of the Law, Jews, guilty and condemned as the Gentiles without the Law (2.1-4, 17-28). Further, pride can subtly tiptoe
into our hearts and make us magnify the faults or deficits of others

---

[6] The practice was not observed by the Philistines (1 Sam. 31.4; 2 Sam. 1.20), but was
common among the Egyptians and Semitic groups, except the Babylonians and Assyrians.
See 'Circumcision', *The Interpreter's Dictionary of the Bible*, vol. I (Nashville: Abingdon,
1980), p. 629.

[7] Paul on many occasions uses 'uncircumcision' as a designation for the Gentiles and
'circumcision' for the Jews.

while minimizing our own. We must make Paul's corrective to the Corinthians the gatekeeper of our hearts. 'What do you have that you did not receive? And if you did receive it, why do you boast as though you did not?' (1 Cor. 4.7).

With an aim to stirring them to a greater gratitude for their new position in Christ, Paul exhorts the Gentiles in v. 12 to remember five[8] deficits or disadvantages from which they suffered in their pre-Christian past. Like the Jews, they were Christless – 'separated from Christ'; but unlike the Jews, they had no hope of the promised Messiah (Gen. 18.15; Dan. 7.13-14; Zech. 9.9-10; cf. Rom. 9.4-5). Second, the Gentiles were stateless – 'excluded from citizenship[9] in Israel'. The Greek term for excluded is used only in two other places in the NT, in each instance in relation to Gentile alienation from God (Eph. 4.18; Col. 1.21). Here it refers to their being 'outside the sphere of God's election'[10] – excluded from the privileges, fellowship, and sense of belonging citizenship afforded in the theocracy of Israel (Rom. 3.1-2; 9.4-5).

The experience of being friendless – 'foreigners to the covenants of the promise' is a third deficiency the Gentiles experienced. Among the number of covenants God made with Israel, the Abrahamic covenant (Gen. 12.1-4; 13.14-18; 15.1-21; 17.1-21), the Davidic covenant (2 Sam. 7.12-17), and the new covenant (Jer. 31.31-34; Ezek. 36.23-36) take center stage. God promised land, seed, and prosperity to Abraham. Israel's future existence was guaranteed through David's Son – the coming Messiah (Ps. 89.3-4, 34-36). In the new covenant God promised to write his laws in the hearts of his people rather than on stone tablets (Jer. 31.31-34; Ezek. 11.19-20). God's great promise behind all the covenants was the sending of the Messiah[11] (Gen. 12.2-3; Dan. 9.25, 27). Not having the promise of messianic salvation, the Gentiles were greatly disadvantaged.

Without the covenants, without divine revelation, the Gentiles were hopeless – 'without hope'. Hardship and hopelessness characterized life for the masses of Gentiles in the first-century Roman Empire. Conversely, Israel's special relationship with God and the hope accompanying it rested upon and was ensured by the covenants. Hope that Messiah alone could give, however (Col. 1.27), messianic blessings that

---

[8] Some of the italicized descriptor designations are borrowed from R. Kent Hughes' *Ephesians* (pp. 90-91) and Stott, *The Message of Ephesians*, p. 96.

[9] The Greek counterpart (πολιτεία) can also be translated 'state,' 'government' or 'commonwealth'.

[10] O'Brien, *Ephesians*, p. 189.

[11] Snodgrass, *Ephesians* (p. 127) opines that the covenants of promise 'focused primarily on the Messiah and the Holy Spirit, the means by which the covenants with Abraham, David, and Jeremiah were fulfilled (see 2 Cor. 3:3-18; Gal. 3:14)'.

he alone could bestow, expectation of future salvation, resurrection, and eternal life – all a part of the faith Gentiles now share in Christ – never crossed the minds of non-Christian Gentiles. Paul states, finally, that the Gentiles were godless – 'without God in the world'. This does not mean they had no god to worship. What Paul said to the Corinthians was true for the whole Gentile world. 'For even if there are so-called gods, whether in heaven or on earth (as indeed there are many "gods" and many "lords"), yet for us [Jews] there is but one God' (1 Cor. 8.5, 6). Gentiles at Ephesus, as elsewhere, were devoted to a pantheon of gods. ἄθεός, from which the English 'atheist' derives and is here translated 'without God', can mean 'ungodly' or 'godless', but here means that the Gentiles were devoid of knowledge of the true and living God, therefore neither believed in nor had relationship with the God of Israel (Rom. 1.18-23; 1 Cor. 8.4, 6; 1 Thess. 1.9).

'But now in Christ Jesus' (v. 13) introduces a drastic and dramatic reversal in the plight of the Gentiles. Reminiscent of the 'but ... God' of 2.4, it means that things are different now. Jesus has made the difference, repealing the 'double alienation' between Jews and Gentiles (2.13-15) and between Gentiles and God (2.16-18), bridging the greatest divide in human history through his death. Once separate from Christ (v. 12), they are now in Christ Jesus (v. 13), sharing with him all the Father's blessings. They who were once underprivileged have now become the privileged people of God. In a final contrast between the pre-Christian state of the Gentiles and their present position of favor, Paul draws particular attention to the fact that they were at one time far away but have now come 'near' (v. 13) – language and images borrowed from Isaiah.

Isaiah had preached 'peace, peace, to those far and near' (57.19), a message probably intended for both home-dwelling and diaspora Jews, but which 'may include also the foreigners'.[12] In the OT the Gentile nations were termed 'far away' because they were far from God and his covenant people (Deut. 28.49; Isa. 5.26; Jer. 5.15). Regarded as being close to God (Ps. 148.14), the Jews were called those who were 'near'. Something of this distinction is intimated in Peter's Pentecost sermon preached to some 15 nations. 'The promise is for you and your children and for all who are far off' (Acts 2.39), and stated clearly in the Lord's charge to Paul. 'Go; I will send you far away to the Gentiles' (Acts 22.21). Gentile separation from the God of Israel was dramatically symbolized in the stonewall barricade in the Jerusalem temple that restricted foreigners to the Court of the Gentiles and prohibited them

---

[12] *Isaiah–Ezekiel*, The Expositor's Bible Commentary, 6 (Grand Rapids: Zondervan, 1986), p. 320. The words were originally addressed to Jews exiled in Babylon, but later applied to proselytes by Jewish rabbis.

access into the sanctuary under pain of death.[13] Jewish rabbis used the term 'to bring near' (Heb. *qareb*, meaning 'accept') of non-Israelite converts (proselytes) to Judaism who, by joining with Israel, came near to God and his people thus entering upon all the privileges of the covenant.

Clearly, Paul's use of the two metaphors in Eph. 2.13 goes beyond a familiar rabbinic understanding. What God has done for Gentile believers is not simply providing entrée into the commonwealth of Israel and the covenant blessings based upon acceptance of the Torah. Rather, he has instituted a new Messianic community, a new humanity, in which Jews and Gentiles as equal members share common access to God and all the privileges he bestows through the sacrificial death of Christ (1.7; 2.19-22; 3.6). The gaping chasm between estranged humankind and God is bridged only by the death of his Son – nothing else. Human redemption and reconciliation were possible only because Christ died to pay the price of sin. This is the bedrock of the Christian faith that it is 'in Christ Jesus' and 'by His blood'[14] that we are saved.

An important section that centers upon Christ's reconciling work, vv. 14-18 continues Paul's treatment of Jew-Gentile estranged relations. The passage divides into two principal parts whose controlling theme is peace: the affirmation of peace (vv. 14-16) and the announcement of peace (vv. 17-18). Prior to Christ's death non-Christian Jews and Gentiles existed as two distinctively separate communities, separated by a dividing wall of hostility (v. 14). Paul explains how through his cross-death Christ brought about peace and reconciliation.

'For he himself is our peace' (v. 14). Mutual hostility characterized relations between Jews and Gentiles without Christ. Though not the central focus of the section, hostility also marked the relationship of unredeemed humankind toward God. Christ's sacrifice reconciled not only Jews and Gentiles, but also humankind alienated from God. The Peace of Rome (*Pax Romana*) instituted by Emperor Augustus brought about a measure of peace in the empire, but it did nothing to improve Jew-Gentile relations. With forceful emphasis in the Greek, Paul states unambiguously that peace is a Person – Christ. He is the embodiment and personification of peace. Without him no lasting peace is possible. Anticipating the type of kingdom the coming Messiah would establish, Micah said of him, 'And he will be their peace' (5.5) and Isaiah, 'And he will be called ... Prince of Peace' (9.6).

---

[13] Josephus, *Antiquities*, XV, 11.5.
[14] D. Martyn Lloyd-Jones, *God's Way of Reconciliation: Studies in Ephesians Chapter 2* (Grand Rapids: Baker, 1972), p. 188.

The peace that Jesus brings is more than the absence of strife. It is more than peace of mind. It entails common concord, mutual acceptance and goodwill, the divine gift of messianic salvation (Lk. 1.79; 19.42), wholeness, total wellbeing, and harmony in personal relationships – accessible to all through the gospel of peace (Eph. 6.15). While one must applaud their efforts, peace organizations and political world leaders will never be able to accomplish lasting peace in the world apart from Christ. In Paul's statement lie both the problem and prognosis of every such human effort: 'the way of peace they do not know' (Rom. 3.17). World peace cannot be found around a conference table. No amount of negotiation and diplomacy can bring it about. Peace is not in an ideology or a philosophical system; it is not in a political or economic theory. It is only in Christ. Whether for the individual or the world, peace is found in embracing the Prince of Peace. Only Christ is able to still the tempest of the troubled heart; only he can remove the inveterate hatred that fuels cruel wars and keeps people and nations apart. Sin brought division, disunity, and hostility. Peace is possible only when sin is dealt with. Christ is the only one who can deal with sin. 'And he will be their peace' Micah prophesied of him (5.5). As with the coming of God's kingdom on earth, so it is with God's promise of peace, however: it is already and not yet. It is only partially present.

Jesus made peace between the Jew and the Gentile, and 'has made the two one and has destroyed the barrier, the dividing wall of hostility' (2.14). Christ's death not only brought an end to mutual hostility between believing Jews and Gentiles. Nor did it simply reconcile two erstwhile enemies. It united them, bringing them into oneness in the church, eliminating class distinctions, racial superiority, social supremacy, and establishing equality. Christ brings people together. All who belong to him, without regard to race, color, gender, class or nationality, live under one banner. All are one family. In uniting the Christian Jew and Gentile, Christ destroyed the barrier which had served as a fence or hedge to keep them apart. It is not the temple balustrade with its posted warnings in Latin and Greek that kept Gentiles from the inner courts and sanctuary to which Paul here refers. Paul identifies the barrier as 'the law with its commandments and regulations' (v. 15). Elsewhere Paul says that by his death Christ has 'canceled the written code, with its regulations, that was against us . . . nailing it to the cross' (Col. 2.14), indicating that the law was a legal note of indebtedness which brought about condemnation. This barrier Christ has destroyed in his flesh (v. 15). How was the law a dividing barrier?

In order to protect the core of the Mosaic law, the rabbis put a broader hedge of regulations around it,[15] which alienated and ostracised the Gentiles. Social intercourse and intermarriage were disallowed, leading to distrust and a settled hostility towards the Jews. Whether the law is understood as a barrier that separated Jews and Gentiles or as a legal instrument of condemnation, by his death Christ brought an end to the hostility it created and nullified it (Rom. 7.4; Gal. 3.13; Col. 2.20) as a covenant and means of salvation for God's new people. Legalism, tribalism, nationalism, denominationalism, ceremonialism, class distinctions, and tradition, therefore, constitute no basis for establishing Christian fellowship. Christ's declaration of unity confronts all cultural myopia, dismisses all narrow ethnocentrism, and dispels provincial claims to social, racial, or gender superiority. He has destroyed the barriers that separate, insulate, and isolate his people from one another (Gal. 3.28-29), his cross forming a bridge that brings them together. He has brought hostility to an end. He has brought disunity to an end. This is God's intention throughout the ages. We should not seek to restore what Christ has destroyed. Unity and equality are validating evidence that we are his and that we are one family. Where there is unity and equality there is no place for superiority or inferiority (cf. Col. 3.11).

1. Creating a New Community through the Cross (2.14–16)

Christ's purpose in tearing down the dividing barrier was 'to create in himself one new man out of the two' (v. 15, NIV); 'to create out of the two races a single new people' (TEV) – a new human race – and 'to reconcile both of them to God through the cross' (v. 16). Just as 'Christian' derives from Christ, so is Christian unity created and centered in him who is both the standard and goal of spiritual unity and Christian maturity. Paul informs the Ephesians that Christian ministers are to equip God's people for works of service 'until we all reach unity in the faith and in the knowledge of the Son of God and become mature, attaining to the whole measure of the fullness of Christ' (4.13). Unity in Christ does not mean uniformity. Paul celebrates both unity and diversity as a gift of the body of Christ (1 Cor. 12.14-26). National, racial, gender, and cultural distinctiveness remains after one becomes a believer. Because Christ has, however, removed the dividing barriers and has reconciled Christians to him and to each other, 'the homogeneous principle – for all its practicality – cannot guide the church. Cul-

---

[15] Mishnah *Abot* 1.1, 2, 3.18; *Epistle of Aristeas*, 139, 142.

tural preferences must take a backseat to unity in Christ ... Christ, not culture, gives the primary definition to life'.[16]

Christians are an entirely new creation, not a renovation or refor-mation of the old. In this new 'experiment' God neither makes the Gentile into a Jew nor the Jew into a Gentile. The church represents a new humanity, a third race – not a blend of the worthiest aspects of the Jews and Gentiles. In the words of Paul, 'Therefore, if anyone is in Christ, he is a new creation; the old has gone, the new has come' (2 Cor. 5.17). Again, in Christ 'Neither circumcision nor uncircumci-sion means anything; what counts is a new creation' (Gal. 6.15). God's first reason for abrogating the law was horizontal – reconciling two hostile races. His second purpose was vertical – 'to reconcile both of them to God'. Horizontal reconciliation between Jew and Gentile could occur only because God had first done the more important work of reconciling estranged humankind to himself. For reconciliation to take place there must be a cessation of hostility. This God accom-plished through the cross by striking a deathblow at the hostility the law created and God's wrath toward sinful humankind. Through the cross, Christians are reconciled both to God and to his redeemed peo-ple. No one can be united to God without also being united to other Christians – no matter who he or she is. Reconciled to God through Christ's death, believers have one God for their Father (1.5; 3.14), Christ as their only Lord (1.22; 4.5) and access to God by the one Spir-it (2.18; 4.4), who brings about unity among the people of God (4.3). Reconciliation and hostility are irreconcilable opposites.

What God desires of the church, he demonstrated in a pilot project at Pentecost. Pentecost was a multicultural, multiethnic, multilingual, and multiracial community where unity celebrated diversity and diver-sity caressed unity. While unity is a mystical given, it is also a goal for the people of God to achieve. To help facilitate cultural diversity ap-preciation with an aim to foster and promote harmony and acceptance, cultural majority churches, on the one hand, need to be aware of the consequences of their cultural imperialism and aver the value of other cultures. Cultural minority assemblies, on the other hand, need to maintain a healthy respect for and affirm the value of their own herit-age and, at the same time seek to broaden their cultural horizons. The world will not be drawn to Christ by our declaration of unity; it will be by a demonstration of it. This entails homogeneous churches com-ing into 'Paul's frame of reference' vis-à-vis unity and heterogeneous

---

[16] Snodgrass, *Ephesians*, p. 153.

people surrendering 'their diversity to the unifying work of the Spirit'.[17]

2. A Shared Peace and Shared Path (2.17-18)

By his death Christ procured peace (2.15), but Paul now echoes the prophetic language of Isaiah (57.19) that Jesus also 'came and preached peace ...' (v. 17). In what sense did Jesus proclaim peace? Some understand this as the incarnate Jesus coming 'with a gospel of peace' (Jn 20.19, 21, 26). The statement cannot, however, refer to any period of the earthly ministry of Jesus, but must allude to the church's missionary activity to both unredeemed Jews and Gentiles. The apostles and all of Christ's preachers and messengers, empowered by the Spirit of Christ, performed this function (Isa. 52.7; Acts 10.36; Rom. 10.15; Eph. 3.5-6). Through his messengers Christ continues to preach peace through the church because the scars, schisms, and hostilities created by sin have not been completely removed.

Verse 18. 'For through him we both have access to the Father by one Spirit'. Common unfettered access to the Father in the one uniting Spirit (cf. Eph. 4.4) is another present benefit of Christ to all the people of God. Jesus himself had said, 'I am the way and the truth and the life. No one comes to the Father except through me' (Jn 14.6). 'Access' appears three times in the NT (Rom. 5.2; Eph. 2.18; 3.12) and translates a Greek word (προσαγωγή), which was used of the introduction of a person to a king, a worshipper's approach to God, or a harbor or haven where ships come in. By way of application, Jesus 'opens the door for us to the presence of the King of Kings; and when that door is opened what we find is *grace*'. And having reached at last the haven of divine grace, 'we know the calm of depending, not on what we can do for ourselves, but on what God has done for us'.[18] Sons of God by grace, believers share with Jesus, the Son of God by nature, the intimate filial language of sonship: 'Abba Father' – language initiated by the indwelling Holy Spirit (Rom. 8.15-16; Gal. 4.6). Jesus makes not only possible the use of the family name, but his death has afforded each individual believer, Jew or Gentile, access to the Father and membership in his family. That the trinity is so vitally involved in our salvation can only fill the heart with gratitude, wonder, love, and praise.

---

[17] Gordon D. Fee, *Paul, the Spirit, and the People of God* (Peabody, MA: Hendrickson, 1997), p. 70.
[18] Barclay, *The Letters to the Galatians and Ephesians*, p. 73.

3. The Prospect of Christ's Work (2.19-22)

> Consequently, you are no longer foreigners and aliens, but fellow citizens with God's people and members of God's household (v. 19).

Emigrating to the New World in search of a better life was an enchanted dream for untold thousands of people in Europe and other parts of the world in the 19th and early 20th century. It still is, to a large extent! As immigrants poured into New York in the 1800s, thousands of children whose parents died aboard ship became abandoned. Unable to speak English, hungry, homeless and jobless, to stay alive they stole and fed on rats and morsels from garbage cans. At night, metal drums and boxes in alleys provided the only beds they knew, their bodies stacked together to provide warmth through many a cold winter's night.

In the hustle and bustle of life, no one seemed to care – until a 26-year-old minister, stricken with compassion at the desperate plight of these orphans, devised a plan to rescue them. Charles Loring Brace's solution became known as the Orphan Train, on which by 1929 about 100,000 children rode westward, finding new parents and new homes at many towns along the way. If the story had ended with this marvelous rescue it would have been enough. But it is sweetened by the fact that two of those orphans became governors, one becoming a U.S. congressman and the other a Supreme Court justice.

Welcoming hopeless spiritual orphans into his family is exactly what God has done for believing Jews and Gentiles. All who have accepted his gracious rescue offer have become 'heirs of God and co-heirs with Christ' (Rom. 8.17). Without qualification, all believers belong to a family and a fellowship in which they share equally. God does not make distinction among his children. He has no favorites.

a. Gentiles and Jews share a common family (2.19)

> Consequently, you are no longer foreigners and aliens, but fellow citizens with God's people and members of God's household' (v. 19).

'Consequently' shows a logical connection between what now follows with what precedes (vv. 11-18), but also draws a reasonable conclusion based upon it – the new relationship believers have with God through Christ in the Spirit. But what does it mean to say that Christians are no longer foreigners and aliens? A foreigner is a stranger, an outsider who has no rights or claims to the benefits of citizenship, except those that may be graciously extended by a host country. An alien is a resident alien who temporarily lives in a foreign country. Though allowed more privilege than the foreigner he, too, has no legal claim to all the rights and privileges of the citizen. As a second-class citizen, he could be expelled from the country or community without right of appeal.

Paul probably uses the two terms to indicate that Gentile Christians are neither homeless, stateless outsiders, nor second-class people in a foreign country. Rather, they are 'fellow citizens with God's people,' the redeemed of all ages (2.19), members of a spiritual theocracy, a new race whose 'citizenship is in heaven' (Phil. 3.20). This is the privilege of all the people of God, without exception. To be fellow citizens with God's people brings with it a sense of belonging and security.

b. Gentiles and Jews form a Spirit-indwelt Community (2.20-22)

The new people of God experience not only full membership in the family of God, but also a vital position in his building, the temple, where the Spirit resides. In vv. 20-22 Paul describes the foundation of the temple (v. 20), its formation (v. 21), and its function (v. 22).[19] Elsewhere Paul calls the church God's building (1 Cor. 3:9). Peter expands this idea to incorporate the idea of temple. '[Y]ou also, like living stones, are being built into a spiritual house to be a holy priesthood, offering spiritual sacrifices acceptable to God through Jesus Christ' (1 Pet. 2:5).

Israel's magnificent temples captured the eyes and heart of the nation, forging their national and religious identity. To the Jews, the temple was a visible symbol of the presence of God among his people, God's house and the only place where he could be worshiped. No Gentile was permitted in the inner sanctuaries. In the new dispensation and in the new spiritual kingdom, Jews and Gentiles constitute God's temple in which the Spirit dwells, the apostles and prophets its foundation, and Jesus Christ its chief cornerstone. Not wood and stone, gold and silver, but an international and interracial people, constitute this temple which is 'built on the foundation of the apostles and prophets, with Christ Jesus himself as the chief cornerstone' (2.20). No part of a building is more important than its foundation. In 1 Cor. 3.10-11 Paul calls himself a master builder who lays Christ as the foundation on which other ministry colleagues are building. Here in Ephesians he presents the apostles and prophets as the foundation and Christ the chief cornerstone of this new temple (2.20). 'The Church's one Foundation is Jesus Christ our Lord', an enduring historic song of the church, rings true. Christ alone is the bedrock on which the church stands (Ps. 118.22; Isa. 28.16).

To a lesser degree, the apostles and prophets are its foundation: they were the inspired conduits of divine revelation, eye-witnesses of

---

[19] Hoehner, *Ephesians*, p. 397.

Christ's saving deeds, and authorized bearers of eternal truth (Eph. 3.4-5). Their teachings are preserved as part of Scripture, and what they taught constitutes the doctrine of the church and the standard by which all truth for all time is determined. They are the exemplars whose lives and deeds model and command conformity by all the followers of Christ.

Like the foundation, the cornerstone is vital to a building, binding two walls together and helping to steady and keep it in line. Similarly, Christ it is that holds the Jews and Gentiles together in his dwelling place – the church. It is in union with him that 'the whole building is joined together and rises' (2.21). We become part of the temple of God in vital and intimate union with Christ. It is in union with him that God's people experience unity and by which growth occurs. The unity and growth of the church are inseparably connected. What is the purpose and function of the new temple Christ is building? It is 'to become a dwelling in which God lives by his Spirit' (2.22).

A temple is a divine residence, the place where God lives. Such was the belief among the common people of the ancient world and of Israel. Ephesus boasted the majestic marble temple of Artemis whose inner sanctuary housed a statue of the goddess; Jerusalem paraded the magnificent temple built by Herod and the inner shrine as God's abode, which provokes the question: if the heavens cannot contain the infinite God, how can any earthly building made by human hands (1 Kgs 8.27)? God's holy people, not sacred edifices, are his true dwelling. His presence is connected to people, not confined to places. God lives in people individually, but also corporately (1 Cor. 6.19), locally but also universally. As God is holy, so must be his people, his temple, in which he dwells. It is the Spirit who makes God's people into a holy sanctuary in which God lives (2.22). The title Holy Spirit describes not only the holy nature of the third member of the trinity, but also his function – that of making people holy.

Reflection and Response (Part 2)

Reflection

The dominant theme of unity and reconciliation in Christ that controls Paul's thought in this chapter (2.11-22) is the topic of our reflection. Alienation from God constitutes the first half of the chapter, and the alienation of humans from each other the second. Paul concluded his eulogistic prayer (1.3-14) with the thought that one day God would unify all things under Christ's headship. This universal unification and reconciliation forms part of the revealed 'mystery of [God's] will' (1.9), fundamental to which is the uniting of Jews and Gentiles in one body, the church (Eph. 3.5-6). The unveiling of this mystery, the union of erstwhile inveterate enemies but now redeemed and reconciled members in Christ's body, is what Paul discusses in 2.11-22 – and will be the focus of our reflection. A vast and seemingly unbridgeable gulf separated the Jews and Gentiles from one another, one larger than the modern world has ever known. The mutual hatred defied description.

In the first of two exhortations of Paul to the Gentiles to 'remember' their pre-Christian past and its deficits (2.11), he reminded them that they were Gentiles by birth and uncircumcised. To the Jews the term 'gentile' intoned derision and disparagement and meant 'pagan', designating one living in moral and spiritual darkness. Paul then directly stated five disadvantages that beset the Gentiles: They were Christless, stateless (without citizenship in Israel), friendless (foreigners to the covenants), hopeless, and godless. Paul does not give the Gentiles' portrait of the Jews, but it was far from flattering. Fact is that the mutual demonizing of each other and the disparities between them created a deep-seated mutual hostility. Shifting from the past, Paul described the present reality of believing Gentiles. What was humanly impossible God accomplished through the death of Christ. Christ the Peacemaker threw down the wall of separation and put to death the mutual enmity. He reconciled believing Jews and Gentiles and made of them one new family, a new humanity (Eph. 2.14-16). No longer aliens, Gentiles have become allies with the Jews in the new community of faith, both having equal 'access to the Father by one Spirit' and becoming 'a dwelling in which God lives by the Spirit'.

The following questions are given to stimulate further reflection on the topic discussed above. In what ways are the mutual attitudes of Jews and Gentiles similar to those expressed among ethnic and racial groups today? In what sense has Christ made of the two erstwhile hostile groups of Jews and Gentiles 'one' (2.14) or 'one new man'? (2.15) What does it mean that the church is united in Christ? What does a united church look like? If the church is united, how do we explain the many different denominations, church communions, discord, and disparities in beliefs and practices that exist today? Is unity a reality or a goal – or both? If it is a goal, how should the unity Christ desires for his people be brought about? Can homogeneous churches and the homogeneous principle of church growth be justified in light of the new community Christ has created and the manifest unity he expects? What does the reconciling work of Christ mean for the fractured homes and communities today? How may this message of reconciliation speak to the cultural myopia, narrow ethnocentrism, and provincial claims to social, racial, and gender superiority current in the church at large?

In order to bring us into the reflection in a personal way, the following questions are raised. How do you view and relate to Christians from cultures, races, and faith persuasions other than your own? How open are you to moving beyond your limited experience and Christian tradition and sampling the rich diversity in other streams of orthodox Christianity? How often and in what context do you seek to fellowship with Christians of ethnicities, nationalities, and belief-systems other than your own? How many close friends of other races and nationalities do you have? Do you pray for Christians in other countries, particularly those who live in countries hostile to the Christian faith? Are you involved in any missions activity in your church?

Response

1. In an effort to answer some of the questions on Christian unity, seek the Lord's wisdom and guidance as to how to proceed. This will involve prayer and the reading of Scripture and Christian literature on the topic.

2. Examine your attitude toward Christians of other faiths, color, and ethnicities and the areas in which you need to grow.

3. Consider the practical implications of unity, the steps you must take, the accommodations you must make.

4. Write down some things you believe you and your local church can do to work toward Christian unity. This should be more than assuming the role of a peacekeeper or peace promoter, but the creation of a positive ambiance in which mutual caring and common partnership can grow.

5. Broaden your circle and deepen your relationship and fellowship with Christians from other denominations and religious affiliations, ethnicities, and nationalities. Whenever possible, join and support them in efforts in their local church and community.

6. Enlarge and sharpen your vision of the church globally; be aware of its progress, plight, challenges and needs. Go online and Google Voice of the Martyrs for a free monthly subscription, or e-mail usa@opendoors.org. Either will keep you abreast of the news about the persecuted church around the world.

7. Get involved in missions efforts around the world, either through your local church or through creditable organizations. Finally, get a map of the world and pinpoint at least three countries where Christians are being oppressed and pray for them often.

D. The Church: A Secret Disclosed (3.1-13)

In 1.15-19 Paul began an intercessory prayer with 'For this reason' (διὰ τοῦτο, v. 15), punctuated with important theological and ecclesiological digressions such as Christ's resurrection and session with his people in the heavenly realms (2.5-7) and the 'double reconciliation' the Gentiles have come to experience through Christ (2.11-22). He now resumes the prayer in 3.1 again with 'For this reason' (τούτου χάριν) only to stray again, for immediately upon making the declaration that his ministry to the Gentiles is the reason for his imprisonment (Acts 21.17-36; Rom. 15.15-21), he digresses from the prayer, not to pick it up again till v. 14, using the same language as in 3.1: 'For this reason' (τούτου χάριν). Verses 2-13 are a formal aside on Paul's ministry to the Gentiles whose focal point is the revelation of the mystery, given especially to Paul, that Gentiles and Jews together constitute the Body of Christ and share equally all Christ's blessings and promises (vv. 2-7). Paul's communication of this mystery, which is central to God's eternal plan and the church's function in God's objective for the universe, are the burden of vv. 8-12. Prompted by the mention of Paul's confinement in Rome (v. 1), the digression, which connects logically with and follows from Paul's reflections on his apostolic ministry to the Gentiles in 2.11-22, is imbued with an appeal that the Ephesians not be disheartened by his present harsh and unfavorable circumstances (v. 13). Even in prison, Paul is mindful of the awesome responsibility that is his as bearer of the revelation of God's mystery. This obligation and his desire to see that the Gentiles understand how deep and boundless is Christ's love for them form a fitting opening to his prayer in 3.14.

1. A mystery disclosed by divine inspiration (3.1-6)

The intent of Paul's prayer begun in v. 1 with 'For this reason' (τούτου χάριν — because of what God has accomplished, explained earlier) is that the Ephesian believers be empowered to put into practice the unique privileges that are theirs as part of God's new people and community of faith. His detour from the prayer to his imprisonment is not without theological significance. The juxtaposition of the forceful self-identification, 'I, Paul', and the self-description, 'the prisoner of Christ Jesus' (cf. 4.1; Col. 1.23; Phlm. 1.9; 2 Tim. 1.8) intimates that Paul is reflecting on his detention theologically, perceiving God's overriding providence in his affairs, thus bringing everything under his lordship – including confinement in Rome. Fierce Jewish opposition to his championship of the Gentile cause has landed him in jail (Acts 21.17-40; 22.21-30), but his physical captivity serves only to express outwardly a greater spiritual thralldom to Christ (he is Christ's prisoner, not Nero's). Missionally, it is both the mark and price for reaching the Gentiles with the gospel and executing his apostleship. Paul's relationship with the non-Jewish believers will certainly benefit from their knowledge of his role in the administration of the divine mystery for the Gentiles.

Not all the Gentile believers in Asia Minor were personally acquainted with Paul, the encyclical Ephesian letter having been written to local assemblies unfamiliar to him; but they were aware[1] of his special commission (οἰκονομία), what is elsewhere termed an 'administration' or 'stewardship/task'[2] (Col. 1.25) entrusted to him. Here in 3.2 (as in 1.10) the word refers to the 'implementation of a strategy' – the enabling equipment to fulfill Paul's missionary assignment to the Gentiles.[3] For the implementation of this assignment, which is to 'make known' the special revelation of the mystery of Christ, Paul has received grace (v. 3). This mystery for him is God's secret plan now revealed of the Gentiles' inclusion in salvation and the Body of Christ (2.16) as equal partners with the Jews (3. 6), a truth he received by means of and in accordance with divine revelation (Gal. 1.12, 15-16). Paul had made a brief statement of this earlier (v. 3; cf. 1.9-10; 2.11-22), and on the basis of his earlier written communication he asks the believers to discern and grasp 'the mystery of Christ' – this truth of which Christ is the center and circumference, and his 'one Jewish-Gentile people'[4] (v. 4).

Knowledge of this mystery was unattainable until God chose to disclose it (Rom. 16.25-27; Col. 1.25-27). Yet, by no means is Paul's gospel a categorically novel idea. In the revelation schema, it is present in the Old Testament in bud – promised by the prophets (Rom. 1.2), attested by the law and prophets (3.21), and preached to Abraham (Gal. 3.8). Furthermore, God's plan to bless the Gentiles through the gospel resounds throughout the OT scriptures (Deut. 32.43; Isa. 11.10; Pss. 18.49; 117.1). The mystery was a new revelation in the manner in which the divine purpose would be fulfilled – by the incorporation and integration of both Jews and Gentiles in the church. This had remained

---

[1] Paul's use of εἴ γε (v. 2), used five times in the NT (2 Cor. 5.3; Gal. 3.4; Eph. 3.2; 4.21; Col. 1.23) does not suggest doubt of the believers' knowledge of his ministry, but asserts a confident assumption: 'surely you have heard'; 'indeed you have heard'.

[2] It is sometimes used of Paul's administration of his apostolic office (1 Cor. 9.17; cf. 4:1) and God's administration of the universe and redemption (Eph. 1.10; 3:9).

[3] Wood, *Ephesians*, p. 45.

[4] Stott, *The Message of Ephesians*, p. 117.

a mystery until the time it was disclosed, Paul the apostle to the Gentiles and primary guardian of this mystery having the honor of 'unfolding its wonder to his readers'.[5] What was but a bud in the OT came to flower in the NT. Revelation of this mystery came by the Spirit to two types of ecclesiastical leadership – God's holy apostles and prophets, both inspired and empowered by the same Spirit[6] who would declare it to the nations (Rom. 16.26).

What Paul has hitherto referred to indistinctly as 'the mystery' on a number of occasions, he now defines with specificity in v. 6, recruiting three parallel, composite terms to that end, each sharing the same prefix, indicating Gentile Christians' complete union with the Jews and the equal partnership they mutually share in all of God's promised blessings to his people. Gentile believers are co-heirs/fellow-heirs (συγκληρόμα) of the same blessings with Jewish believers (Rom. 8.17; Gal. 3.29; 4.7), fellow-members of the same body – 'concorporate'[7] (σύσσωμα), and co-sharers/joint-sharers (συμμέτοχα) of the promise (Eph. 2.12; Gal. 3.22, 29), all this being made possible in Christ and the gospel.

2. A mystery declared through human instrumentality (3.7-13)

To God's grace Paul attributes both the revelation of the gospel plan and his commission to share it among the Gentiles. 'I became a servant of this gospel by the gift of God's grace...' (v. 7). Only a mighty demonstration of God's power and grace could so transform a persecutor into a preacher (1 Tim. 1.12-14) and grant him such divine privilege. This gracious dispensation, fraught with a shuddering responsibility, Paul accepts with a sense of cringing unworthiness that wrings from him a personal self-designation expressed by a double diminutive found nowhere else in the NT: 'less than the least [ἐλαχιστοτέρῳ] of all the saints' (NIV uses 'God's people' for 'saints', v. 8; cf. 1 Cor. 15.9; 1 Tim. 1.15). In this posture of humility lies one of the great secrets of Paul's ministry. His weakness was his strength (2 Cor. 12.10).

Paul's life and experience of grace are laden with salutary lessons. His checkered past notwithstanding, God called him to ministry (Eph. 3.8, the Greek lays stress on God's action to him specifically) – teaching us that in God's sight no one is denied ministry based solely upon the deficit of his or her past. Further, the call to ministry depends not upon the superlative quality of one's gifts, but upon the superabundance of God's grace. God redeems our past and presses it into the service of his kingdom.

---

[5] O'Brien, *Ephesians*, p. 232. Italics author's.
[6] Bruce, *Colossians, Philemon, Ephesians*, p. 315.
[7] Stott, *The Message of Ephesians*, p. 117.

With Christ as its sum and substance, Paul sees the good news he is called to declare to the Gentiles as so bafflingly vast and inscrutably mysterious that he calls it 'the unsearchable riches of Christ' (v. 8). 'Unsearchable', 'fathomless', 'untraceable', and 'infinite' are among the English terms that translate the Greek (ἀνεξιχνίαστος) which is used elsewhere in Scripture to describe the mystifying nature of creation (Job 5:9; 9:10) and the plan of salvation (Rom. 11.33). As Paul had mentioned earlier (3.3, 5-6), God's plan to incorporate the Gentiles into his people in Christ would have remained hidden unless God had revealed it to him, the apostles, and the prophets. The term may also indicate that the wealth in Christ's treasury of salvation is as immeasurable as it is inscrutable.

Paul knew that God had given him a priceless gift and a special assignment. That gift was the gospel, and the gospel, at one time securely hidden in God and beyond human discovery (v. 9), was no longer classified information. God had lifted the veil that once shrouded it. His assignment was to proclaim it to the Gentiles and dispel the spiritual darkness (φωτίσαι, throw light upon, make plain) that draped the whole human landscape (v. 9). In his *Nunc Dimittis*, Simeon had said of the Messiah-child: He is 'a light for revelation to the Gentiles and for glory to your people Israel' (Lk. 2.32). That is the revelation Paul now brings to the Gentiles and the whole world, constrained by a sense of moral indebtedness to share it (Rom. 1.14-16; 1 Cor. 9.16).

Whatever God does in the world, he does primarily through the church. But the influence of the church universal extends beyond this world. It impinges upon and impacts 'the rulers and authorities in the heavenly realms'[8] (v. 10) — good and evil angels (cf. Job 1.6; Dan. 10.13, 21; 1 Pet. 1.12), with emphasis upon the malevolent powers. Paul has already mentioned that as God's divine masterpiece, the church is destined to be God's 'exhibit A' to the heavenly hosts throughout the endless years of eternity (Eph. 2.7). But now he tells us here in 3.10 that in this present time she is the showcase — 'object-lesson'[9] — a classroom and theater — of God's multifaceted wisdom to the world of angels. As the church's message spreads throughout the world, its sweet, swelling melody echoes to the distant world of spirits, arresting the eyes and ears, holding in awe and rapture an audience of befuddled angelic hosts (1 Pet. 1.12). What is it that captures their attention? Paul says it is God's multicolored wisdom God displays in the church.

---

[8] G.B. Caird's idea that the rulers and authorities here refer to political and economic systems staggers under the weight of its own incredulity. See his *Principalities and Powers, A Study in Pauline Theology* (Oxford: Oxford University Press, 1950).

[9] Bruce, *Colossians, Philemon. Ephesians*, p. 320.

'Multicolored'[10] or 'manifold' (v. 10, NIV) translates πολυποίκιλος, a
term used to describe woven carpets, flowers, crowns, and embroidered cloth. Contemporarily it is employed as a technical term in geol-
ogy to identify uncommonly assorted crystals.[11] The word may allude
to 'the intricate beauty of an embroidered pattern'. Here, however,
'beauty and diversity' may be its main emphasis.[12] God's multicolored
or manifold wisdom is expressed in his eternal purpose achieved in
Christ – that of reconciling and uniting in one body two seemingly
irreconcilable enemies, the Jews and Gentiles. God's variegated wisdom certainly reflects the diversity of races, languages, cultures, and
nationalities that make up the church.

Conceived in eternity (v. 11) this reconciliation that discloses God's
many-splendored wisdom through the church manifests presently his
intention for his people, but also anticipates the ultimate reunification
of all things in Christ (Eph. 1.9, 10). It is a proclamation of the present
defeat of all evil powers at the cross, but also a prophetic preview of
the final overthrow of Satan and his diabolical forces. As God's 'pilot
scheme for the reconciled universe of the future', the church is both
God's model of present reconciliation and his 'agency ... for the bringing about of the ultimate reconciliation'.[13] The effect of God's work in
and through the church ripples across boundless space and echoes
throughout the world of angels and spirits.

It should come as no surprise, but rather great encouragement, to
believers that God has chosen that which to the world appears insignificant and irrelevant to exhibit his surpassing wisdom. What Paul said of
the Corinthian believers he says of the followers of Christ today. 'Not
many of you were wise by human standards; not many were influen-
tial; not many were of noble birth. But God chose the foolish things of
the world to shame the wise; God chose the weak things of the world
to shame the strong. He chose the lowly things of this world and the
despised things – and the things that are not – to nullify the things that
are, so that no one may boast before him' (1 Cor. 1.26-29).

All God does fits into an eternal plan and purpose. His wisdom displayed in the church was no afterthought. Nor was the church's role in
his program of redemption and reconciliation accomplished in Christ
(v. 11)!

Having set forth God's eternal plan of redemption and reconciliation
achieved by Christ, Paul now turns to the present privilege believers

---

[10] Bruce has noted that the Greek equivalent was first attested in Euripides, *Iphigeneia
in Tauris* 1149 where it refers to 'many-colored cloaks', p. 320, n. 64.

[11] Wood, *Ephesians*, p. 48.

[12] Vaughan, *Ephesians* (Bible Study Commentary; Grand Rapids: Zondervan, 1977),
p.76.

[13] Bruce, *Colossians, Philemon, Ephesians*, pp. 321, 322.

enjoy through Christ – freedom to address God and fearlessness to approach his presence (παρρησία, v. 12). This Greek term that means 'freedom of speech', was first used of the legal right of every citizen of democratic Athens to speak publicly with freedom and frankness. When used in association with preaching in the NT, it describes a fearless boldness to declare the good news (Acts 4:31; Eph. 6:19). The writer of Hebrews employs it to teach that Christ has made it possible that through faith in him his followers can address God this way without fear of rejection or reprimand (Heb. 4.16; 10.19).

'Approach' – better 'access' – translates προσαγωγή, which carries the notion of introduction. Used always of Christ in the NT (Rom. 5.2; Eph. 2.18; 3.12), it denotes him as the only one that can bring us into God's presence. With one article governing 'address' (speech) and 'access' (admission) and the word 'confidently' also modifying both, Paul may simply mean that because of their close relationship with the Father both Jews and Gentiles can come to him with assured confidence at all times. This confident access to God is made possible 'through faith in him [Christ]' (διὰ τῆς πίστεως αὐτοῦ). A group of interpreters view the pronoun *autou* (αὐτοῦ) as a subjective genitive meaning 'his' [Christ's] and 'faith' as a synonym for 'faithfulness'. 'Christ's faithfulness', in dying on behalf of believers, then, is what provides the means of access to God.[14] While not denying the necessity of Christ's obedient death in salvation, most interpreters (and translations) understand the word as an objective genitive representing Christ as the object of faith. This means that confident access to God comes through faith in Christ.

Verse 13 concludes the lengthy parenthesis Paul began in v. 2. Gentile believers have unfettered freedom to approach and address God. This privilege was part of God's plan for them, a privilege Paul had made known in the gospel he had preached to them. But Paul, their champion, is himself in chains in Rome as he writes this letter, which could result in some losing heart. Rather than leading to their dismay, Paul wants them to see his sufferings as God's providential plan and purpose at work in their favor – for their benefit – and for bringing God glory (cf. 2 Cor. 1.6; 4.17; Col. 1.24; 2 Tim. 2.10).

E. Paul's Prayer for the Church (3.14-19)

Breaking away to discuss the Gentiles' place among the people of God and the church's function in his universal plan (vv. 2-13), Paul now resumes his petitionary prayer begun in v. 1, an intercession anchored in God's purpose of fashioning a new humanity in Christ (2.11-22) and

[14] O'Brien, *Ephesians*, p. 249.

inspired by the apostle's desire to see Gentile believers fully experience their remarkable privilege in Christ (3.2-13).

Paul's prayer offered with intensity and urgency, intimated in the posture of kneeling (κάμπτω τὰ γόνατά μου, 'I bend my knees', v. 14), can be tendered with confidence because it is presented to one who is Father. Standing to pray was the customary position for the Jews (Mk 11.25; Lk. 18.11, 13) and early Christians. Kneeling signified great reverence, deep solemnity, or unusual earnestness (Ezra 9.5; Lk. 22.41; Acts 7.60; 21.5; Phil. 2.10). The one before whom Paul kneels is described as 'Father, from whom the whole family in heaven and on earth derives its name' (v. 15). 'Family' is to be understood to mean any group that shares a common forebear or ancestor (people, clan, tribe, nation).

At issue, however, is whether the Greek term (πᾶσα πατριά) should be translated 'whole family' (AV, NIV) or 'every family' (RV, ASV, RSV, NEB). If understood as 'the whole family', then all the redeemed both in heaven and on earth — the church triumphant and the church militant — are here represented as constituting one large family. If the rendering 'every family' is adopted, the idea suggested is that every group of intelligent beings both of angels — described in rabbinic literature as the higher family — and humankind take the name 'family' from the one archetypal Father. God is a family of three — Father, Son, and Holy Spirit and reveals his tripartite nature through a variety of family imagery. The absence of the Greek article notwithstanding, Paul's emphasis on oneness rather than plurality throughout lends the translation 'the whole family' contextual support (e.g. 2.18, 19; 3.6).

Some scholars see a larger picture here than family, based on a word-play by Paul — 'father' (πατήρ, v. 14) and family (πατριά, v. 15). While the latter does not ordinarily designate fatherhood, but rather family, such scholars urge that the concept of paternity is, however, strongly present. This has led to the conclusion that Paul may be saying more than that the whole Christian family 'is named from the Father, but that the very notion of fatherhood is derived from the Fatherhood of God'.[1] To say that the Christian family and/or the concept of fatherhood derives from God, Paul intends more than the mere conferring of the title 'family' or 'father'. Rather, the term 'signifies [God's] bringing them into existence, exercising dominion over them ... and giving each their appropriate role', affirming the sovereign power of God and human dependence on him for existence.[2]

On behalf of those who have become members of this large family Paul now prays. His tripartite intercession proceeds in stair-step fash-

---

[1] Stott, *The Message of Ephesians*, p. 134.
[2] O'Brien, *Ephesians*, p. 256.

ion, each introduced by the words 'so that' (ἵνα, see vv. 16, 18, 19). As in 1.17, 18, its goal is to show that believers acquire God's abundant resources, commensurate with their inexhaustible supply, through the Spirit who is the agent of divine power (Acts 1.8; Rom. 1.4; 1 Cor. 2.4). Paul wants the people of God to be lavishly empowered by God's immeasurable power in the inner being (v. 16) so as to experience Christ more fully, to allow his full lordship and its attendant blessings to become an ever-growing reality in their lives. Perhaps concerned about the discouraging effect of his imprisonment on the Gentile believers (3.13) and conscious of their own suffering for the faith, Paul intercedes that they 'be strengthened with power through/by his Spirit' (δυνάμει κραταιωθῆναι διὰ τοῦ πνεύματος αὐτοῦ). The sphere of this Spirit-imparted strengthening is 'in your inner being' (εἰς τὸν ἔσω ἄνθρωπον). For one to hold up under the pain, stress, and hardships of life the Spirit's strength is needed in the interior life. This inner strengthening by the Spirit results in Christ dwelling in the heart (v. 1).

To the extent that the Spirit empowers believers, to that degree they are transformed in the likeness of Jesus. The measure of God's bestowal is according to (κατά) – his glorious wealth, 'which corresponds to the inexhaustible wealth of his radiance and power available to humanity'.[3] God not merely gives a portion ('out of') his vast resources; he gives a proportion ('according to') commensurate with his enormous supply[4] and incredible generosity.

This fuller experience Paul describes as Christ's dwelling in the believers' heart (v. 17a), which is equivalent to their inner being (v. 16). As Christians, the Ephesian believers already had Christ dwelling in their hearts, but a life may be genuinely Christian and yet far from entirely Christian. Put another way, 'in some Christ is just present, in others He is prominent, and in others again, He is preeminent'.[5] As intimated by the Greek, Paul's prayer for the Ephesians is that Christ may exercise preeminence and permanent settlement (κατοικῆσαι, used also in Col. 1.19; 2.9) *in* their lives rather than a casual or temporary stay (παροικῆσαι, used in Lk. 24.18; Heb. 11.9). Christ will do this through faith – their personal trust in him.

Believers are strengthened in their inner person when Christ is fully at home in their lives, when he takes up full and permanent residence and controls their spiritual faculties – thoughts, attitudes, and actions. As the outward person, the body, which is wasting away daily (2 Cor. 4.16), needs constant renewal to discharge its physical duties, so the

---

[3] Lincoln, *Ephesians,* p. 204.

[4] Warren W. Wiersbe, *The Bible Exposition Commentary,* vol. II (Wheaton, IL: Victor Books, 1989), p. 32.

[5] Graham Scroggie, *Paul's Prison Prayers* (London: Pickering and Inglis, n.d.), p. 70.

inner self where Christ seeks to take up residence needs daily Spirit-imparted renewal and empowerment to succeed at living an abundant Christian life.

The second petition in Paul's prayer is that believers be immovably established in God's love (v. 17b) and, as a result, love one another deeply. In Ephesians, love is central to the nature and purpose of God (1.4; 2.4; 5.2, 25; 6.23 and is a distinctive attribute of his children (1.15; 5.28; 6.24). Two metaphors – one horticultural and the other architectural – are recruited to show the significance of this divine virtue, mentioned earlier in 1.4. Love is the soil in which believers are planted and the foundation on which they are built. Of utmost importance to the survival of a tree or plant is its root system. Its sustenance and stability derive from and depend upon its root system. Deep taproots in the soil will guarantee that the tree will neither topple in the storm nor wither in the sun. No tree can live or flourish without firm and deep roots.

Similarly, believers are strengthened inwardly by God's Spirit so that they might be deeply rooted in Christ's love (Col. 2.7) – a love that not only holds them securely and sustains them, but also provides the soil for them to grow and bear the mature fruit of a deeper experiential knowledge of him. Paul's horticultural metaphor is complemented by an architectural one (v. 17). No part of a building is more important than its foundation. A good foundation ensures solidity and stability. To go high, a building must first go deep. Christians are to anchor their lives upon the strong and firm foundation of the bedrock of Christ's love (Col. 1.23; see Mt. 7.24-29). Established on any other foundation, their lives will buckle in the storm.

Paul's final petition is that believers, enabled by God, be enlightened to grasp together with all the saints some immeasurable spiritual reality, but Paul does not actually state what it is. Some scholars suggest that it refers, among other things, to the mighty power of God, the mystery of salvation, or the manifold wisdom of God.[6] The NIV's preference for Christ's love as the object of Paul's request invites the strongest scholarly and contextual support. In v. 17b Paul anchors the entire petition in the love of Christ, and in Rom. 8.35-39 he links two of the dimensions (height and depth) mentioned in Eph. 3.18 with the love of Christ.

It is God who enables believers both to love and to grasp spiritual truths, but these truths are discovered and learned in the fellowship of the family of God – 'together with all the saints' (v. 18), not in solitary contemplation or in isolation from the Christian community. There is no place for spiritual elitism in the Christian community. Isolated and

[6] O'Brien, *Ephesians*, pp. 261-63.

private knowledge or experience, while important, is limited and subjective and fails to grasp fully the limitless love of God. No Christian
can attain spiritual maturity in isolation.

The knowledge or understanding referred to includes mental apprehension, but goes beyond it to the experiential, a point expressed in
the Greek term found here (καταλαβέσθαι), which means to seize
something so as to make it one's own or to know by experience. In
Phil. 3.12 Paul uses the indicative form of the word – (καταλάβω) to
describe his earnest desire to 'take hold of that for which Christ took
hold of me'. This desire is certainly far more than a mental understanding of Christ. Paul wants the saints to know Christ's love in four dimensions – width, length, height, and depth – that is that they may
experience the vast immensity, the all-encompassing and boundless
character, and totality of this love – a love that is central to God's nature and purpose.

Having described the vast dimensions and unfathomable expanses of
Christ's love (v. 18), Paul now entreats paradoxically that the Ephesians
may 'know this love that surpasses knowledge' (v. 19a). By no means
does the entreaty suggest that Christ's love is unknowable. Rather, it
implies that no matter how immense one's knowledge of Christ's love
or how fully one enters into that love, no one can ever 'plumb its
depths or comprehend its magnitude' because 'there is always more to
know and experience'.[7] Our finite mind can never fully grasp the infinite love of God for his children. We will spend eternity probing in
vain to fathom its inexhaustible depths.

A bold petition for the fullness of God climaxes Paul's entire intercession: 'that you may be filled to the measure of all the fullness of
God' (19b). 'No prayer that has ever been framed has uttered a bolder
request. It is a noble example of παρρησία, of freedom of speech, of ...
"boldness and access in confidence"'.[8] 'Fullness' features prominently
in Ephesians and Colossians. Whereas in the latter Paul states that
God's fullness resides in Christ, and that believers are given fullness in
Christ (Col. 1.19; 2.9-10; cf. Eph. 1.23), in the former he exhorts us to
a life of growth in Christ (Eph. 4.13-16; 5.18). Continual transformation and growth into the likeness of Christ is a part of the maturing
process of believers. 'And we, who with unveiled faces all reflect the
Lord's glory, are being transformed into his likeness, with ever-
increasing glory, which comes from the Lord, who is the Spirit'
(2 Cor. 3.18). Paul adds in Ephesians that the goal of God's gifts to the
church is 'to prepare God's people for works of service, so that the

---

[7] O'Brien, *Ephesians*, p. 264.

[8] Armitage Robinson, *St. Paul's Epistle to the Ephesians* (London: James Clarke, n.d.),
p. 89.

body of Christ may be built up until we all reach unity in the faith and in the knowledge of the Son of God and become mature, attaining to the whole measure of the fullness of Christ' (4.12-14).

To be 'filled to the measure of all the fullness of God' (3.19b) can hardly mean that believers can contain the inexhaustible totality and attributes of the divine essence, for the highest heavens themselves cannot contain God (2 Chron. 6.18). Nor should it be applied only to an eschatological final perfect state in heaven. Rather, as we are commanded to be perfect as our heavenly Father is perfect, and to be holy as he is holy (Mt. 5.48; 1 Pet. 1.15-16), so Paul's prayer invites us to a present experience of growth and transformation into the image of Christ – a life fully yielded to him and filled with his presence, power, blessings, and mature fruits of the Spirit. Paul is not fearful that he may have asked too much. That is impossible, for God's 'capacity for giving far exceeds his people's capacity for asking – even imagining'.[9] Positionally, believers are complete in Christ (Col. 2.9-10), but practically we experience only the grace we apprehend by faith.[10] We must be willing to receive all that God wishes to bestow.

Paul had earlier implored the Father for spiritual blessings of amazing and immeasurable value (3.16-19). Now after pondering God's awesome power and love, the incredible things he had done for his people, and the wonder and grandeur of his eternal plan and purpose for the church, Paul erupts in a lofty doxology, an apt, effusive benediction to his prayer (vv. 20-21).

More than a conclusion to Paul's prayer, the doxology is a climax both to all that the apostle has stated in chs. 1–3 concerning God's plan and purpose in redemption and to the first half of the Epistle. It acknowledges God as the one 'who is able to do immeasurably more than all we ask or imagine' (v. 20a). The phrase 'immeasurably more' translates ὑπερεκπερισσοῦ, a compound adverb coined by Paul. Called one of Paul's super-superlatives, it denotes the highest degree of comparison possible – infinitely in excess of all expectation ('superabundance').[11] Without question, the term alludes to the matters Paul has discussed in this section, but is not limited to them. The superlative teaches that God's capacity to answer prayer exceeds not only our oral requests, but 'far surpasses even such thoughts as are too big for words, and too deep for utterance'. Furthermore, 'those desires which are

---

[9] Bruce, *Colossians, Philemon, Ephesians*, p. 330.

[10] Wiersbe, *Ephesians*, p. 33.

[11] According to E.K. Simpson, the word, perfectly classical, is a Platonic combination that means 'beyond comparison'. *Ephesians*, p. 84, n. 34.

dumb from their very vastness, and amazing from their very boldness, are insignificant requests compared with the power of God'.[12]

God's resources are inexhaustible and his ability is immeasurable. We lack because we limit him by our faithless praying, our feeble thinking, and our petty asking, our uncertain expectation. What noble privilege that we who cannot comprehend God's power are the channels through which it actively operates (see 1.19-21)! At work in every believer is the same power that raised Christ from the dead and seated him in heavenly places. This power working in even the humblest believer is not only to transform us; it is also to empower us to become transformers of our homes, our communities, and our world.

Since it is God who has acted to save and bless bountifully, He alone is worthy of all praise (v. 21). This praise or glory, occasioned by 'the incomparable riches of his grace, expressed in his kindness to us in Christ Jesus' (2.7), must be unceasing throughout time and eternity – 'throughout all generations, for ever and ever'. Though unusual to find 'in the church' and 'in Christ' in any doxology, both the occurrence and sequence find support in the earliest and most reliable manuscripts. For Paul, God's presence-in-power resides in both Christ and his church, the church being inseparably associated with him (1.22-23; 4.15-16). Paul's aim here is simply to honor God for the church in which, surprisingly, Jews and Gentiles share fraternal oneness, and also to extol him for sending Christ the church's head through whom such union was achieved (cf. 2.14-19). We can add nothing to the intrinsic splendor and grandeur of God, but we fulfill the purpose of our existence when we glorify him and manifest his glory to others in word and deed.

Reflection and Response (Part 3)

Reflection

By far the most intensely personal section of the Epistle, this chapter comprises an intercessory prayer (1, 14-21), cut short by an extended digression in which Paul explains his apostolic ministry to the Gentiles and his longing to see Gentile believers fully realize their marvelous privilege in Christ (3.2-13). A most majestic request of Paul for the church, it contains two principal petitions – inward strengthening through the Holy Spirit, and an apprehension of Christ's love complemented by an experience of the fullness of God. The intercession reveals more than Paul's desire for the Ephesian Christians; it expresses

---

[12] J. Eadie, *Commentary on the Epistles to the Ephesians* (Grand Rapids: Zondervan, 1979), p. 261.

God's will in redemption for all his people. Its intensity and urgency is intimated in the posture of kneeling (3.14). The Jews and early Christians stood to pray. Deep solemnity and unusual earnestness were associated with kneeling. The petition can be made with confidence because it is presented to one who is Father and offered on behalf of members of his family.

Paul's prayer proceeds in a stair-step manner. He wants the believers to have spiritual strength, spiritual depth, and spiritual comprehension. An ever-broadening and ever-deepening experience of Christ, his lordship becoming an ever-growing reality in their lives, and an acquisition of God's abundant spiritual resources are the burden of the prayer. Paul's petition is primarily for spiritual, not material, blessings. Knowing God better, experiencing him more intimately and more fully is its aim. Our reflection will focus on this prayer of Paul in 3.1-21. The following questions are raised to stimulate further reflection on this magnificent prayer.

What role does prayer play in the churches you know? How seriously do they take the prayer of Paul? What fills the agenda and content of prayers you hear in church? What do prayer groups you know make the focus of their prayers? Generally, how effective are the prayers you hear? How may Paul's prayer inform how Christians pray? What difference may praying prayers like Paul's make in the lives of individual Christians and the church?

In an attempt to inspire reflection of a more personal nature the following questions are offered. What role does prayer play in your life? How seriously do you take this prayer of Paul? What absorbs most of your time, attention, and energy in prayer? Do you see the pursuit of intimacy with God as vital to your faith and Christian life? What is the usual target of your prayers? How much of your praying is self-focused and how much is focused on the needs of others?

Response

Among the many responses that could be given to the questions above, the following are worthy of consideration.

1. Inserting your name at the appropriate places, write in your own words and then pray audibly Paul's petitionary prayer in Eph. 3.14-21.

2. When you pray examine the focus and motivation of your prayers, noting in what ways you may need to make your praying more reflective of Paul's.

3. Compare how much time you spend in prayer with time given to other activities, for example television and the inter-

net, and say what you will relinquish to increase your devo-
tional time.

4. Make a list of the things you see as obstacles to prayer in your
   life and another list of the things that give you incentive to
   pray.

5. Write down how you are going to eliminate the obstacles
   and harness the incentives to pray.

6. Join a prayer group and connect with prayer partners who
   feel the same way you do about cultivating closer intimacy
   with God.

Ephesians 4

A striking transition in the Epistle begins with this chapter. Not un-characteristic of the writings of Paul, there is a shift in emphasis where-by ethics succeeds doctrine, exhortation follows exposition; how one ought to behave/live replaces what one ought to believe (cf. Rom. 12.1-2; Col. 3.1). Though they exude an air of prayer, praise, and thanksgiving, chs. 1–3 are principally doctrinal, unfolding and elucidat-ing God's eternal redemptive plan and purpose for his creation (1.3-14). Believers are raised from the dead and seated with Christ in the heavenlies (2.1-10); Jew and Gentile are reconciled in an equal frater-nal relationship in the church (2.11–3.13). God is progressively moving all things toward the goal of summing up all things in Christ. A mag-nificent eulogistic attribution of glory to God concludes ch. 3. While it can never be said that chs. 4–6 are totally bereft of doctrinal content and 1-3 devoid of ethical implication, nevertheless, with the retrospec-tive 'therefore' (οὖν) of 4:1, Paul signals a distinct shift from the theo-logical to the practical, i.e. from the believer's wealth in Christ to the believer's walk in Christ.[1] Pagan vices are to be denounced, Christian virtues demonstrated. God's new community must live by a new standard. This transition may imply that right doctrine ought to lead to right conduct. What one believes often determines how one behaves. The walk of individual believers, how they live, has much to do with the unity of the community – a theme that resounds in 2.11-22, 3.2-13, and 4.1-6.

III. The Church's Duty: Live Worthily of God's Call (4.1–6.24)

The master key that unlocks the structure of the Epistle, 4.1, serves as a vital link that connects the theme of divine call embedded in chs. 1–3 to the exhortations in 4–6. Its summons to a reconciled community of believers to 'live a life worthy of the calling you have received' is both retrospective and prospective. The adverb ἀξίως means appropriately, in balance. Paul's appeal, then, is that believers bring into balance their conduct with their call. 'Call' or 'calling' here, while losing nothing of its meaning of divine summons to salvation by election (Rom. 11.29; Eph. 1.18; 4.4; 1 Cor. 1.26; 2 Tim.1.9), includes believers' union into one corporate body.

---

[1] It is instructive that the imperative occurs only once in the first half of Ephesians (2.11) and forty-two times in the rest of the Epistle. The hortatory nature of chs. 4–6 is heightened by the repeated use of 'walk/live' (περιπατέω) in 4.1, 17; 5.2, 8, 15.

Responsible living, which to Paul is a logical corollary to divine benefits graciously bestowed (Rom. 12.1), is in harmony with one's vocation and is the only fruit worthy of persons divinely chosen and richly blessed by God. The privilege of being objects of divine call must impinge upon everything believers do, serving as 'the standard for Christian living' and putting the Christian life 'on the highest plane'.[2] What it means to live worthy of one's calling is what Paul extrapolates more fully in the exhortations in the second half of the Epistle. The estimate of this type of life is determined by how believers relate to the believing community (4.2-16), to society (4.17-5.21), to their family (5.22-6.9), and to the unseen dark forces of evil (6.10-20). In ch. 4 Paul's appeal to the Ephesian believers to live a life worthy of their calling both defines the nature of the church, of which they are a part, and describes its duty in a four-fold way: the church is and is to be a society dedicated to divine purpose (4.1-16), a society that practices purity (4.17-24), a society that promotes integrity (4.25-29), and a society that propagates forgiveness (4.30-32).

A. The Church: A Community Called to Divine Purpose (4.1-16)

Verses 1-16 stress the spiritual qualities constitutive of the life of those called of God, and serve as a preview of what follows in 4.17-6.20. These verses can be divided into three parts. In addition to their admonition that the readers live a life worthy of their calling, vv. 1-6 depict the believing community as a body called to exercise the unity the Spirit produces – a unity that sallies from and reflects the nature of God. Verses 7-11 describe it as a society called to encourage the diversity Christ provides, and vv. 12-16 portray it as chosen to embrace and exemplify the maturity both unity and diversity beget.

1. Called to exercise the unity the Spirit produces (4.1-6)

Flying in the face of prevailing Greco-Roman culture, in v. 2 Paul enumerates five spiritual virtues generally associated with the cringing and submissive temper of slaves in the first century, but qualities also illustrative of the life of Jesus (Mt. 11.29; Phil. 2.8; cf. Gal. 5.22-23), to distinguish believers who walk worthily of their calling: humility, gentleness, patience, forbearance, and love. Humility renders ταπεινο-φροσύνη, which literally means 'lowliness of mind' and depicts a disposition shaped by a proper estimate of oneself and the intrinsic worth of others, while gentleness – disciplined strength – conveys the

---

[2] Leon Morris, *Expository Reflections on the Letter to the Ephesians* (Grand Rapids: Baker Books, 1994), p. 112.

idea of tenderness toward people and surrender to God. The term translated 'patience', μακροθυμία, connotes having a long fuse in dealing with people. It literally means 'long-tempered' – what James calls being 'slow to become angry' (1.19). It describes the power to withstand provocation and not strike out or strike back at the wrongdoer. Forbearance (patience magnified) means tolerance – the ability to endure or put up with, to make allowance for the faults and weaknesses of others. Love is the final and crowning grace. 'In love' (Eph. 4.2c; cf. Col. 3.14) means love must be the source, conduit, and controller of this behavior for 'Love is patient, love is kind' (1 Cor. 13.4).

More than being characteristics of a life worthy of the Lord, these five graces help the believer protect and preserve the unity of the Spirit, a matter Paul will now address. Turning to the significance of Christian unity, Paul exhorts his readers to 'Make every effort to keep the unity of the Spirit through the bond of peace' (v. 3). 'Make every effort' translates σπουδάζοντες, a participle which means diligence, eagerness, and urgency (see 2 Tim. 2.15; 4.21; Heb. 4.11; 2 Pet. 1.10). It may also be rendered, 'Spare no effort; make it a priority'.[3] As a present participle issuing a command, it urges continuous effort. Christian unity is not the achievement of believers; it is the gift and work of the Holy Spirit preserved by the behavior of its recipients. It is not primarily an undertaking to be accomplished or a goal to attain. It is a present reality bestowed in the gospel, innate in the constitution of the church and its membership, and 'guaranteed by the one Spirit who inspires it, the one Lord who governs it,' and 'the one God who is the source of its life'.[4] The church is invisibly and indivisibly one, just as God is one, Christ is one, and the Spirit is one. It is, however, the task of believers to preserve and exhibit visibly what the Holy Spirit produces, and the virtues listed in v. 2 are a great asset toward this goal. While the hostility and division between Jew and Gentile, which Paul addressed earlier (chs. 2-3), may serve as a backdrop to this exhortation, the desired unity which Paul invites the community of faith to maintain is not limited to that centuries-old problem. Its appeal resounds with contemporary relevance and urgency in a church fractured by doctrinal and denominational strife.

This unity, 'the ground of the Church's existence',[5] makes neither ecclesiastical uniformity nor organizational unity its aim. Christ-like relationships and togetherness among believers are its central thrust, and peace its binding and bonding factor. The church's unity serves both an existential and eschatological purpose. Existentially, the

---

[3] Lincoln, *Ephesians*, p. 237.
[4] G.B. Caird, *Paul's Letters from Prison* (Oxford: Oxford University Press, 1976), p. 71.
[5] Caird, *Paul's Letters from Prison*, p. 71.

church's unity is 'the means by which the manifold wisdom of God is being displayed to the universe'. Eschatologically, the church is 'the eschatological outpost, the pilot project of God's purposes', and his people 'the expression of this unity that displays to the universe his final goal'.[6] Denominations and various Christian communions have their place and, arguably, individually and collectively serve the cause of Christ. They fail Christ's unity test, however, when rivalries, strife, and internecine enmity are allowed to grow within and between them. Their visible witness is weakened when peace and harmony are sacrificed on the altar of a myopic and narcissistic conceit. Christian unity is not negotiated around an ecclesiastical conference table; nor can it be mandated by church councils. It springs from the unity of the triune God, and rests upon seven fundamental unities which form the pillars on which the Spirit erects genuine oneness among the people of God (vv. 4-6). Its unity is reflective of the unity of the Godhead. Just as there can be no other gods or lords, 'so there cannot be other churches'.[7] This unity is as enduring as the oneness of God himself. Therefore, it is 'no more possible to split the church than it is possible to split the Godhead'.[8]

How may the Trinity's involvement in the church be conceived? First, the one family is created by the one Father God. Secondly, the one faith, hope and baptism are created by the one Lord Jesus. Thirdly, the one body is created by the one Holy Spirit.[9] Paul begins this incipient creed, 'there is one body' (4.4; cf. 1.23; 2.16) – which refers to the universal church comprising both redeemed Jews and Gentiles – and there is 'one Spirit'. There is only one church, so there can be only one Spirit. As a body bereft of the vivifying spirit is but a lifeless corpse, so is the church without the Holy Spirit. The Holy Spirit indwells the church and vitalizes, energizes, and unifies it (1 Cor. 12.13). Every local assembly is a visible manifestation of the universal one, and shoulders the responsibility of making Christ's vision of oneness a reality locally. Fourthly, believers 'were called to one hope' – the common future guaranteed by the Spirit (Eph. 1.14) of ultimately sharing in God's glory (Rom. 5.2; Col. 1.23, 27; 1 Jn 3.2). Moving on from a series of unities associated with the Spirit, Paul turns his attention to a second trio of unities related to Christ: 'one Lord, one faith, one baptism'. Hitherto, he has referred to Jesus as 'Lord' no fewer than twenty times in this Epistle, a title used of Yahweh in the Old Testament.

---

[6] O'Brien, *Ephesians*, pp. 285, 286.
[7] F.W. Beare, *The Epistle to the Ephesians* (The Interpreter's Bible Commentary, 10; Nashville: Abingdon, 1953), p. 686.
[8] Stott, *The Message of Ephesians*, p. 151.
[9] Stott, *The Message of Ephesians*, p. 151.

On the basis of his resurrection and exaltation, Jesus now sits at the place of highest honor and authority (cf. Rom. 14.8-9; 1 Cor. 8.6; Phil. 2.9-11) as unrivaled Savior and Sovereign, and is the sole object of faith (Acts 4.12; Rom. 3.30; 10.9). While 'faith' is sometimes used in the NT of the gospel message or the corpus of Christian belief (Gal. 1.23; Phil. 1.27; 1 Tim. 3.9; 4.1; Jude 3), the absence of the corresponding definite article 'the' strengthens the case for its denoting personal trust in Christ as Savior and Lord. To Christ alone all Christians owe absolute allegiance. For this non-negotiable truth many early believers were willing to – and did – pay the ultimate price. 'Baptism' is the third unity in the second triad of unities. At once the means and expression of the oneness all believers share (Gal. 3.26-28), it is not only the seal of our incorporation into the body of Christ and a symbol of spiritual union (1 Cor. 12.13) but also identification with Christ in his death, burial, and resurrection (Rom. 6.3-5; Col. 2.12). Paul brings his list of spiritual unities to a climax in a 'Christian reworking of the Shema of Deut. 6:4'[10] in which he praises the 'one God and Father of all, who is over all and through all and in all' (v. 6), placing this sovereign God as the eventual source of all spiritual unity, and affirming his 'transcendent sovereignty' – his rule over all – and his 'immanent pervasiveness'[11] – his working through and indwelling all. There is a sense in which this sovereign and transcendent God is universal Father (Mal. 2.10), but in this context where the unity of the church is foremost, the 'all' of which Paul speaks can allude only to Christians, members of the church, referred to subsequently as 'each one of us' (v. 7). All believers, irrespective of race, color, class, or country of origin, share a common father (Gal. 3.26-29). To speak of God as 'father' is to acknowledge his immanence, winsome approachability, warm love, and tender care. Having an equal stake in the same family, sharing the love of the same father, afforded the same privileges to serve, believers have every incentive to promote unity in the Christian family – a family over which he rules, through which he works, and in which he dwells.

2. Called to encourage the diversity Christ provides (4.7-11)

Paul ended his discussion on believers' unity (4.1-6) by explaining that the one God who is Father of all transcends all, rules over all, and indwells all. In this section, beginning with the phrase 'But to each one of us' (v. 7), he now turns from the theme of unity to the diversity of each individual part and Christ's allocation of grace to each believer in the body (4.7-11). This means that each Christian possesses a particular gift and individuality for a unique function in the church, a fact which

---

[10] O'Brien, *Ephesians*, p. 284.
[11] Wood, *Ephesians*, p. 57.

should stifle the spirit of competition, envy or gift valuation that makes one member feel inferior or superior to another. As he also argues elsewhere (Rom. 12.3-8; 1 Cor. 12.4-31), far from being an enemy of unity, diversity is instead its ally, working for 'the common good' – the benefit of the whole church (1 Cor. 12.7; see also Eph. 4.16) – in the cause of bringing the church to full maturity in Christ (Eph. 4.13).

No member possesses all the gifts; nor is any member without a gift: 'But to each one of us grace has been given as Christ apportioned it' (v. 7). In the same way the Spirit 'distributes' spiritual gifts 'to each one, just as he determines' (1 Cor. 12.11), so Christ has 'apportioned' (Eph. 4.7) grace for ministry to each person in varied measure (κατὰ τὸ μέτρον). This means that Christ bestows the assignment and ability – both encompassed in the term translated 'grace' (χάρις) – and the proportion of power necessary (μέτρον) to accomplish the assigned task (cf. v. 16; Rom. 12.6). Such ministry assignment and attendant capability are not only for the clergy, but also for every individual Christian.

Verse 8 relates the conferral of these gifts to an OT prophetic declaration of which Christ is fulfillment: 'This is why it says …' (διὸ λέγει) occurs only here, in 5:14, and in Jas 4.6 in the NT. Paul does not specify the source of his reference, but many scholars believe it derives from Ps. 68.18 (68.19 MT; 67.19 LXX). A song of triumph, Psalm 68 in its earliest context is a call of Israel to God to deliver them from their enemies, as in former days (vv. 1-3). God wins a resounding victory and ascends Mount Zion. Like a military conqueror, on returning home he leads captives in procession laden with the spoils of war. Paul sees the passage as a prophetic preview of the overwhelming victory Christ achieved at the cross and ascension. Even a cursory comparison of Eph. 4.8 and Ps. 68.18 reveals both striking similarities and dissimilarities, leading some scholars to conclude that Paul is not citing a single verse but 'summarizing all of Psalm 68'.[12] Others have presumed that Paul, as he has done elsewhere (cf. Hab. 2.4 and Rom. 1.17/Gal. 3.11; Deut. 30.12-14 and Rom. 10.6-8), by divine inspiration, has adapted the Greek rendering to serve his theological purpose.

Rabbinic theology interprets Ps. 68.18 as Moses' ascent up to Mount Sinai to receive the Law ('gifts') so that he might give it to the people (e.g. *T. Dan* 5.10, 11; *Midr. Tehillin* on Ps. 68.11; *Abot R. Nat.* 2.2a).[13] A textual tradition different from the MT and LXX is, however,

---

[12] John F. Walvoord and Roy B. Zuck, eds. *The Bible Knowledge Commentary* (Colorado Springs: Cook Communications Ministries, 2000), p. 634.
[13] Walter Liefeld suggests that Ps. 68.18 alludes to Num. 8.5-19 where God sets apart the Levites to serve the priests. In the NT, however, all believers are called and gifted by God to serve the church, which is a royal priesthood (1 Pet. 2.9). See *Ephesians* (IVP New Testament Commentary Series; Leicester, UK/ Downers Grove, 1977), p. 102.

reflected in the Syriac Peshitta, which renders the verse 'you have *given* gifts', and the Aramaic Targum, which reads 'you gave'. Both the Masoretic Text (MT), the traditional Hebrew Old Testament, and the LXX (Septuagint), the Greek version of the Old Testament, render Ps. 68.18, 'You ascended to the height; ... you received gifts among humankind'. One attempt to resolve the apparent conflict between the two renditions is to translate 'among' (Heb. ב, Gk ἐν) with 'for', i.e. Moses went up to Mount Sinai and received the Law 'for' humankind.

As seen in the book of *Jubilees*, Pentecost, the most important Jewish festival, is further prominently associated with the covenant at Sinai. The contrast between Moses and Christ and Law and grace, whether or not Paul consciously intends it here, is obvious in the text. Moses ascended Mount Sinai; Christ ascended 'far above the heavens' (v. 10). Moses gave the people Law; Christ gives his people grace (v. 7) and divinely ordained leaders (vv. 11-13). 'For Paul, as for the early Jewish Christians before him (cf. Acts 2:33), Christ's ascension to heaven and subsequent gift of the Spirit at Pentecost had trumped Moses' ascent to heaven and subsequent mediation of the law to Israel'.[14] However one may view Ps. 68.18, the theological direction of the psalm serves well the Christological interests of Paul to show the triumph of Christ over the evil spiritual forces arrayed against God and his people.

Before he enumerates and identifies some of the gifts that Christ has apportioned, Paul introduces vv. 9-10 as a parenthetical and Christological explication of v. 8, accentuating the fact that the ascension of the divine person (Christ) alluded to in the Psalm is preceded by his prior descent from the heavenly realm. The phrase 'to the lower parts of the earth' (v. 9), which gives the locale of Christ's descent, is variously understood. The early church fathers, connecting it with 1 Pet. 3.19, took the genitive (of the earth) as comparative or partitive, and translated it as 'parts lower than the earth' – the underworld of the dead. In this view, which is theologically and grammatically viable (Acts 2.25-35; Rom. 10.7), Christ who ascended to the highest part of heaven also descended into the lowest part of the earth, *hades/sheol*, making his triumph total and all-encompassing. Christ's going to the earth's lowest region, according to exponents of this view, was to afford the dead an opportunity to hear the gospel or release from the devil's prison (limbo) the saints who had died under the old covenant.

Other interpreters understand the genitive as appositional or definitional, rendering it 'the lower parts, namely, the earth'. Here Christ's descent refers to his incarnation and cross death (humiliation, Phil. 2.5-11), his ascent to his exaltation (Acts 2.31-36). This is the view of most expositors by far. In Ephesians Paul advocates that it was at his ascen-

---

[14] Thielman, *Ephesians*, BECNT, p. 266.

sion that Christ vanquished the evil spiritual powers, not at his descent into *hades/sheol* (1.19-21). A third and least popular view is that Christ's descent alludes to his coming in the Spirit at Pentecost to impart gifts to the church. Though attracting a few modern proponents, the notion of Christ's 'harrowing of hell' associated with the early church fathers has little theological or contextual support. In keeping with his cosmological dualism, Paul's contrast here is likely 'not between one part of the earth and another, but between the whole earth and heaven'.[15] Christ is exalted 'higher than all the heavens' (v. 10). Whether Paul here implies the idea of three (cf. 2 Cor. 12.2) or seven heavens (the Jewish view), he is clearly showing Christ's elevation to the place of ultimate honor and supremacy, the goal of Christ being 'to fill the whole universe'.

An obvious echo of 1.23, the statement means that the aim of Christ's exaltation is that he might permeate the universe and exercise sovereign rule over it – a prerogative predicated of God in the OT (cf. Jer. 23.24). The train of thought introduced in v. 7 – that of Christ apportioning gifts to his people – but interrupted by the excursus on the descent and ascent of Christ (vv. 8-10), is resumed in v. 11, Paul now armed with the knowledge that the exalted Lord is the one who has endowed the church with his gifts of grace. Christ exercises his lordship on earth primarily through the church. Gifts bequeathed to his body, the church, therefore, are to that end. Christ's will and purposes for the world are accomplished and his sovereign rule extended as his people grow and mature and attain ultimate unity in him.

Having set forth Christ's cosmic triumph over malevolent spiritual forces, Paul will now show how the gifts the sovereign Lord bequeathed upon the church advance its growth in unity, Christlikeness, and maturity (4.11-16).

Verse 11. This verse is an elaboration on the gifts the exalted Christ gave (and gives) to his people, alluded to in v. 8. Paul reveals that these gifts are chosen and gifted leaders. The NT records five lists of gifts given to the church (Rom. 12.6-8; 1 Cor. 12.8-10, 28-30; Eph. 4.11-12; cf. 1 Pet. 4.10-11). These gifts are divergent yet complementary, and representative rather than exhaustive. Trinitarian in origin, they reveal a rich diversity with a goal of uniting and maturing the body of Christ for greater usefulness. They are all 'spiritual' though they are not all exclusively 'gifts of the Spirit'. What is distinctive about the Ephesians passage (cf. 1 Cor. 12.28-30) is that it designates the gifts not as

---

[15] Calvin, *The Epistles of Paul the Apostle to the Galatians, Ephesians, Philippians and Colossians* (trans. T.H.L. Parker; Edinburgh: Oliver & Boyd, 1965), p. 176; cited by Bruce, *Colossians, Philemon, Ephesians*, p. 343.

divine abilities or ministries, as in other passages, but as gifted ministers – persons, not enablement to minister. These ministers equip and enable others to utilize their own particular ministries so that the body is 'brought to maturity, wholeness, and unity'. These equippers are agents of the word 'through whom the gospel is revealed, declared, and taught'.[16]

Because of the overlapping of functions with these early ministers and the situational and organizational structure that characterized the early church, it is risky to attempt a neat, water-tight definition or categorization of duties and responsibilities. Equally difficult is to extrapolate the roles of contemporary ministers from the fluid and ancient categories they represent. With the emphatic-intensive pronoun αὐτός in v. 11, Paul calls attention to the fact that these ministers – and all true ministers – are first chosen by Christ, who 'gave some to be ...' (v. 11). They are not self-appointed; nor does the church bestow ministry upon them. The church appoints and commissions them for service only in recognition and confirmation of the divine call.

'Apostles' and 'prophets' appear first in every list in which they are paired and were mentioned earlier in the foundation of the church (2.20; 3.5; cf. 1 Cor. 12. 28). They were 'the authoritative recipients and proclaimers of the mystery of Christ'.[17] The noun 'apostle' occurs only once in the Septuagint (1 Kgs 14.6), but 80 times in the NT. The verb, which means 'to send', appears 79 times in the NT, at times in a restricted or specific sense to describe the twelve disciples/delegates of Jesus, and at other times in a broader sense for other commissioned messengers (Acts 14.4, 14; 2 Cor. 8.23; 10.12-15; Gal. 2.12; Phil. 2.25). The verb ἀποστέλλειν carries the resonance of its Hebrew counterpart שׁלח, which in the first-century Jewish world denoted the sending of an emissary with a special commission to act with the full authority of the sender.

As 'witnesses to the event of God's mighty act of self-revelation and human redemption at the center of which was the Lord Jesus Christ',[18] apostles held the highest authority in the church, a prerogative seen in the primacy of place Paul gives them in his writings (1 Cor. 12.28; Eph. 2.20; 4.11), the attesting miraculous signs and wonders that attended their ministry (2 Cor. 12.12), and the special deference Paul commanded from the churches he established (1 Cor. 4.15-16; 9.1-2). Paul employs the term 'apostle' 25 times. Without assigning rank or classification to any, he includes in the primary circle of those he deems apostles The Twelve (1 Cor. 15.5), James (1 Cor. 15.7; Gal.

---

[16] O'Brien, *The Letter to the Ephesians*, p. 298.
[17] O'Brien, *The Letter to the Ephesians*, p. 298.
[18] Frank Stagg, *New Testament Theology* (Nashville: Broadman Press, 1962), p. 258.

1.19), himself (1 Cor. 15.8), Andronicus and Junias (Rom. 16.7), and presumably Apollos (1 Cor. 4.6, 9), and Barnabas (1 Cor. 9.6).

Some scholars believe, however, that two categories of apostles are mentioned in Paul's writings: 'Apostles of Christ' and 'apostles of the churches'.[19] The apostles of Christ comprised the twelve who were chosen, discipled (Acts 1.21-22), and commissioned by Christ himself (Mt. 28.19-20; Acts 1.8), and were eyewitnesses of his resurrection. The number twelve, symbolic of the twelve tribes of Israel (Gen. 35.22; 42.13, 32; Num. 1.44), was adopted as a title given to those Jesus appointed to be with him and whom he designated 'apostles' – representatives sent out 'to preach and to have authority to drive out demons' (Mk 3.14, 15; cf. Mt. 10.2; Lk. 6.13). Though predominantly called 'disciples' in Matthew and Mark,[20] 'The Twelve' became the most popular designation of this group in the Gospels,[21] and endured throughout the life of the early church (Acts 6.2; 1 Cor. 15.5), Peter and the other disciples with the 120 taking pains to preserve that number of members in the apostolate after the death of Judas (Acts 1.12-26). It would appear that this distinctive group (himself included) is what Paul has in mind in Eph. 4.11. These apostles assumed a place of prominence above all other Christian leaders 'by virtue of having received a divine commission for their task, and by the range of spiritual gifts at their disposal'.[22]

Clearly, the office and function of the Twelve (and Paul) are irreplaceable and unrepeatable. Because they lived in closest proximity to the historical Jesus and the events of redemptive history and were uniquely endowed by the Spirit to receive, interpret, and transmit divine revelation, 'There was and is no independent access to Jesus Christ except through them'.[23] Further, their teachings and lives have defined and determined for all time what was to be normative doctrine and behavior for the individual believer and Christian community universally (1 Cor. 5.6; Gal. 1.8-9; 1 Tim. 1.3; 6.3, 4; 1 Pet. 2.18). They were 'the charter-witnesses of Christ's resurrection, clothed with

[19] Michael Green, *To Corinth with Love* (Waco, TX: Word Books, 1988), p. 179; Stott, *The Message of Ephesians*, p. 160; Stagg, *New Testament Theology*, p. 260. The apostles of Christ were chosen and sent out by Christ himself; the apostles of the churches were chosen and sent out by the churches.

[20] They are called 'disciples' 69 times in Matthew and 43 times in Mark, 'the Twelve' 9 times in Matthew and 11 times in Mark.

[21] Collectively and individually, Matthew designates them 'disciples' 69 times and Mark 43 times.

[22] David E. Aune, *Prophecy in Early Christianity* (Grand Rapids: Eerdmans, 1983), p. 202.

[23] Green, *To Corinth with Love*, p. 180.

life-long and church-wide authority over life and doctrine'.[24] Eschato-logically, they will 'sit on twelve thrones, judging the twelve tribes of Israel' (Mt. 19.28) and have their names written on the twelve founda-tions of the New Jerusalem (Rev. 21.14).

It is not without significance that while the NT has provisions, in-structions, and stipulated requirements for the appointment of bish-ops/elders and deacons (1 Tim. 3.1-13; Tit. 1.5-9), after the replacement of Judas no instruction is given for the appointment of apostles. No attempt was made to replace James the brother of John who died at the hands of Herod (Acts 12.2). Some believe that in 1 Cor. 15.6-8 Paul regards himself as the last apostle and restricts the office of apostle to those who had seen the risen Lord during the 40-day sojourn before his ascension (Acts 1.3).

Paul's use of 'apostle' is not ironclad or definitive of only The Twelve and the others named above. In Phil. 2.25 he speaks of Epaph-roditus as 'your messenger' (ὑμῶν δὲ ἀπόστολον) and in 2 Cor. 8.23 of the two delegates accompanying him as bearers of the collection for the Jerusalem church as 'representatives[25] of the churches' (ἀπόστολοι ἐκκλησιῶν). The designation of Epaphroditus and the two brothers as apostles of their churches, coupled with the unique and singular role the 'Apostles of Christ' have played in the church's doctrine, canon, history, and tradition, not to mention the need to demarcate the boundaries of claimants to the gift/office of apostleship, has led to the justification of this second category of apostles. A closer examination will reveal that whereas the apostles of the churches possessed only the gift and not the office of apostleship, the Twelve and Paul possessed both gift and office.[26]

Though he nowhere claimed to be one of the Twelve nor was pre-sent for Christ's post-resurrection appearances, Paul uniquely qualifies both as an apostle of Christ (1 Cor. 15.8-9; Gal. 1.1; 2.6-9) and an apostle of the church (Acts 13.3). His distinctive call to apostleship came through a later vision of the risen Christ (Acts 9.1-19; 22.4-16; 26.9-18; Gal. 1.12). In 1 Cor. 15.8 he calls himself 'one abnormally born' (ἔκτρωμα), which means that his calling to be an apostle came

---

[24] William Hendriksen, *Ephesians* (New Testament Commentary, 10; Grand Rapids: Baker, 1978), p. 196.

[25] The word ἀπόστολος, translated elsewhere 'apostle', is rendered 'messenger' and 'representative' respectively in most translations.

[26] Walvoord and Zuck, eds., *Ephesians*, p. 635. Among the secondary were Paul, Bar-nabas, James, Andronicus, Junias, and Epaphroditus who had not followed Jesus from the time of John's baptism (Acts 1.22). Paul, however, though not one of the Twelve, func-tioned uniquely both as a primary and secondary apostle, having been commissioned into ministry both by the risen Lord and the church. As bearer of delegated authority, an apostle had no power to transfer such authority.

rather late – a fact his enemies exploited on more than one occasion to challenge and even discredit his apostolic authority (1 Cor. 9.1, 2; 2 Cor. 11.21-33; Gal. 1.6–2.18). Yet, he regarded his conversion to be comparable to the Twelve's experience of Christ's resurrection (1 Cor. 15.3-8), and insisted that he had seen the risen Lord (1 Cor. 9.1) and was directly commissioned by him (Rom. 1.1; 1 Cor. 1.1; Gal. 1.1, 15-24). Paul possessed all the authority and prerogatives of an apostle of Christ (1 Cor. 15.9-11; Gal. 1.8-9) and was received and recognized by the other apostles as one of them (2 Pet. 3.15).

Prophets are Christ's second gift to the church. The title 'prophet' (προφήτης) occurs 144 times in the NT. Its Hebrew equivalent in the OT, נביא, denoted one who received messages from God and was divinely authorized to proclaim them on his behalf (cf. Exod. 7.1-2; Num. 12.6-8). The *navi* also functioned as 'seer' (רֹאֶה) – of what was hidden – an earlier pre-monarchical designation. Agabus, one of the few prophets named in the NT, stands out for his foretelling (Acts 11.28; 21.10-11). Patterned after their OT counterparts, NT prophets were both God's authorized spokespersons who proclaimed a relevant word from God to the contemporary life situation (1 Cor. 14.3-40) and ones specially endowed by the Spirit to predict future events (Acts 11.27-28; 21.10). Moses' desire for God's people (Num. 11.29) is fulfilled in the prophethood of every believer (Acts 2.17-18; 19.6; 1 Cor. 14.31). Prophets, however, were an identifiable group of 'specialists' called and gifted by God as channels of divine information. Though they served in a subservient role to the apostles, with the apostles they constitute the foundation of the church (2.20; 3.5), utilizing their prophetic gift to edify, comfort, encourage the saints (1 Cor. 14.3, 31), interpret and communicate the mysteries of the faith (1 Cor. 12.10; 13.2; 14.23, 30-31), and equip believers for ministry (Eph. 4.11). While the reception and diffusion of divine revelation was their primary function, some prophets itinerated – while others ministered solely in their local communities[27] – preaching and teaching the word with spontaneity and power (1 Cor. 14.6, 26).[28] As with the primary apostles, these 'canonical prophets' have no successors. No provisions or instructions are given for any would-be successors (cf. Acts 14.23; 20. 17, 28, 38; 1 Pet. 5.2). However, the prophetic gift and functions continue in contemporary 'charismatic prophets'.

The evangelist (εὐαγγελιστής) is the third gifted person Christ has bequeathed to the church. Meaning 'bearer of good news', the title appears on only two other occasions in the NT: as a description of Phil-

---

[27] Aune, *Prophecy*, pp. 211-12.

[28] Walter Elwell, ed., s.v. 'Spiritual Gifts', *Evangelical Dictionary of Theology* (Grand Rapids: Baker, 1984), p. 1044.

ip (Acts 21.8) and of the work Timothy is encouraged to do at Ephesus (2 Tim. 4.5). The pervasiveness of the verb (εὐαγγελίζομαι) underscores the important fact that sharing the gospel is central to the life and mission of the Christian and church. It is also significant that whereas the term 'to preach' (κηρύσσειν) implies a method – a public verbal proclamation as a herald – the verb from which 'evangelist' derives (εὐαγγελίζομαι) is restricted to no method of sharing the gospel, but rather indicates the nature of the message to be communicated – good news. This leaves room for much creativity, flexibility, and adaptability. Similar to the apostle and prophet, the evangelist is a gifted person given by Christ with the task of spreading the gospel. This likely involves traveling from place to place (Acts 8.4-5, 35, 40; 21.8).

Pastors and teachers are Christ's last gift to the church. Because the two titles share one article there has been an ongoing debate for many years as to whether two distinctly gifted persons are represented or one person with two sets of skills. The former view was held by some earlier interpreters who regarded the ministry of pastors and teachers as modal and local, whereas that of the apostles, prophets, and evangelists was itinerant. The latter perspective understands the article as explanatory, identifying the pastor and teacher as one person (pastor-teacher). This approach ignores 2.20, where the one article connects 'apostles' and 'prophets' but recognizes them as two separate groups. A third and more popular option is to view pastors and teachers as two distinct groups with overlapping gifts and functions. The text, therefore, calls for neither an absolute distinction between pastors and teachers nor an absolute integration of both but an intersection of skills and duties. Teaching was required of all pastors (1 Tim. 3.2), but shepherding was not part of the portfolio of the teacher.[29]

In the NT three interchangeable terms are used to describe the duties and functions of the leader who fills the office of shepherd: pastor, bishop, and elder (Acts 20.28; 1 Pet. 2.25; 5.1-2). 'Pastor' (ποιμήν), a term used in the OT of the leaders of Israel and laden with Middle Eastern culture, can also be rendered 'shepherd', and designates the caring, feeding, leading, and protecting duties of the gifted leader Christ has given to the church. The overall well-being of the Christian community was the responsibility of the pastor. When 'bishop' (ἐπίσκοπος) is used (5 times), the pastor's role as overseer (guardian) is in view. 'Elder' (πρεσβύτερος), used 70 times in the NT, corresponds to the OT *sab* ('grey-headed') and *zaqen* ('aged' or 'bearded'). In the Middle East age was highly regarded. With age came experience, status, and special respect and honor. Leadership of the community was

---

[29] Daniel Wallace, *Greek Grammar Beyond the Basics* (Grand Rapids: Zondervan, 1996), p. 284; Thielman, *Ephesians*, p. 275; Hoehner, *Ephesians*, pp. 543-44.

therefore accorded to older men (Exod. 18.12; Num. 11.16-17; 22.7; Deut. 27.1). The church perpetuated this practice[30] (Acts 11.30; 21.18).

Under unrelenting threat by false teachers and false teachings, the early Christian communities needed gifted individuals who would both protect believers and bring them to a place of Christian maturity. Teachers provided this critical service. While teaching would have been part of the function of the four earlier groups of leaders, there was a special group of people in the church whose task it was to teach (2 Tim. 1.13-14; 2.1-2; Tit. 1.9). Teaching would entail an exposition and application of Scripture and a faithful and accurate communication of the doctrine and tradition of the apostles.

3. Called to exemplify the maturity both unity and diversity beget (4.12-16)

In this section Paul discloses the purpose and goal for the gifted persons Christ has given to the church which are mentioned in v. 11. Their purpose is twofold, one urgent or immediate – 'to prepare the saints to serve in building up Christ's body' (v. 12), and the other ultimate or final – 'that we might no longer be infants', an aim in which proper growth is emphasized (vv. 14-16). Attainment to mature adulthood measured by Christ's full stature is the stated goal of the building up of the body (v. 13). Are the special ministers in v. 11 the ones who carry out the total task of equipping the saints, doing the work of ministry, and building up the body of Christ? Or is the task of these ministers to equip/train (καταρτίζω) the saints to do the work of ministry? One's interpretation will be determined by how one punctuates the three prepositional phrases used in v. 12. At issue here is the organizational structure of the church and how it conducts ministry. Does the NT church represent a structure in which an elite clergy monopolizes ministry or a more democratic one in which all the people exercise their gifts for the common good? (1 Cor. 12.7).

By placing a comma after each prepositional phrase, the KJV and RSV yield an interpretation which places the total operation of the church in the hands of ministers with the laity playing a spectator role.[31] The more acceptable approach is to see a progression in the prepositions which leads to the conclusion that Christ assigned gifted people to the church for the purpose of equipping all the saints, with the immediate goal of equipping them for the work of the ministry, and 'the final goal

---

[30] Later in the church's life the title referred to a function without any necessary inference of age.

[31] In his commentary on Ephesians, James Dunn favors this view, arguing that 'opting for the other view is too often motivated by a zeal to avoid clericalism and to support a "democratic" model of the Church' (p. 253).

of building up the body of Christ'.[32] It is only when God's people are equipped, with each member effectively playing his or her divine role, that the church will be built up and proper growth achieved.

'Until we reach ...' (v. 13) sets forth the progressive, prospective, and final goal of Christ's giving gifted people to the church (v. 11) to prepare God's people for building up the body of Christ (v. 12). What is this goal to which both equippers and the equipped must collectively and unceasingly work? It is twofold,[33] with Christ as the object: unity and maturity. Unity is a present reality Christ has obtained for the church (2.11-22), but in 4.3 Paul urges the Ephesians to maintain 'the unity of the Spirit', and here to attain unity 'in the faith and in the knowledge of the Son of God' (4.13). Like unity, the faith (4.5) and knowledge (1.9-10) have already been given, but are yet to be fully realized (cf. 3.18-19). This juxtaposition of actuality and aspiration, gift and goal, calls attention to the eschatological tension between the 'already' and the 'not yet' of Christian unity.

Rich diversity exists among Christ's followers in regards to spiritual gifts and functions, but such diversity is to promote unity. In view of and in opposition to the presence of false teachings and the deceitful scheming of false teachers, which results in spiritual immaturity and instability (vv. 14-15), Christian believers are called to unity in the faith. Whether theological or practical, insular individualism and hermetic isolation are marks of immaturity, and find no support in the New Testament. A maverick Christian is unheard of in the New Testament. Paul invites here to a collective confidence in and commitment to the whole corpus of orthodox Christian teaching 'that was once for all entrusted to the saints' (Jude 3) and centers upon Christ. His call is to a corporate acceptance of the accurate knowledge (ἐπίγνωσις) of what God has revealed about his Son. The church's object is 'not Christ but its own maturity in unity which comes from knowing, trusting and growing up into Christ'.[34]

Full maturity, which is the ultimate goal to which the church must aspire, means literally 'becoming a mature man' ('become mature', NIV), which is measured and defined by the 'whole measure' (NIV) or 'full stature' (NEB) of Christ. 'Becoming a mature man' translates εἰς ἄνδρα τέλειον. ἄνδρα (from ἀνήρ) is the word for 'male', Paul probably comparing a mature adult male with a boy. It has the same idea as the generic ἄνθρωπον used in 2:15, where Paul calls the unification of Jews and Gentiles in the church 'one new man' (ἕνα καινὸν

---

[32] Hoehner, *Ephesians*, p. 549. See also Stott, *The Message of Ephesians*, p. 168.
[33] Hoehner sees one goal – that of attaining maturity, but three aspects to that goal ('Ephesians', p. 553).
[34] Stott, *The Message of Ephesians*, p. 169.

ἄνθρωπον). The use of the singular depicts the corporate body of be-lievers as a single organism. The adjective τέλειον designates something that has reached its goal or end (τέλος), and may refer to fully-grown animals or persons, unblemished or perfect sacrifices or persons, and mature in contrast to immature. Moral perfection (KJV) has no support in the context, but maturity finds a strong contrast with 'infants' in v. 14. Working to build up the body of Christ until all the people of God reach unity in the faith and in the knowledge of Christ and until the church arrives at full maturity is the task of all believers.

If maturity to full adulthood is the ultimate goal for the church, then Christ's full stature is the standard by which that goal is measured. The noun ἡλικία refers principally to physical stature (height) in the NT (Lk. 2.52; 19.3), but also to age (Mt. 6.27; Lk. 12.25; Jn 9.21) and maturity (full age, Jn 9.23). Both imageries of stature and maturity have contextual support. Christ is the ultimate height to which his people must grow spiritually; his perfection is that to which the church (and every Christian) must aspire (Rom. 8.29). But Christ is also the stand-ard of spiritual maturity and completeness to which the people of God must conform (cf. v. 14). The 'corporate Christ cannot be content to fall short of the perfection of the personal Christ'.[35] Christ's bequest of gifted people (v. 11) for preparing the saints for the building up of the church (v. 12) enables God's people along their journey toward escha-tological unity and maturity. Attainment to Christ-like stature and maturity (v. 13) will progressively bring an end to all immature childish behaviors, spiritual infantilism, selfish individualism, juvenile instability, puerile ignorance, and protect the church against negative forces that seek its destruction (v. 14; cf. 1 Cor. 13.11; 2.6; 3.1-2).

With a variety of metaphors, in v. 14 Paul illustrates the marks of spiritual infantilism in contradistinction to Christ-like maturity (v. 13). His concern is the 'vulnerability of the spiritually immature to false teaching'.[36] To the extent the church or individual believers mature in the faith to that degree they are able to ward off heresy and not fall victim to it. 'Children/infants' (νήπιοι) in v. 14 sets up a double con-trast[37] with the 'mature man' of v. 13. Silliness, immaturity, and igno-rance characterize infants, wisdom and experience traits of the mature adult. But the plural 'children/infants' over against the singular 'mature man' suggests that individualism is 'a sign of childishness, unity a sign of maturity'.[38] Paul further describes the instability, helplessness, aim-less, and potentially perilous roving of an infantile believer as a boat or

[35] Bruce, *The Epistles to Colossians, Philemon, Ephesians*, pp. 350, 351.
[36] Thielman, *Ephesians*, p. 283.
[37] Lincoln, *Ephesians*, p. 257.
[38] Lincoln, *Ephesians*, p. 257.

driftwood tossed about by angry waves and ferocious variable winds (cf. Jas 1.6). Such a person is 'tossed back and forth' by each new wave of doctrine (κλυδωνιζόμενοι) and 'swung around' (περιφερόμενοι, used of spinning tops or making dizzy), by every furious gust of false teaching that blew through. The false teaching here was likely incipient Gnosticism which plagued the Asian churches at the time of Paul's writing (cf. Col. 2.8). A mélange of a meager skeleton of Christian doctrine, Oriental mysticism, and Jewish ritualism, it undermined the person of Christ, Christian living, and salvation by faith.

Paul unmasks with three carefully chosen words (κυβεία, πανουργία, μεθοδεία) the treacherous disguise behind the heretics and their heresy, stealthily calculated to deceive and entrap unstable and immature believers (v. 14). 'Cunning' or 'trickery' translates κυβεία, which refers to dice-playing and the cheating associated with it.[39] The gullibility of the spiritually immature to the wholly human and devious games of the heretics is clearly what Paul has in mind. The term rendered 'craftiness' or 'deceitfulness' (πανουργία), literally means 'doing any- or everything'. Always bearing an evil connotation in its five occurrences in the NT (Lk. 20.23; 1 Cor. 3.19; 2 Cor. 4.2; 11.3; Eph. 4.14), it bespeaks here 'unscrupulousness that stops at nothing'[40] to achieve its devious end. Such was the work of those who intentionally misrepresented the gospel (2 Cor. 4.2), and Satan's shrewd deception of Eve (2 Cor. 11.3). The heresy's organized and premeditated process of deception is cradled in the word μεθοδεία, whose negative meaning here echoes in 6.11 (its only other NT appearance), where it describes 'the devil's schemes' (NIV), devisings, or strategies to destroy believers. Derived from an older cognate (μέθοδος), it is used in the LXX twice of military cunning (Esth. 16.13; 2 Macc. 13.18), and denotes a method, procedure, process[41] – a deliberate, organized, and methodical plan of action to deceive.

Whether in the first century or in the twenty-first, behind every error and every heretic stands the devil whose calculated plan is to deceive. He devises and schemes ways to undermine the truth, to lure, entrap, confuse, and manipulate infantile followers of Christ. Now as then, he uses scripture to this end, and the ignorant, immature, and unstable become easy prey. With the adversative 'but' (δέ), in v. 15 Paul sets forth a new positive course of action for the believers as they move toward the goal of growing up into Christ. Unlike the false

---

[39] The slave philosopher Epictetus used the verb κυβεύω to describe 'philosophical cheating' whereby a philosopher's lifestyle belied his claim. See Thielman, *Ephesians*, p. 283.

[40] Wood, *Ephesians*, EBC, p. 59.

[41] Hoehner, *Ephesians*, p. 563.

teachers who pander false teaching through deception, God's children must grow by 'speaking the truth in love' – literally, 'truthing in love'. Truth and love are here lifted up as prerequisites to Christian spiritual growth. Speaking the truth (ἀληθεύοντες) entails more than speech; it encompasses speech and corresponding attitudes and actions (Jn 3.21). Love, an attribute of Christian maturity, denotes the manner by which truth is to be expressed (Eph. 5.2), and is 'the criterion for an assessment of the church's true growth'.[42] The counter-balancing of truth with love is important, because truth without love is cold orthodoxy, and love without truth is maudlin sentiment. 'Truth becomes hard if it is not softened by love; love becomes soft if it is not strengthened by truth'.[43] As a living organism, the church is not static but dynamic. Living things grow. God's living temple comprised of Jews and Gentiles 'rises' (αὔξει, 2.21), and here as believers lovingly speak the truth they 'grow up' (αὐξήσωμεν) into Christ the head (v. 15).

Paul connects the church's wide-ranging growth ('in all things, or in every way', v. 15) toward maturity into Christ its Head to its willing adherence to the truth (cf. 6.14), i.e., the practice of transparency and integrity. Not only is Christ the goal of all Christian growth (v. 15), but as v. 16 indicates, he is also its supreme source (ἐξ οὗ, from whom) of growth, who progressively and deftly fits the church together (construction; cf. 2.21 συναρμολογούμενον), holding it together (cohesion, συμβιβαζόμενον; see also Col. 2.19), connecting it (ἁφῆς), and supplying all that is essential for its growth and harmonious operation. While Christian growth is into Christ (v. 15) and from Christ (v. 16), Paul sees the interconnectedness and efficient interaction of the whole body of believers as vital to the ultimate goal of Christian maturity and the building of the church (1 Cor. 12. 14-16). Malfunction and dysfunction, immaturity and instability, will prevail in a church out of sync. Only as believers find their proper place and minister in their individual gifts will the church arrive at full maturity.

B. The Church: A Community that Practices Purity (4.17-24)

Unlike the Colossian Epistle that launched verbal missiles against a virulent heresy infecting the churches, Ephesians is irenic and non-combative and gives no hint of a moral or doctrinal crisis in the assemblies. References to Christian ethical conduct to this point have, therefore, been occasional (2.10; 4.1-3). Paul's practical admonition to holy conduct, which begins at 4:1 with 'I urge you to live a life worth of the calling you have received', had Christian harmony and its constitu-

[42] O'Brien, *Ephesians*, p. 316.
[43] Stott, *The Message of Ephesians*, p. 172.

ent elements as its focus (4.2-6). At v. 17 a clear break from the theological and a centering upon moral and ethical behavior is discernible, highlighted by Paul's fourfold use of the word 'walk' or 'live' (appearing first in 4.1, but now in 4.17; 5.2, 8, 15).

Comprising the larger paraenesis (ethical portion), 4.17-5:21 may be subdivided into smaller units. (1) In the first (4.17-24), Paul exhorts the believers to make a complete and radical break with their pagan past (vv. 17-19) and, in stark contrast, as new persons, to let their new lives in Christ set the pattern for how they conduct their lives (vv. 20-24). (2) A list of vices to shun and virtues to embrace constitutes the next subdivision (4.25-5.2). (3) The radical difference between the new life they have received in Christ is contrasted with the old under the imagery of light and darkness (5.3-14). (4) A final ethical summons is given in the 'summary climax' of 5.15-21. 'Be very careful, then, how you live – not as unwise but as wise' (v. 15). Christianity is more than belief; it involves how God's people ought to live. The two are inseparably connected. Ethics is belief put into practice, and is the fruit of a life worthy of one's calling. Far from being an individualistic and private matter, however, it is lived out in the community of faith and the harmony of the community as a primary goal. Christian ethics is not principally 'an individualistic ... brand of personal holiness'. On the contrary, it concerns living the Spirit-filled life 'in Christian community and in the world'.[1]

1. Putting off the old life of reckless lusting (4.17-22)

Paul's ethical appeal to the believers to 'no longer live as the Gentiles do' (v. 17; cf. Col. 3.7) – a decadent and morally bankrupt lifestyle described extensively in Rom. 1.18-32, but here more briefly in vv. 18-19 – is accompanied by divine sanction (in the Lord), signaling its solemnity and urgency. A new existence, as Christians are, demands a new and corresponding conduct (2 Cor. 5.17; Eph. 2.10; Col. 3.10). Pagan vices (vv. 17-19) must be renounced and replaced with Christian virtues (vv. 20-21). The umbilical cord to the past must be cut. The standard of living Paul enjoins upon the Gentile believers is based on the instruction they had received, and which was reflective of the life and character of Jesus (v. 21). The instruction, which establishes the quality of life they should lead, is further defined in vv. 22-24 by three infinitives: 'to put off' (ἀποθέσθαι, v. 22), 'to be renewed' (ἀνανεοῦσθαι, v. 23), and 'to put on' (ἐνδύσασθαι, v. 24). Scholars differ as to whether these infinitives are being used as imperatives, as indicatives that explain the content of the teaching the Ephesians had received, or as denoting the lifestyle that results from the teaching.

[1] Fee, *Paul, the Spirit, and the People of God*, p. 99.

Although these infinitives are cradled in a larger ethical section of the Epistle, not until v. 25 does Paul use the first of eleven imperatives in the chapter (vv. 25-32). While both grammar and context favor viewing them as indicatives that explicate the substance of what the believers had been taught, it is argued that in this exhortatory milieu the three infinitives also seem to have 'implied imperatival force', urging the Christians to continue 'to live out the implications of their mighty break with the past'.[2] The tension between the imperative and indicative moods here and elsewhere in Paul's writings is illustrative of the tension between the 'already' and the 'not yet' which may be summarized in the exhortation: 'Be what you are'![3] Irresponsible and reprehensible Gentile behavior sallies from worthless thinking (v. 17) and darkened understanding (v. 18). 'Worthless' or 'futile' (μάταιος) means aimless, meaningless, or failing to accomplish the designed purpose. A cognate term is used with a different word for 'thinking/reasoning' (διαλογισμός) in Rom. 1.21 for the fruitless and destitute speculation that stemmed from rejection of the knowledge of God which resulted in the degradation of creation. 'Thinking' (νοῦς) in Eph. 4.17 bespeaks mindset, thinking capability, and disposition. 'Darkened' describes a permanent state in which rational cognition has taken flight (cf. Rom. 5.8, 11), resulting in a condition of inability to grasp 'the truth of God and his gospel'.[4] The process of reasoning (διανοία), sometimes equated with 'heart' (Heb. לֵב) – the center of human perception – is translated 'understanding' in v. 18. Far from the mental acuity and growing sophistry of enlightenment of which the modern secular mind is wont to boast, what Paul describes here is mental and moral capacity so compromised that it is no longer in tune with reality and is 'left fumbling with inane trivialities and worthless side issues'.[5]

Quite the opposite is true of believers whose spiritual eyes have been opened to divine truth (1.17, 18). Alienation from the life of God (the term, used also in 2.12, suggests a persistent state of being) – a reality of Gentile existence – means to be devoid of a relationship with God (2.12), who is the source of life (Jn 17.3). Begun with an unyielding rejection of divine truth, this tragic descent results in spiritual death (2.1, 5). The internal cause of their estrangement is twofold: 'because of the ignorance that is in them' and 'the hardening of their hearts' (v. 18). Abbreviating Rom. 1.18-23, Paul in speaking of ignorance here has in mind more than lack of knowledge or unawareness of God. As knowledge of God refers to an intimate relationship with him, rather

---

[2] O'Brien, *Ephesians*, p. 327.
[3] Bruce, *Colossians, Philemon, Ephesians*, NIC, p. 357.
[4] O'Brien, *Ephesians*, p. 321; cf. Lincoln, *Ephesians*, p. 277.
[5] O'Brien, *Ephesians*, p. 320.

than mere intellectual cognition or consciousness of him, so, conversely, ignorance of him depicts a determined unwillingness to obey his
demands rather than lack of information about or awareness of him.
This conscious refusal to obey God makes one culpable (Rom. 1.23;
2:1). Scripture resolutely testifies to the power of ignorance and falsehood to corrupt, and truth's power to set free, dignify, and refine.[6] In
addition to being willfully ignorant, pagans are alienated from God and
eternal life because of the hardening of their hearts. 'Hardening' translates πώρωσις, a medical term used of a callus formed after a broken
bone was reset − a protuberance harder than the bone itself[7] and resulting in loss of sensitivity to pain. As calloused skin becomes insensitive
to pain, so the Gentiles with hardened heart − a resolute refusal to hear
and obey God − have become numb to moral shame. Morally insensate
and undiscerning, their conscience unable to register inner stings of
guilt, they cast off all ethical restraint and fearlessly plunge headlong
into ever more repugnant practices, with an ever-increasing appetite
for more (4.18-19). In v. 19 Paul uses two words to describe this moral
bankruptcy − ἀπαλγέω and ἀσελγεία. The former speaks of the loss of
ability to experience 'shame or embarrassment',[8] the latter of 'freedom
with no boundaries'[9] and 'the performance of blatant acts with no consideration of personal standards or social sanctions'.[10]

'But you' (ὑμεῖς δέ) at the beginning of v. 20 in the Greek text
shows a stark contrast between the pagan past of the believers and their
present life in Christ, and emphasizes the fact that Jesus offers a better
life. Far from the reckless and wanton conduct that characterized the
Gentile way of life, believers lived 'in accordance with the truth that is
in Jesus' (v. 21). Behavioral transformation finds its source and inspiration in a dynamic relationship with the living Christ. Their acceptance
of the gospel and discipleship in Christ meant renunciation of unholy
vices and the prosecution of a life of holiness (cf. 2 Cor. 5.17). Paul
portrays this change of life under an imagery common in the ancient
world, especially in Gnosticism and the mystery religions: putting off
and setting aside clothes − the old worthless, unregenerate self (v. 22;
Rom. 6.6; Col. 3.9), and putting on clothing − the new self (v. 24).
The old garments represent an earlier lifestyle/behavior (ἀναστροφή)
being progressively corrupted by deceitful desires and assigned to ruin;
new clothing symbolizes new conduct demonstrating ethical virtues,

---

[6] Stott, *Ephesians*, p. 176.
[7] Wood, *Ephesians*, p. 61.
[8] O'Brien, p. 322, quoting Louw and Nida § 25. 197.
[9] Hoehner, *Ephesians*, p. 590, quoting Plato *Republica* 4 §424e.
[10] Hoehner, *Ephesians*, p. 590.

such as holiness and righteousness (v. 24). Changing clothes means changing identity, cutting loose from the old regime.

2. Putting on the new life of righteous living (4.23-24)

In addition to abandoning the old sinful self (v. 22) and approving the new transformed self (v. 24), the readers had been taught the need for inward spiritual renewal (v. 23). It is noteworthy that in respectively describing the doffing of the old way of life and the donning of the new that Paul uses two aorist infinitives (ἀποθέσθαι, v. 22 and ἐνδύσασθαι, v. 24), contextually denoting a definite, once-and-for-all completed past action. However, when correspondingly describing the ruin or decay to which the sinful conduct leads (v. 22) and the inward renewal believers experience (v. 23) Paul employs the present infinitive (φθειρόμενον and ἀνανεοῦσθαι), implying that, though an established fact, both ruin and renewal are an ongoing process. The inference is: reprehensible heathen behavior springs from worthless thinking (v. 17) and darkened understanding (v. 18); exemplary Christian conduct depends upon a progressively renewed mind. By employing the passive infinitive (ἀνανεοῦσθαι), Paul intimates that the ongoing transformation in God's people is not humanly initiated. Rather, God is the change agent who effects it (cf. Rom. 12.2) in 'the spirit of [the] mind' (v. 23) – an expression without comparison in ancient Greek literature.[11] Since all references to 'spirit' in Ephesians (except 2.2) allude to the Holy Spirit, who works in the lives of the people of God (1.17; 3.16; 4.3; 5.18; 6.18), and since Tit. 3.5 expressly refers to the Holy Spirit as the medium of spiritual renewal, some have urged that 'spirit' here refers to the Holy Spirit. Against this position it may be argued that nowhere in the NT is the Holy Spirit called the 'Spirit of your mind'. 'Spirit of holiness' (Rom. 1.4), 'Spirit of God' (Rom. 8.9; 1 Cor. 2.12), 'Spirit of adoption' (Rom. 8.15), and 'Spirit of the Lord' (2 Cor. 3.18) are common titles for the Holy Spirit. Further, in Rom. 8.16 Paul distinguishes between the Spirit of God and the human spirit, and in 1 Cor. 14.14 between the mind and the human spirit. Contextually, it is far more reasonable to accept 'spirit' as referring to the human spirit.

Yet, one should 'recognize the Holy Spirit as hovering nearby'[12] as the agent of spiritual renewal (Jn 3.3-7; 2 Cor. 3.18; Tit. 3.5), bringing about internal change 'in mind and spirit'.[13] In v. 24 Paul calls the process of inward renewal a putting on of the new person (cf. 2.15; 3.16), which may apply to both the individual Christian and the church

---

[11] O'Brien, *Ephesians*, p. 330.

[12] Fee, *God's Empowering Presence*, p. 712.

[13] Morris, *Expository Reflections*, p. 140.

composed of believing Jews and Gentiles living as persons belonging to the new creation. This new self is 'created to be like God' (κατὰ θεὸν κτισθέντα), a statement that echoes not only the Genesis creation language (Gen. 1.27), but also depicts God as the source and standard/pattern of the new creation/self. To possess the divine image has ethical implications, which Paul identifies as true righteousness (δικαιοσύνη, moral uprightness) and holiness (ὁσιότης, personal piety and reverence before God; cf. Lk. 1.75). Acknowledging the Holy Spirit as the architect of moral change and spiritual revitalization is not to encourage human passivity in the process. We must create the environment and cultivate the soil in which God can achieve his will. This involves divine-human cooperation.

C. The Church: A Community that Promotes Integrity (4.25-29)

The opening inferential conjunction 'therefore' in v. 25 logically and integrally connects specific exhortations Paul is about to make (vv. 25-32) with his preceding statements regarding the believers' repudiation of the unworthy and disruptive behavior of the old way of life and their embracing the virtues of the new (4.17-24). It specifically recalls v. 24 and Paul's idea of believers being 'created to be like God in true righteousness and holiness'. Strong ethical conduct required of the Christians, but stated in general terms in that earlier section, is now enjoined upon them with direct hortatory and unambiguous specificity. Each of five admonitions whose aim is to promote unity in the community has a negative prohibition offset by a positive exhortation and the purpose for giving it. For example, discontinuing lying, stealing, and losing one's temper is not enough; telling the truth, working hard, and being kind to others must become a lifestyle. This new section, which gives a code of conduct[14] for daily life (see Rom. 1.29-31; 1 Cor. 5.10-11; Gal. 5.19-23; Col. 3.8-14), explicates the practical fundamentals of Christian behavior, emphasizing the necessity of speaking the truth, managing anger, honesty, kindness in speech, forgiveness, love, and sexual control.

Verse 25. All falsehood or deception – the lying/the lie (τὸ ψεῦδος) – which represents the old person (v. 22) and is contrary to 'the truth that is in Jesus' (v. 21) and 'true righteousness and holiness' (v. 24), is the first thing Paul's readers are instructed to put off (cf. Col. 3.8-9). Rather, since they have put on the new self with its God-like qualities,

---

[14] Scholars do not agree on the ultimate origin of such ethical catalogue of virtues and vices, found also in the Old Testament, Qumran Literature, Judaism, Stoicism, and Greco-Roman ethical philosophy.

and are members of one body (v. 25), they belong to each other, depend on each other, and are held together in a covenant relationship that calls for mutual transparency. Therefore, 'each of you must . . . speak truthfully to his neighbor' (v. 25; cf. 4.15, 16). Striking 'salvation-historical and typological connections'[15] between Zechariah 8 and Ephesians 4 and the religious communities each addresses are apparent here. In Zechariah 8 'Speak the truth[16] to each other' commences a series of exhortations (vv. 16-19) flowing out of promises God made about the new Jerusalem (vv. 1-15). God's remnant people will dwell in Zion, which will be called 'the city of Truth', and represent to their neighbor the attributes of truth, righteousness, and holiness of the God whose presence abides there.

Verses 26-29. Along with deception, anger militates against harmonious relationships within the community of faith. Therefore Paul, borrowing language from the LXX (Ps. 4.4), where David laments his unjust accusation, yet encourages his enemies to surrender exasperation or anger to God who answers prayers, commands, 'Be angry, and do not sin' (NKJV; ὀργίζεσθε καὶ μὴ ἁμαρτάνετε). Some translators see the imperative (ὀργίζεσθε) as functioning conditionally or concessively, and translate it, 'If you are angry' or 'although you are angry'. At issue is whether permission is being given to be angry or anger is being allowed with restriction.[17]

The likelihood of anger is clearly intimated in v. 26b and its danger in v. 27. In v. 31 Paul encourages renunciation of it (cf. 6.4). While anger is not encouraged, the thrust of v. 26 is on sinning because of the coddling of anger. The translation, 'In your anger do not sin' (NIV), acknowledges this and upholds the NT pattern of dealing with anger and sin (Jas 1. 19-20; cf. Mt. 5.21-22; Gal. 5.20; Col. 3.8; 1 Tim. 2.8; Titus 1.7). The destructive consequence to which festering and uncontrolled anger may lead – sin (v. 26) and giving the devil ('slanderer') a foothold (v. 27; cf. Acts 25.16) to exploit the situation – demands prompt and speedy action in dealing with it. This promptness is seen in what may be a common ancient proverb,[18] 'Do not let the sun go

---

[15] O'Brien, *Ephesians*, p. 337.

[16] O'Brien (*Ephesians*, p. 338, n. 274) notes that there are six references to 'truth' in Zechariah, and with the exception of 7.9 all occur in ch. 8 (vv. 3, 8, 15, 16, and 19). Similarly, six of the seven uses of the 'truth' appear in the paraenesis of chs. 4–6, with four occurring in ch. 4 (vv. 15, 21, 24, 25; cf. 5.9; 6.14).

[17] Thielman avers that justifiable anger is 'outside the purview of the admonition' (*Ephesians*, p. 313).

[18] According to Plutarch, the Pythagoreans had a custom of joining right hands and reconciling disputes among the parties involved before sunset (*Moralia: De fraterno amore* 17 §488c). The *Damascus Rule* records a similar practice by the Essenes: 'They shall rebuke each man his brother according to the commandment and shall bear no rancor from one day to the next' (CD 7.2.3).

down while you are still angry' (v. 26). Instead of giving way to anger, believers are encouraged to 'leave room for God's wrath' (Rom. 12.19).

A third way Gentile believers are to show passage from the old life to the new (vv. 22-24) is to work hard at what is useful (cf. Rom. 12.13; Gal. 6.10; Eph. 2:10) rather than steal, so they may have something to share with the destitute (v. 28). Condemned in the Decalogue (Exod. 20.15; Deut. 5.19; cf. Isa. 1.29; Jer. 7.9; Mk 10.19; Rom. 13.9) and the Holiness Code (Lev. 19.11), stealing reflects the type of people who responded to the gospel.[19] Theft has no place in the Christian life. As with modern society, the ancient world condemned stealing. Poor people with meager incomes, however, tried to increase their lot by furtive pilfering. The thief (ὁ κλέπτων), instead of stealing, Paul exhorts, must engage in hard, diligent, and honest toil (κοπιάω) 'with [his] own hands' – an expression that refers not only to manual labor, but emphasizes the undertaking of strenuous work for gain with the hands once used to steal. Paul then states the purpose of such work: Engaged in honest work, the thief now not only provides for his own family but also for 'those in need' (v. 28), hence demonstrating the generosity that characterizes the Christian lifestyle (Acts 2.45; 4.32-35; Rom. 15.26-27; 2 Cor. 8-9).

The words 'useful', 'share', 'need', 'helpful', 'needs', and 'benefit' connect vv. 28 and 29, the first triad in v. 28, and the second in v. 29 (NIV). The thief ceases stealing and performs useful or beneficial work that he/she might have something to share with those in need in the community of faith (v. 28). No unwholesome word should be spoken, rather only that which is helpful, caters to the needs of others, and may benefit the hearers. Both verses focus on the interests of the community, v. 28 through upright action and v. 29 through uplifting speech.

As bad action (v. 28) can have disruptive and destructive consequences so can unwholesome speech (v. 29; cf. Mt. 15.11). The word 'unwholesome' (σαρπός)[20] is used of rotten wood, rancid fish, and withered flowers. In this context it could be rendered 'unprofitable', 'putrid', or 'foul'.[21] The word may not be limited to bad language, 'but malicious gossip and slander' or any conversation that 'injures others and sparks dissension' is included.[22] The word approximates one which Paul uses in Col. 3.8 (αἰσχρολογία, cognate used in Eph. 5.4) for abu-

---

[19] E.A. Best sees the thieves alluded to as seasonal laborers or skilled tradesmen who had no source of income to sustain their families when unemployed. See his 'Ephesians 4.28: Thieves in the Church', *Irish Bible Studies* 14 (January 1992), 2-9.

[20] This adjective is used in Matthew of a decayed or rotten tree bearing rotten fruit (7.17-18) and rotten fish (12.33-34).

[21] Hoehner, *Ephesians*, pp. 628, 629.

[22] Wood, *Ephesians*, p. 65. O'Brien comes to the same conclusion (*Ephesians*, p. 344).

sive, vulgar, or contemptuous speech. Filthy or vulgar speech, which often accompanies anger, may be one reason why admonitions about speech are combined in ancient Jewish exhortatory literature. Paul will allow neither dishonest deed nor derogatory speech among the community of believers.[23] Conversely, whatever is beneficial for 'building others up', whether physical (deed, v. 28) or spiritual (speech) is encouraged (v. 29).

D. The Church: A Community that Propagates Forgiveness (4.30-32)

'And do not grieve the Holy Spirit of God' (v. 30) does not begin a new injunction in this section but is a coordinate of the previous prohibition, linked by the coordinating conjunction 'and'. The two clauses could be rendered: 'Do not let any unwholesome talk come out of your mouths ... and do not grieve the Holy Spirit of God'. Unwholesome speech uttered against another member of the church community grieves the Holy Spirit, whose mission is to bring about unity and reconciliation in the body (2.18, 24; 4.3-4). The admonition against grieving the Spirit is not limited to distasteful speech, but to any action or speech which disrupts the Spirit's work and gives the devil a foothold (v. 27) to attain his ignoble aims, hence all the negative matters in 4.25-5.2. Holy by nature, the Holy Spirit is always grieved by unholiness or impurity; and being one Spirit (2.18; 4.4), disharmony and disunity will also grieve him. Indeed, 'anything incompatible with the purity or unity of the church is incompatible with his own nature and therefore hurts him'.[24]

References are made in the NT to behaviors that militate against the desires or purposes of the Holy Spirit, such as lying to the Holy Spirit (Acts 5.3), testing the Spirit of the Lord (Acts 5.9), resisting the Holy Spirit (Acts 7.51), and quenching the Spirit (1 Thess. 5.18). The concept of grieving the Holy Spirit is not unique to Paul, but is found in the OT and extra-biblical literature.[25] It is not to pseudepigraphal sources that Paul turns in dealing with this topic but to Isaiah 63, where he finds typological correlation and from which he recruits language (v. 10) nearly verbatim and applies to his ecclesiastical context (Eph. 4.30). Isaiah 63 recapitulates events of the exodus in which

---

[23] The Greek construction in both vv. 28 and 29 may suggest putting a stop to behavior and speech already taking place.

[24] Stott, *Ephesians*, p. 189.

[25] The *Damascus Document* speaks of the Israelites defiling their Holy Spirit and blaspheming the ordinances of God with the tongue (CD 5.11, 12; 7.4). The idea of grieving the Holy Spirit is found in Hermas, *Mandates* 10.2.4; 10.3 2 and the *Testament of Isaac* 4.40.

Yahweh as their mighty redeemer delivered Israel out of Egypt, entered into covenant relationship with them, and led them by his presence into rest (Exod. 33.8-10, 14; cf. 23.20-23). For all God's gracious actions toward an undeserving people, and in defiance against his explicit command (Exod. 23.21), Israel rebelled against the Lord and grieved his presence – which in Isa. 63.10 the prophet clearly interprets as the Holy Spirit.

Placing the church within a new exodus typology, Paul views the people of God as a new (Eph. 2.15) covenant and redeemed (1.7) community, a holy temple where God dwells by his Spirit (2.21-22). Drawing application from Isa. 63.10, he cautions the Ephesian believers not to grieve the Holy Spirit as Israel had done in the desert, especially since they were sealed by the same Spirit until the day of eschatological redemption (4.30). That day is called elsewhere 'the day of the Lord' (1 Thess. 5.2; 2 Thess. 2.2; 1 Cor. 1.8; 5.5; 2 Cor. 1.14) or 'the day of Christ' (Phil. 1.6, 10; 2.16), and refers to the final day of salvation for the righteous and judgment for the wicked. The sealing by the Spirit of believers (an incentive for Paul's injunction) indicates his stamping of his character on them as his very own purchased possession (Eph. 1.14) and his guarantee to protect them until that final day (2 Tim. 1.12).

Verses 31-32. The Holy Spirit's presence in the believer is reason enough to clean up one's speech (and behavior). Not only is the Spirit by nature holy, and is distressed by anything inconsistent with his character, but his function is to make people holy. Furthermore, as Paul reminds us in v. 30, the Spirit is the one who seals believers until the day of redemption.

With a final appeal in this chapter, Paul urges his readers to let their conduct demonstrate their new life in Christ. As with the earlier part of the paraenesis (vv. 25-29), a three-fold pattern appears in this section. A negative admonition (a summons to eliminate anger and other associated vices, v. 31) is balanced by a matching positive one to exhibit mutual kindness, mercy, and forgiveness (v. 32), and concluding with the reason or motivating clause ('just as in Christ God forgave you').

Paul's list of negative speech and attitudes to be laid aside begins with the adjective 'all' (v. 31), suggesting every form of the five vices associated with rage, which itself may sally from bitterness and culminates in abusive public speech against a fellow Christian. 'Bitterness' or 'resentment' ($\pi\iota\kappa\rho\iota\alpha$) means something 'sharp', 'piercing', or 'bitter' (Acts 8.23; Rom. 3.14; Heb. 12.15) exemplified in 'a sour spirit and sour speech'.[26] This is followed by 'rage' (θυμός) and 'anger' (ὀργή), which may be taken as synonyms (cf. Col. 3.8). If a difference is in mind, then the former connotes a sudden outburst of passion (2 Cor. 12.20; Gal. 5.20), and the latter deep-seated and settled anger (1 Tim. 2.8; Jas 1.19, 20).

'Brawling' and 'slander' are addressed next. The first translates κραυγή, which means 'screaming', 'yelling', or 'shouting'. It may denote joyful shout – as with the announcement of the bridegroom's arrival (Mt. 25.6) or Elizabeth's receiving news of Mary's conception (Lk. 1.42); or it may describe the mournful weeping of Jesus in prayer (Heb. 5.7) or loud clamoring (Acts 23.9). The present context, however, invites the connotation of strife or rowdy face-to-face altercation, hence 'brawling' (NIV), 'angry shouting' (NEB). 'Slander' ('cursing', NEB) renders βλασφημία, which in both the OT and NT often bespeaks profane speech (blasphemy) against God (Ezek. 35.12; Mt. 12.31; 15.19; Rev. 13.1, 5, 6; 17.3), vilifying or abusive speech (Mk 7.22; 1 Tim. 6.4) – a meaning which aligns well with the parallel passage in Col. 3.8 and serves this context best. The final vice, 'malice' (κακία), is a generic term with a range of meaning from a concern that causes human distress (Mt. 6.34) to spite, to a vicious disposition. When used in a context where malicious speech is in view (cf. Col. 3.8; 1 Pet. 2.1), it refers to 'a mean-spirited or vicious attitude or disposition'.[27] It denotes 'the deep unkindness of the self-centered, Christless heart'.[28] Paul avers that no form of it or any of the other negative behaviors has any place among the people of God. With the aorist imperative (ἀρθήτω) Paul enjoins that a clean sweep be made of them (v. 31).

Verse 32. Genuine Christianity is more than a list of prohibitions, so Paul now enjoins three virtues that must replace the five vices he mentions in v. 31 (cf. Col. 3.12-13). His Christian readers must be kind, compassionate, and forgiving towards each other always (implied by the Gk. present imperative). In so doing they will maintain harmony in the community, but more so show the character of the Spirit within them. 'Kind' (χρηστός; 'generous', NEB) means to be good (Jer. 24. 2-3, 5; Lk. 5.39), pleasant (Jer. 52.32; Mt. 11.30), genuine or precious (Ezek. 27:22; 28:13), and kindly. Such a disposition toward each other reflects God's gracious attitude and acts toward repentant sinners (Eph. 2.7; cf. Rom. 11.22; Tit. 3.4).

---

[26] Stott, *Ephesians*, p. 190.
[27] Thielman, 'Ephesians', p. 319, quoting BDAG 500.
[28] H.C.G. Moule, *Ephesians Studies* (New York: Fleming H. Revell, n.d.), p. 235. Stott opines that malice may comprehend all five preceding vices (*Ephesians*, p. 190).

'Compassionate', εὔσπλαγχνος, derives from σπλάγχνον, and refers to the liver, kidneys, heart, and larger viscera, since the Greeks regarded the internal organs as the seat of feelings and emotions. Appearing only in the plural in the NT, it is used of Judas's insides gushing out (Acts 1.18), human compassion (Phil. 1.8; 2:1; Col. 3.12) and God's tender mercies (Lk. 1.78). It carries the idea of feeling sympathy or pity toward the weaknesses, needs, or miseries of others. 'Forgiving' (χαρί-ζομαι) is the rendering of a word built on the same Greek root as the word 'grace' (χαρ-), and means 'to be gracious', 'exercise grace', hence to 'give freely', 'pardon', and 'forgive'. Mutual forgiveness is a feature of genuine Christian fellowship and necessary for harmonious relationships in the community of faith. By adding 'just as in Christ God forgave you' (cf. Col. 3.13), Paul makes God's supreme example the motivation, model, and measure of the forgiveness believers ought to exercise toward each other.

Reflection and Response (Part 4)

Reflection

This chapter reveals a distinct shift from the doctrinal and theological teaching in chs. 1–3. It begins the ethical portion of the Epistle in which Paul presents practical ways Christians ought to live in view of their spiritual transformation and the teaching they received. On becoming Christians, some Ephesian believers struggled in completely letting go of their old way of living. With an appeal to holy living as God's standard for his people, Paul shifts his focus and emphasis on doctrine to how God's new people ought to live. The inescapable message in this transition is that God demands a new and loftier standard of living from his redeemed people than he does from the unregenerate. The aim of ethical Christian living for Paul is more than personal holiness; it includes believers maintaining communal unity and attaining maturity measured by the stature of Christ. It is also an expression of gratitude for all that God has done in Christ for believers and a way of living a life worthy of one's calling (4.1).

Further, unlike the heathen who have become alienated from God because of intellectual obtuseness and moral bankruptcy, Christians have received the illuminating and liberating truth in Christ and a new life whose goal is purity. Incompatible with the unrighteous deeds of darkness, such a life demands a radical break with the old pagan way of living, a stripping-off of it as one does an old or dirty garment and a putting-on of the new garment of righteousness. Pagan vices must be renounced and replaced with Christian virtues. Negative attitudes and behaviors that conduce to disunity must be shunned; they grieve the Holy Spirit, the divine agent of reconciliation, and give place to the

devil to divide, breed disharmony, and destroy the body of Christ.
Positive and unity-building virtues must be encouraged and promoted.
The questions that follow are offered to facilitate further reflection on
the call for purity in 4.1-32.

What is the prevailing attitude of Christian colleagues about sin and
the need for biblical purity? How is this disposition similar to or different from that which is described in Ephesians 4? How important is
biblical purity to the life of the church today? How sincerely and pas-
sionately is the church committed to Paul's injunction to ethical purity?
What might an ethically pure church look like? How well are churches
you know living up to this image? Can a church demand purity from
its membership? If so, how should a church go about enforcing that
requirement? What attitudes or sins do you see as potentially most
damaging to unity in the church? How can they be curbed?

In an effort to provoke further reflection on the text and thereby
make Paul's ethical admonition more personal, the questions below are
asked. What is my perspective on personal holiness? How seriously do
I take the biblical exhortation to personal ethical purity? In the midst
of a prevailing culture that is inimical to and cynical regarding Christian teaching about morality, how am I able to live the Christian life
without embarrassment and compromise? How do I seek to be pure
without being legalistic? How do I integrate my faith and experience,
my theology and ethics? What practical steps do I take to deal with
sinful behavior in my personal life and that of my Christian brothers
and sisters? What do I think are personal and communal consequences
of unholy living? What should my attitude be toward Christian brothers and sisters who struggle to live pure lives?

Response

1. With the reflection questions as an adjutant, scrutinize your
   own life for sinful dispositions and behaviors that may lie
   below the surface. Catalog specific things the Spirit may reveal to you.

2. Solicit the help of a trusted Christian friend or two in showing you areas unknown to you that may need your attention.

3. Having ascertained areas of sin for which you need to repent and seek forgiveness, confess those sins to God and by
   faith accept his forgiveness and power to change you.

4. Commit to regular participation in worship and Bible study
   by establishing 'accountability' relationships are vital to

maintaining a life that is pure and a love aglow to please God.

5. Participate in a footwashing service. Allow this physical act of humble submission to Christ's command to be a sign of spiritual cleansing from sin.

E. The Church: A Spirit-filled Community (5.1–6.9)

With his third use of the term 'walk' or 'live' (περιπατέω) in the paraenetic section that sets forth moral guidelines (4.1, 17; 5.2), Paul continues to plead for practical application of the doctrines he expounded in chs. 1–3. Hitherto, he has admonished the believers to walk in unity (4.1-16) and purity (4.17-32). The church's witness is inseparably connected to its unity and purity. In a more urgent way than in Colossians, Paul here is trying to solidify the boundaries between the church and the world 'and to make the audience aware of the need to do so'.[1] Paul's admonition in this third section, i.e. that the Christians walk in love (5.1-6), continues and builds upon 4.17-32, but more immediately upon v. 32, where believers are urged to forgive each other 'just as in Christ God forgave [them]'. To forgive this way is part of what it means to be imitators of God – a life to which Paul enjoins his readers. In 5.1–6.9 he sets forth a standard of moral living of which the pagan world had never dreamed, lifting Christian behavior to the level of imitation of God and the sacrificial, self-giving love of Christ (vv. 1-6). Forbidding a return to unholy indulgences of their pagan past, he encourages a life of inner integrity and outward uprightness, demonstration of divine wisdom, and the Spirit's fullness which should brim over into worship, and into social and domestic relationships.

1. Living in love (5.1-6)

Verses 1-2. In v. 1 Paul challenges the Christians to 'follow God's example' (NIV) – 'always be imitators of God' (γίνεσθε ... μιμηταὶ τοῦ θεοῦ). Such ethical endeavor, inspired by God's gracious and forgiving action wrought in Christ on the believers' behalf (4.32), is consistent with and an expected family trait of children who know the Father's precious love (5.1). As children delight in imitating their earthly parents so believers should seek to imitate God who is their heavenly Father (cf. Mt. 5.48). In v. 2 Paul shifts the object of emulation from God the Father to Christ his Son. The notion of identification with

---

[1] Witherington, *The Letters to Philemon, the Colossians, and the Ephesians*, p. 304.

and imitation[2] of Christ is not alien to Paul. To him, every believer identifies with Christ in death, burial, resurrection, enthronement, and advent (Rom. 6.4-8; Eph. 2.5-7; Col. 3.1-4), and should likewise imitate him (1 Thess. 1.6) or Paul himself (1 Cor. 4.16; 10.31-11.1; Phil. 3.17; 2 Thess. 3.7, 9) in demeanor.

In v. 2 Paul requests that the believers 'live a life of love'. In his last use of 'live/walk' (4.17) he insisted that they 'no longer live as the Gentiles'. Here in 5.2 his admonition constitutes a positive and distinctive contrast – 'to live a life of love'. To live a life of love includes thinking, speaking, and acting in love, and positively summarizes his earlier exhortations. This way of life marked by love finds its ground and model in Christ, whose supreme example resulted in his substitutionary (ὑπὲρ ἡμῶν, cf. Eph. 5.25) and sacrificial death[3] (cf. Rom. 3.25; 8.3; 1 Cor. 5.7; Heb. 10.10, 14). Christ's self-giving sacrifice was well-pleasing (fragrant offering; cf. Phil. 4.18) to God and fully accepted[4] as an atonement for sin. By implication and intended application, Paul anticipates John, who admonishes the children of God: 'Jesus Christ laid down his life for us. And we ought to lay down our lives for one another' (1 Jn 3.16). The idea of imitating God is not unique to Christianity; it is present in Hellenistic and Jewish ethics. What is unique to the Christian faith is the selfless and sacrificial self-giving of God's Son, inspired by love, on behalf of sinners, whose loving action his followers are admonished to exemplify.

Verses 3-4. Verses 3-14 continue but change the trajectory of Paul's ethical instruction from the believers' wardrobe (4.22, 24-25) and emulating God or Christ (4.20, 24, 32; 5.1-2) to placing behavior in the binary categories of what is 'fitting' and 'not fitting/shameful' for the people of God (vv. 3-4) and what is 'hidden' (darkness) and what is 'exposed' (light, vv. 8-14). In vv. 3-14 Paul warns believers on the one hand to steer clear of sexual immorality and greed endemic to the Gentile world and lifestyle; on the other hand he urgently appeals that

---

[2] The notion of being imitators of God is found in middle Platonism and Hellenistic Judaism, represented most expressly by Philo. No explicit reference to the concept occurs in the OT and only in Eph. 5.1 in the NT.

[3] Here Paul capitalizes on two words borrowed from the Jewish sacrificial system: 'offering' and 'sacrifice'. 'Offering' (προσφορά) is a cognate of its verb form which means 'to bring,' as in presenting 'sacrifice' (θυσία). The two terms are used of animal and non-animal sacrifices. Occurring together in Ps. 40.6, they may refer to a single gift (as a hendiadys), the costly self-giving of Christ for our sins.

[4] The fragrant smell of various sacrifices, whether the burnt offering (Lev. 1.9), meal offering (Lev. 2.2), peace offering (Lev. 3.5), or sin offering (Lev. 4. 31) portended their acceptance by God. Christ's self-offering was fragrant and perfect, well-pleasing, and fully accepted by God.

believers illuminate the morally and spiritually benighted Gentile world
with the gospel and ardently seek the conversion of non-believers.

The term 'but' (δέ) in v. 3 signals a strong contrast between the topic of self-sacrificial love Christians are challenged to exhibit (vv. 1-2)
and the self-gratifying sensuality of non-believers that follows (a
throwback to the prohibitions of 4.17-24) behavior Paul subsequently
calls 'fruitless deeds of darkness' done in secret (vv. 11, 12) – conduct
that incurs the wrath of God and results in exclusion from the kingdom of God (vv. 5, 6). So frightfully commonplace in the Gentile
world yet so alien to the Christian character are the vices catalogued in
vv. 3-6 (cf. Col. 3.5) that Paul says 'there must not be even a hint' (v.
3) of them among the believers, which may mean they are unworthy[5]
topics even for conversation, let alone practice, or that there should
not be the slightest insinuation or suspicion of their presence among
God's holy people. As elsewhere (1 Cor. 6.18; Gal. 5.19; 1 Thess.
4.13), sexual immorality[6] tops the list and may encompass a variety of
aberrant sexual activity, but especially adultery or fornication. Impurity
(moral indecency) and greed ('ruthless greed', NEB) appeared earlier in
4.19, Paul equating the latter with idolatry (v. 5; Col. 3.5). Greed be-
tokens extreme selfish gratification, no matter what the cost to others,
and may carry the idea of sensual indulgence. All such behavior con-
tradicts the character of God Christians are expected to imitate and the
love of Christ they must demonstrate.

Turning from addressing immoral sexual conduct (v. 3), Paul then
gives attention to three other kindred sins of indecent speech[7] which
members of the sanctified community must avoid (v. 4): obscenity,
foolish talk, and coarse joking. Earlier in 4.29 he inveighed against
'unwholesome talk' because of its devastating effect upon the believing
community. Now he assaults it both for its utter incongruity with and
usurpation of grateful praise in the life of the Christian. 'Obscenity'
(αἰσχρότης), while used here particularly of disgraceful or shameful
speech (cf. Col. 3.8), sometimes carries a wider meaning of disgraceful
speech or behavior. 'Foolish talk' (μωρολογία) or 'silly talk' (RSV)
encompasses coarse vulgarity and the words of fools devoid of any
decency. 'Coarse joking' (εὐτραπελία) which literally means 'an easy
turn of speech' – 'flippant talk', NEB) was used in classical Greek in a
good sense to mean 'wittiness'[8] or negatively to connote the midpoint

---

[5] Paul says they are 'not fitting' – ἀνῆκεν – for the people of God (v. 4).

[6] The injunction carries all the more weight as sexual immorality was sacralized in
Ephesus, where orgies were performed in worship of the goddess Artemis (Diana).

[7] The three words used appear only here in the New Testament – obscenity, foolish
talk, and coarse joking.

[8] Plato *Republica* 8.14 §563a. Regarded as essential to good social intercourse, Aristotle
refers to it as the love for laughter distinctive of youth (*Rhetorica* 2.12.16 §1389b. 11).

between buffoonery and boorishness.[9] While the notion of witty repartee may be present, the context suggests 'jesting that has gone too far,' 'humor in bad taste, or 'dirty jokes'.[10] These forms of speech 'refer to a dirty mind expressing itself in dirty conversation'.[11] Over against the self-centered vices of sexual immorality and obscene speech listed in vv. 3-4, Paul exhorts the people of God to thanksgiving – a fitting response for God's greatness and goodness (Rom. 1.21; cf. Col. 3.15-16) and a life filled with the Spirit (Eph. 5.18), but probably also gratitude for sex over against the pagan dishonoring and vulgarizing of it.

Verses 5-6. In v. 5 Paul reiterates the triad of sins he disallows in v. 3, this time warning of the serious consequences to those who practice them, namely, exclusion from the eschatological kingdom (v. 5) and experience of God's wrath (v. 6). The gravity and certainty of the caveat is underscored by two emphatic phrases: 'of this you can be sure' (v. 5) and 'Let no one deceive you' (v. 6).

As in Col. 3.5 Paul here identifies (sexual) greed with idolatry (v. 5), a common custom in Judaism that condemns both sins as distinctive of stark heathenism.[12] Avarice is idolatry because the object desired displaces God from the center of one's life and place of first priority and replaces him with something or someone else (cf. Rom. 1.25). The persons described in v. 5 are barred[13] from 'the kingdom of Christ and of God' – a unique phrase in the NT which shows the present conjoint reign of Messiah with God (but see Rev. 11.15) – because their character and conduct are incompatible with the nature of the kingdom into which only the regenerate are granted entry (Jn 3.3). Any teaching to the contrary, Paul avers, is empty deception to be avoided (v. 6). This is no matter for debate. Furthermore, contra Gnosticism, the sexually permissive, who are called 'disobedient' (literally 'sons of disobedience' – a Semitism which depicts the predominant trait of a person as disobedience, and therefore unwillingness to surrender to God's authority), are candidates for God's holy and righteous anger in both its present and future manifestations (cf. Rom. 1.18-32).

2. Living in light (5.7-14)

Because of the everlasting separation and punishment that awaits the disobedient – most likely unbelieving Gentiles (vv. 5-6), Paul warns

---

[9] Hoehner, *Ephesians*, p. 655; see Aristotle *Ethica Nicomachea* 2.7.13 §1108a. 24-27.

[10] Hoehner, *Ephesians*, p. 656.

[11] Stott, *The Message of Ephesians*, p. 192.

[12] *Testament of Judah* 19.1.

[13] See 1 Cor. 6.9-10 and Gal. 5.21 for a similar list of persons excluded from the kingdom.

the readers, 'Therefore do not become their partners/fellow-sharers/participants' (literal translation). The prohibition does not disallow contact or association[14] (cf. 1 Cor. 5.10), as the NRSV intimates. The word translated 'partners', 'fellow-sharers', or 'participants' (συμμέτοχοι, cf. 3.6) indicates partnership, participation, deep involvement – even identification with – and in context refers to the non-Christians and their sinful deeds mentioned above. Partnership with the unrighteous may lead to one becoming an accomplice of their profligate deeds, and participation with sinners in their evil deeds means sharing in their everlasting doom (cf. 2 Cor. 6.14–7.1).

Moving on from depicting the awful future that awaits unbelievers and their accomplices (vv. 6-7), using the 'once-now' schema introduced in 2.1-10, 11-22 and the ethical symbolism of light and darkness, in v. 8 Paul states another reason why believers ought not to be partners with them and their dissolute activities: their dismal past has given way to a dazzling present – 'But you were once darkness, but now you are light in the Lord.' Paul has already described the distinction between the Christian and non-Christian under the metaphors of the old person and the new person (4.22, 24), but the representation of darkness and light[15] heightens the contrast. Metaphorically, darkness connotes death,[16] ignorance, error and evil;[17] light represents life, happiness, revelation, truth, and righteousness.

John states that the non-Christian person loves darkness rather than light (3.19) and that every evildoer hates the light and avoids it for fear of exposure (3.20). The followers of Jesus who himself is the light of the world (Jn 8.12; 9.5; 12.46), are children of God who is light and in whom is no darkness (1 Jn 1.5; cf. Jn 12.35-36). God's children, therefore, cannot live in darkness. As darkness and light can never coexist (Isa. 5.20; Amos 5.18; Mic. 7.8; Mt. 6.23; Jn 3.19), so are the values and conduct of the believer and those of the unbeliever in diametric opposition. Darkness bears corresponding fruit (Eph. 4.25, 31); so does light. The fruit of light Paul describes as a manifestation of all goodness, righteousness, and truth (Eph. 5.9; cf. Gal. 5.22; Eph. 2.10), virtues

---

[14] Such was the case with members of the Qumran community who were enjoined a radical separation from all outsiders (1QS 1.4, 5; 5.10, 11; CD 6.14, 15), but never the church (1 Cor. 5.10). The RSV rendering unfortunately propagates this understanding.

[15] The light/darkness image occurs frequently in the OT (cf. Ps. 27.1; Isa. 9.2; 10.17; 42.6, 16; 49.6; 60.1), Qumran literature (cf. 1QS 1.9, 10; 3:13, 19-21, 24, 25) and the NT, particularly in the writings of John (cf. Mt. 4.16; Lk. 1.79; Jn 3.19; Acts 26.18; Rom. 2.9; 2 Cor. 6.14; Eph. 6.12; 1 Pet. 2.9; 1 Jn 1.6).

[16] Homer, *Iliad* 4.461; Euripides, *Phoenissae* 1453.

[17] Stott, *Ephesians*, p. 199. The imagery of darkness permeates Qumran literature, often depicting the path of sin and evil (cf. 1QS 2.7; 3.19, 21; 1QM 15.9; 4Q177 3.8). It also occurs frequently in the OT.

also advocated in the OT (2 Chron. 31.20; Mic. 6.8) and partly in Qumran (1QS 1.5), and are weighted with a wide range of ethical and metaphorical meaning.

For believers to live consistently as children of light they must 'find out what pleases the Lord' (v. 10). 'Find out' (δοκιμάζοντες) shows how children of light ought to walk (v. 8) – namely, by discovering what pleases the Lord. Used of the testing of metals, δοκιμάζω means 'to prove' or 'approve after testing'. But, it was also used of witnesses for a trial who had to be 'put to the test' before approval and candidates to the priesthood who had to be 'proven fit', and thus 'approved' after examination. In Rom. 12.2 Paul tells the believers that obedience to his appeal that they be transformed by renewing their minds will result in their being able to 'test and approve [δοκιμάζω] what God's will is', the NIV extracting and combining the two ideas of trial and approval from the single Greek verb.

A single idea is maintained in Rom. 2.18, where Paul concludes that because the Jews have God's law and know his will they are able to approve things that are excellent. Paul's prayer that the Philippians 'may be able to discern [δοκιμάζω] what is best ...' also reflects a single idea (1.10), as does 1 Thess. 5.21 where Paul urges the believers to 'test everything' and 'hold on to the good'. The context of Eph. 5.10 argues for the single idea of 'discerning' or 'ascertaining' since determining what the Lord's will in every situation is necessary for living a life that pleases him.

Not only will persons who desire to please the Lord walk as children of light (v. 8) and produce the fruit of light (v. 9), they will 'have nothing to do with the fruitless deeds of darkness, but rather expose them' (v. 11) – a prohibition which accentuates absolute incompatibility, expressed earlier in the 'once-now' dichotomy in 2.1-10, 11-22, the old person/new person antinomy in 4.22, 24, and the light/darkness dualism in 5.8. 'Have nothing to do with' translates an imperative (συγκοινωνεῖτε)[18] and its negative indicator, and harks back to v. 7 where Paul urged, 'Therefore do not be partners with them', literally translated, 'Therefore do not become their partners/fellow-sharers/participants' (συμμετοχοί). Whereas in v. 7 Paul prohibits partnership with evildoers, here in v. 11 his proscription is against participating in their unfruitful deeds. In both cases the preposition 'with' (σύν) denotes participation or sharing.

The proper Christian response to the unfruitful deeds of darkness is not only to avoid them, but also to expose them. 'Expose' renders

---

[18] This verb is used three times in the NT: here, in Phil. 4.14 of the Philippians' compassionate sharing in Paul's afflictions, and in Rev. 18.4, where the saints are urged to come out of fallen Babylon so as not to share/participate in their sins.

ἐλέγχω,[19] which generally means 'convince' or 'reprove' when used of persons, but 'to bring to light' or 'expose' when used of deeds, actions or things. The Christian life must blaze like a summer sunrise in the darkness, exposing sin for what it is.

In v. 12 Paul gives the reason for both the negative and positive injunction in v. 11. 'For it is shameful even to mention what the disobedient do in secret' – a tacit reference at least to sexual vices mentioned earlier (vv. 3-4). So unspeakably abominable are the deeds pagans practice under the cloak of secrecy that Christians should not even mention them (cf. 5.3), let alone participate in them. Rather, exposing them is what Christians are called upon to do.

Owing to their obscure nature vv. 13-14a have resulted in a variety of interpretations.[20] The adversative 'but' (δέ) in v. 13 contrasts 'the things done in secret' (what the disobedient do in secret, NIV) and light that exposes them. A fair measure of clarity is achieved if one sees Paul's argument as moving from the exposure of works of darkness (v. 11), through their illumination by the light (v. 13), to a concentration on the light itself (v. 14) – an outline of the process by which darkness is changed into light. The darkness-light motif is not used in abstraction, but depicts ethical conduct. Christians who were at one time darkness are now light in the Lord (v. 8), and by their godly way of life expose the deeds of darkness for what they truly are (v. 11). But light does more than make visible: it also transforms (cf. Col. 1.13). The light's transforming effect is what Paul has in mind by 'But everything exposed by the light becomes light' (v. 13). A debated issue here is: who is the object of transformation – non-Christian outsiders or compromising Christians? It is maintained by some that the context has nothing to do with the conversion of unbelievers, but rather the restoration of believers who partner with unbelievers in the fruitless works of darkness.[21] While this view finds a parallel in the Qumran community's dealing with errant members,[22] a more common view is that the convicting and ultimately transforming effect of believers' lives on the unbelieving, moving them to 'respond to the light in such a way that

---

[19] In the NT the word is used also in Eph. 5.13; Mt. 18.15; Lk. 3.19; Jn 3.20; 8.46; 16.8; 1 Cor. 14.24; 1 Tim. 5.20; 2 Tim. 4.2; Tit. 1.9, 13; 2.15; Heb. 12.5; Jas 2.9; Jude 15; Rev. 3.19.

[20] See O'Brien, *Ephesians*, p. 373.

[21] Hoehner, *Ephesians*, p. 685. John Eadie, in agreement with Olshausen, questions whether light always has a transforming influence since the devil and many wicked people have been exposed to the light without any such change occurring in their lives (*Epistle to the Ephesians*, Grand Rapids: Zondervan, 1979), p. 386. J. Moritz holds a similar view. See *A Profound Mystery: The Use of the Old Testament in Ephesians* (Leiden: Brill, 1966), pp. 113-15.

[22] CD 20.3-5.

they are themselves light'[23] (i.e. become like believers, v. 8), is what Paul has in mind.

Paul seals his argument with a fitting quotation. 'Wake up, O sleeper, rise from the dead, and Christ will shine on you' (v. 14b). It is unnecessary and untenable to connect these lines with Gnostic thought in which the spark of light in the slumbering soul trapped in a material world is urged to recall its eternal heavenly home,[24] or with the mystery religions' reveille for an initiate's induction into a mystery cult.[25] The introductory 'this is why it is said'–literally, 'therefore it says' (διὸ λέγει, v. 14) seems to signal a citation from an OT passage (cf. 4.8), and draws an inference from v. 13. The origin[26] of the poetic lines, however, is an issue of much scholarly debate. Most scholars opine that, if biblical at all, they are mere echoes of Isaianic passages (9.2; 26.19; 51.17; 52.1), not direct quotation of them. Rather, the lines are a fragment of an Easter[27] baptismal hymn, or liturgical chant addressed to baptismal candidates (cf. 1 Tim. 3.16).

Understood in the context of the preceding discussion on darkness and light (5.8-13) and the subsequent exhortations on Christian conduct (5.15-33), the entreaty to 'wake up' from (moral and spiritual) sleep and 'rise from the dead' (v. 14b) may refer to the public renunciation of the 'fruitless deeds of darkness' (v. 11) – what Paul earlier called putting off the old self (4.22) – and the putting-on of the new self (v. 24), which baptism represents. The idea,[28] supported by others,[29] that the early church perceived baptism as an enlightenment strengthens that argument. The conclusion that these words spoken at believers' baptism serve now to remind the readers of 'the power of the light, of the transformation to their new status that has taken place, and of its ethical implications',[30] is a common one.

The hymnic piece should be interpreted in the context of 5.8-14 which deals with believers' behavior and its possible consequence on those living in darkness. Moreover, although 5.14b has no direct corre-

---

[23] Lincoln, *Ephesians*, p. 331. Cf. Stott, *Ephesians,* pp. 200-201.

[24] *Acts of Thomas,* 110.43-48; *Odes of Solomon* 8.3-5; *Corpus Hermeticum* 1.27.

[25] Aristophanes, *Ranae* 340-342; *Orph. Hymn* 50.90; Firmicus Maternus, *On the Error of Profane Religions* 18.1.

[26] Some scholars conjecture that Paul composed the poem, or that he cites OT scripture from memory. It is even speculated that Jesus is the source of its composition.

[27] 'Rise from the dead' clearly suggests a resurrection context, but resurrection and baptism share a close connection.

[28] Woods, *Ephesians*, p. 71.

[29] Martin, *Ephesians, Colossians, and Philemon* (Interpretation; Atlanta: John Knox, 1991), p. 63.

[30] Lincoln, *Ephesians*, p. 332. Bruce observes, 'a tristich, best interpreted as a primitive baptismal hymn, in which the congregation greets the new convert as he or she emerges sacramentally from the sleep of spiritual death into the light of life (*Ephesians*, 376).

spondence with any OT passages, 'it nevertheless has structural, linguistic, and conceptual connections with Isaiah 26.19 and 60.1-2'.[31] The verbal parallels in Eph. 5.14b and Isa. 26.19 are inescapable, both verses using 'rise', 'wake', and 'dead', while 'sleeper' in Ephesians finds a counterpart in 'those in the tombs' in Isa. 26.19. Isaiah 60.1-2 yields additional connections, the light/darkness dualism being the most dominant. Contextual interpretation of the Isaianic passages and their influence upon the hymn implies that the poetic piece more likely refers to conversion rather than baptism,[32] sleep, death, and darkness describing the state of the non-Christian person (cf. Rom. 13.11-14; Eph. 2.1, 5; 1 Thess. 5.5-8).

The summons to wake up and rise from the dead describes the radical about-face at conversion which includes being transported out of darkness into the transforming light of Christ. This interpretation is consistent with Old Testament passages where the imagery of God's light shining upon his people refers to his salvation: 'make your face shine upon us that we may be saved' (Ps. 80.3, 7, 19; cf. Deut. 33.2; Ps. 50.2). Alluding to the Christian hymn or his own composition rooted in the Old Testament, Paul takes believers back to their conversion in which they were awakened out of the sleep of spiritual death and the glorious light of Christ shone upon them and saved them, summoning them to values and standards diametrically opposed to the world.[33] To live out the implications of that transformed life Paul now calls the believers; in that process, 'Christ will shine on you' – probably meaning that like the shining sun (cf. Job 31.26[34]) Christ will illumine their way and approve their walk (cf. Prov. 4.18).

3. Living in wisdom (5.15-20)

The imperative walk/live (περιπατέω) and the inferential conjunction 'therefore/then' (οὖν) in combination appear five times in the practical half (paraenesis) of the Epistle (chs. 4–6), serving to depict the superlative ethical lifestyle members of the community of faith are expected to conduct and also as a clue to the main breaks in the section. In 4.1 Paul challenges believers to live in unity by reason of their exalted position in Christ described in chs. 1–3, and in 4.17 to live in purity and not as unbelieving Gentiles. In 5.1-2 believers are exhorted as imitators of God to live in love, and in 5.7-8 to live in light as children of light. A

[31] O'Brien, *Ephesians*, p. 375. Another passage with such connections is Isa. 51.9, 17.

[32] O'Brien, *Ephesians*, p. 376. Cf. Martin, *Ephesians*, p. 63.

[33] O'Brien, *Ephesians*, p. 377. See also Hendriksen, *Galatians and Ephesians* (NTC; Grand Rapids: Baker, 1979), pp. 235, 236.

[34] In 5.14 the Greek word for 'shine', ἐπιφαύσκω, is also used in Job 31.26 for the shining of the sun.

plea to walk in wisdom in 5.15 governs a series of admonitions that run through 6.9, centering on life within the Christian community and more specifically its worship. Hitherto, Paul has mainly contrasted the believers' pre-Christian past with their new life in Christ (4.17–5.14), placing much emphasis on the profligate lifestyle of the pagans. Using 5.15-18 as a point of transition, in 5.15–6.9 he engages in an extensive description of the wise life the Spirit-filled believer is expected to live. The household code regulating family and communal relationships making up the lion's share of the section (5.22–6.9) flows directly from the entreaty of v. 21 for mutual submission 'out of reverence for Christ'.[35] This reciprocal submission is possible only by being filled with the Spirit (v. 18).

Some have called 5.15-21 a 'summary climax'[36] of the ethical section (chs. 4–6), the goal of the whole paraenetic section being a depiction of what it means to live a life that pleases God, or believers walking worthily of their calling. It begins with the governing word 'live', which further explains and defines what Paul means in 4.1 by 'live a life worthy of the calling you have received'. Paul's final entreaty to his readers to 'be very careful, then, how you live' (5.15; cf. Col. 4.5), requires being wise (v. 15), taking full advantage of every opportunity (v.16), an intelligent grasp of the Lord's will, and being filled with the Spirit (v. 18). In contradistinction to the life of the unbeliever, out of the Spirit-filled life flow praise and worship that honors God (vv. 19-21).

'Then, watch how carefully you live/walk' is a literal translation of the first part of v. 15, some interpreters viewing 'then' as a bridge linking v. 15 with 5.8-14, i.e. an admonition to the awakened and converted sinner to live discreetly, not as unwise, but as wise. It seems more likely, however, that Paul is beginning a new section. A translational problem encountered here is whether the adverb 'carefully' is modifying 'watch' or 'live/walk', i.e. should it be translated as 'watch carefully' or 'live/walk carefully'? Over against the AV which adopts the latter, most modern translations (e.g. NASB, NEB, RSV, JB) follow the former based upon the order of NA[27] and UBS[4] and stronger manuscript evidence.[37] A better translation, then, is 'Watch carefully, then, how you live/walk'. The command 'watch' or 'take heed' is in the present tense and suggests habitual behavior. Coupled with 'carefully'

---

[35] Verse 21 actually contains the last of five participles begun in v. 18 that illustrate how the Spirit-filled person ought to live. The last participle (ὑποτασσόμενοι), however, takes Paul's discussion in a new direction.

[36] Snodgrass, *Ephesians* (NIV Application Commentary; Grand Rapids: Zondervan, 1996), p. 286.

[37] Bruce Metzger, *Textual Commentary on the Greek New Testament* (Stuttgart: Deutsche Bibelgesellschaft, 1994), p. 608.

(ἀκριβῶς can also mean 'accurately'), it 'indicates that this admonition regarding godly behaviour is both important and urgent'.[38] Some have opined that Paul's strong emphasis on believers being careful how they live may indicate his awareness of efforts to dupe believers into 'harmless' participation in sexual immorality and greed.[39]

How believers should live Paul now explains: 'not as unwise but as wise' – contrasting behaviors rooted not only in the sapiential tradition (cf. Prov. 4.10-14; 9; 10.8, 14) but also in Qumran literature where the sons of light are said to walk in wisdom and the sons of darkness walk in imprudence.[40] The contrast here is between the life of the Christian, who is light and walks in light (5.8, 13), with that of the Gentile who is darkness and walks in darkness (5.8-12). There is a difference between being smart and being wise. To be smart could mean nothing more than possessing knowledge, but to be wise in biblical terms is to possess the skills to live life that pleases God and in turn be fulfilled and blessed in the process. This calls for an understanding of God's will (v. 17; cf. Prov. 1.1-7; Col. 1.9-10), which is more than intellectual knowledge or living in conformity with Torah.[41]

Paul's fondness for the terms 'wise' and 'wisdom' is very apparent, the former appearing sixteen times in this Epistle. The latter appeared earlier in 1.8 where Paul reminds the believers that God had lavished on them 'all wisdom and understanding' by revealing 'the mystery of his will' (v. 9). It occurred also in the intercessory prayer (1.17-19), Paul praying that God may grant them 'the Spirit of wisdom and revelation' so that they may know him better (v. 18), and also that they grasp the mystery of his plan 'which he purposed in Christ' (1.9). A third occurrence of the term is in 3.10 where it describes the 'manifold wisdom of God' in his uniting Jews and Gentiles in Christ, an act which Paul elsewhere calls 'the mystery that has been kept hidden for ages' (Col. 1.26). Wisdom and mystery go together. It takes wisdom to understand the mystery, committing the people of Christ to 'bringing their lifestyle into conformity with God's wonderful plan of saving men and women in Christ. To be wise is to grasp the significance of the Lord's will.'[42]

Wise people are able to read the signs of the times, have a certain mental attitude, and make lifestyle adjustments as to how they use time, an adjustment depicted in the phrase 'making the most of every opportunity' (ἐξαγοραζόμενοι τὸν καιρόν). The verb (ἐξαγοράζω) is a

---

[38] O'Brien, *Ephesians*, p. 380; also see Lincoln, p. 341.
[39] Thielman, *Ephesians*, p. 356.
[40] See 1QS 3.19-25; 4.24.
[41] Cf. *T. Naph.* 8.10.
[42] O'Brien, *Ephesians*, p. 381.

commercial term of the marketplace. In classical Greek it meant 'to purchase', and was used of the buying of items or the freedom of slaves.[43] It is used in Daniel 2.8 of the Chaldeans who, failing to interpret Nebuchadnezzar's dream, were 'attempting to buy time' (καιρὸν ὑμεῖς ἐξαγοράζετε) in order to delay their certain death. It appears four times in the NT – all in Paul's writings (Gal. 3.13; 4.5; Eph. 5.16; Col. 4.5). In Galatians it refers to redemption from the curse of the law. Here, as in Col. 4.5, it may mean that Christians, who live in the last days, 'should attempt to buy or gain time' in order to live lives that please God.[44] The more common term for 'purchase' or 'buy' (ἀγοράζω) appears here. With the attached prefix *ex-* intensifying the force of the verb, it more likely implies 'to buy up intensively', 'to snap up every opportunity that comes',[45] which intimates eagerly seizing and exploiting at any cost each opportunity presented to do good. This may suggest making up for lost time 'when one was a sinner, or to make the most of the time one has to bear witness and live well, probably the latter'.[46]

The reason for living this way is: 'because the days are evil' (v. 16b), a perspective reflective of the two-age motif in Hebrew eschatology wherein this present evil age (עולם הזה) is contrasted against the perfect coming age (עולם הבה). The present age is evil because it is under the control of the evil one (Eph. 2.2; 6.13; cf. 1 Cor. 2.6, 7; Gal. 1.4), but believers who have become 'light in the Lord' (5.8) and share the life of the age to come (Jn 17.3) are charged to snap up every opportunity during this acceptable day of salvation (2 Cor. 6.2), do good works to which they were preordained (Eph. 2.10), and live lives that please God (Eph. 4.1-32; Col. 1.10).

Verse 17a is essentially a restatement and expansion of v. 15b. The unwise (ἄσοφος) are now called fools (ἄφρων), a harsher term that intimates senseless imprudence. References to fools are common in wisdom literature (e.g. Prov. 1.22; 10.18, 23; 14.26; 17.18; 21.20). Among a fool's many negative traits are failure to acknowledge reliance on God and lack of insight into practical living. Believers are exhorted

---

[43] Diodorus Siculus 36.2.2. The middle voice (as used in the text) being used of buying a slave's freedom has led Thielman to the conclusion that Paul is here urging his readers to 'buy the present time out of its slavery to evil and to use it instead in ways that are "pleasing to the Lord" (5:10)'. This should take place 'moment by moment, in the practical decisions of everyday life' (*Ephesians*, pp. 356, 357).

[44] O'Brien, *Ephesians*, p. 382; cf. Lincoln, *Ephesians*, p. 341.

[45] David H. Field, 'Buy, Sell, Market [ἀγοράζω, ἐξαγοράζω, πωλέω]', *NIDNTT* I (1975), p. 268.

[46] Witherington, *The Letters to Philemon, the Colossians, and the Ephesians*, p. 310.

'not to be foolish' (4.17b), but[47] as wise they should 'understand what the Lord's will is' (5.17a). To 'understand' (συνίημι) means more than grasping facts; it refers to 'the ability to bring things together and see them in relation to one another'[48] – tantamount to the modern expression, 'getting it together'. Practical, life-changing insight is what Paul has in mind. This kind of insight has the Lord's will as its object (cf. Rom. 12.2), and includes believers' election (1.4, 5), God's plan to bring together all things in heaven and earth under the headship of Christ (1.9, 10), growth in Christ (4.15), and Godlikeness (4.24). While this is probably not entirely ruled out, personal guidance for one's life is not what Paul has in mind. God's great plan for the universe and his people is.

Verses 18-21. These verses, which comprise one long sentence in Greek, provide the third and final contrast,[49] broadening the scope of what it means for believers to live wisely and circumspectly (v. 15). In v. 18, still contrasting the behavior of the unbeliever and that of the believer, Paul adduces a twofold entreaty to this end, one negative and the other positive: 'Do not get drunk on wine'; rather, 'be filled with the Spirit'. The former indicates 'never do so,' the latter 'always be so'.[50] The latter both concludes the chain of admonitions that began in 4.17 and guides and governs the rest of the passage, centering in upon the Spirit-filled life as being key in Christian relationships. Paul's emphasis is not referring to getting drunk – forbidden conduct taken for granted by ones walking in the light – rather, he is 'urging them continually to live in/by the Spirit'.[51] Wine's influence upon a person is drastically different than the Spirit's influence. The one results in senseless and shameful behavior, the other to a life of praise to God and healthy relationships. No evidence exists to substantiate the claim[52] that the situation in the Corinthian assembly (cf. 1 Cor. 5.11; 11.21) is here replicated, or that Gentile Christians had imported elements of pagan mystery cult celebrations into the church, provoking Paul's prohibition in 5.18a. Such proscription is common in wisdom literature (cf. Prov.

---

[47] 'But' translates ἀλλά, which denotes a strong contrast between fools and wise persons.

[48] Cleon Rogers and Rogers, *Linguistic and Exegetical Greek New Testament* (Grand Rapids: Zondervan, 1998), p. 444.

[49] The verses show a radical distinction between two lifestyles – the praiseworthy lifestyle of the Spirit-filled Christian and the profligate lifestyle of the drunkard. See A.W.D. Hui, 'The Concept of the Holy Spirit in Ephesians and Its Relation to the Pneumatologies of Luke and Paul' (Ph.D. dissertation, University of Aberdeen, 1992), p. 311.

[50] Fee, *God's Empowering Presence*, p. 720.

[51] Fee, *God's Empowering Presence*, p. 720.

[52] James D. Dunn, *Jesus and the Spirit* (London: SCM, 1975), p. 238.

23.31).[53] As mentioned earlier, Paul is recapitulating and expanding earlier contrasting behaviors of believers and unbelievers, a contrast that began in 4.17. Since God's people have a renewed mind (4.23), they are encouraged to live wisely (5.15) as ones who understand what God's will is (5.17).

In 5.8-15 Paul further characterizes the antithesis between Christians and non-Christians under the primary imageries of light and darkness, but also sleep and wake (v. 14) and wise and fool, exhorting believers in v. 11 to 'have nothing to do with the fruitless deeds of darkness' because such conduct is a manifestation of the senseless imprudence of fools[54] (v. 15). Intoxication is one of the principal features of darkness, which Paul describes elsewhere as taking place at night (Rom. 13. 12, 13; 1 Thess. 5.6-8). Believers who have become 'light in the Lord' (5.8) should not participate in works of darkness, such as getting drunk on wine (a darkness/night activity); rather, they must be filled with the Holy Spirit who inspires wholesome and Godly conduct befitting children of the day.

'Do not be drunk' (v. 18a) translates a present imperative (μεθύσκεσθε) with a prohibition (μή), a construction that normally commands the cessation of a behavior or action in progress. In keeping with this understanding, some interpreters have deduced that the Dionysian cult with its idiosyncratic cultic intoxication and wild behavior has infiltrated and infected the Christian community. Paul is therefore putting a stop to that lifestyle, pointing out its incongruence with the Spirit-filled life believers are supposed to live. Other commentators believe that pagan debauchery has degraded the Christian 'agape feast' (2 Pet. 2.13; Jude 12; cf. 1 Cor. 11.17-34), thus courting Paul's forceful injunction. Since there is, however, no indication that the Ephesian church was guilty of the misconduct for which Paul chastised the Corinthian assembly (1 Cor. 5.11; 11.21) or the presence of Dionysian bacchanalia among the Ephesian believers, that seems less likely here. Furthermore, if Ephesians is a circular letter such a specific judgment would seem inappropriate. The prohibition more likely intimates Paul's concern that discourages such conduct from ever becoming habitual in the lives of the people of God.[55] The reason for the ban

---

[53] Jewish ethical writings are replete with prohibitions against drunkenness (cf. *Testament of Judah* 11.2; 12.3; 13.6; 6.1; *Testament of Issachar* 7:2-3), but Paul most likely depended upon canonical wisdom tradition.

[54] A.J. Köstenberger sees intoxication with wine as equivalent to the foolish imprudence mentioned in 5.15. See his article, 'What Does It Mean to Be Filled with the Spirit? A Biblical Investigation', *Journal of the Evangelical Theological Society* 40 (1997), p. 232.

[55] Hoehner, *Ephesians*, p. 700; Daniel Wallace, *Greek Grammar beyond the Basics: An Exegetical Syntax of the New Testament* (Grand Rapids: Zondervan, 1996), pp. 714-17. μή,

follows immediately: drunkenness 'leads to debauchery' (ἀσωτία), a term which along with its cognates, carries in classical Greek, the LXX, and the New Testament (Lk. 15.13; Tit. 1.6; 1 Pet. 4.4) something of the notion of profligacy, casting off restraints, lack of self-control, dissipation, and sexual excesses – behaviors that lead to ruin. Paul, then, lifts up Spirit-filled living as worthy and wise living.

What may appear surprising at first blush is that Paul does not merely enjoin abstinence on his readers; rather,[56] he urges them to 'be filled with the Spirit' – an experience some in the crowd misconstrued as drunkenness (Acts 2.4, 12-15). The ancient Jewish philosopher Philo observed remarkable similarities between the intoxicated person and a person possessed by God.[57] Any meager outward similarities both God/Spirit-possessed and intoxicated persons may share are drastically outweighed by the acutely divergent outcomes of each experience. As a depressant alcohol leads to dissipation, and removes a person's self-control, judgment, discernment, balance, and wisdom. In the end neither the drunkard nor others benefit from the overindulgence. On the contrary, the Spirit-filled life bears the fruit of self-control, peace, patience (Gal. 5.22-23), healthy relationships, fashioning the beneficiary more into the likeness of Christ.

Spirit-infilling, not intoxication with wine, receives emphasis in 5.18, Paul recruiting five participles to aid unpacking what the Spirit-filled life looks like. Nor is 'ecstasy' Paul's concern; the Spirit's controlling presence is. Because of the close similarity between Col. 3.15–4:1 and Eph. 5.18–6.9, it is very likely that both passages essentially carry the same meaning, i.e. to be Spirit-filled means to be under God's control, which leads to praise and healthy and happy mutual relationships.

The Greek term which is rendered 'be filled' (πληροῦσθε) is a present imperative, denoting a continuing, ongoing fullness – not a once-for-all experience.[58] In 3.19 Paul had prayed that the Ephesian believers 'be filled to the measure of the fullness of God', and in 4.13 stated that the goal of the 'gifts' Christ gave to the church is to help it attain to

---

followed by the present imperative generally stops an action in progress – but not always. It may simply command refraining from an action or activity (e.g. Eph. 4.30; 5.17; 6.4).

[56] The word ἀλλά (but) draws a strong contrast between the wine-intoxicated lifestyle and the Spirit-filled lifestyle believers should embrace.

[57] 'Now when grace fills the soul, that soul rejoices and smiles and dances, for it is possessed and inspired, so that to many of the unenlightened it may seem to be drunken, crazy, and beside itself ... For with the God-possessed not only is the soul wont to be stirred and goaded as it were into ecstasy but the body also is flushed and fiery ... and it is true that these sober ones are drunk in a sense.' Philo, *De Ebr.* 146-148, quoted in Lincoln, *Ephesians*, p. 344.

[58] Gerhard Delling, 'πληρόω', *TDNT* VI (1968), p. 291.

'the whole measure of the fullness of Christ'. The Trinitarian nature of the ecclesiology of Ephesians is unmistakable. 'With the Spirit' (ἐν πνεύματι, v. 18) may be construed as both a dative of means (by) and a dative of content (with), thus deducing the meaning 'being filled by the Spirit and thus also filled with the Spirit'.[59] Spirit-fullness signifies being 'completely controlled and stamped by the powers'[60] with which one is filled. In light of the subsequent verses the infilling of the Spirit cannot be viewed solely as the transformation of believers into the image of God and Christ.[61] The emphasis is 'being filled to the full by the Spirit's presence',[62] which is another way of saying, 'live in/by the Spirit' (Gal. 5.16). The Spirit-filled life is a vital necessity for the Christian, for it is the Spirit that imparts wisdom to walk in the will of God (vv. 15, 17), inspires authentic Christian worship (vv. 19-20), and helps to create genuine Christian relationships (vv. 21-33).[63]

In the wake of the explosive and ever-expanding transnational, transethnic, and transcultural global advance of the Pentecostal and Charismatic renewal movement[64] with its emphasis on Spirit-baptism and glossolalia, it is appropriate to inquire what relation, if any, exists between the Pentecostal-Charismatic experience of Spirit-baptism and Paul's characterization of Spirit-fullness in Eph. 5.18. Are Luke and Paul speaking about the same experience? And how do the marks and distinctives of a Spirit-filled life (from the Pentecostal-Charismatic perspective) correspond to those in the Pauline passage? Each of the three NT writers who focus on the Spirit's ministry emphasizes one of the three dimensions of the Spirit's work. Luke in his Gospel and Acts stresses the Pentecostal, charismatic, service-oriented aspect of the Spirit's work. John focuses on his paschal, conversion-centered work, and Paul on his purifying and consecration work.[65] If Paul accentuates the purifying and sanctifying work of the Holy Spirit, should one extrapolate the same idea from Paul's command to be filled with the Spirit (Eph. 5.18)? Or is Spirit-baptism and Spirit-empowerment what Paul has in mind?

---

[59] So Lincoln, *Ephesians*, p. 344. See also Fee, *God's Empowering Presence*, pp. 721, 722.
[60] Gerhard Delling, 'πληρόω', *TDNT* VI (1968), p. 291.
[61] O'Brien, *Ephesians*, p. 392. Cf. Lincoln, *Ephesians*, p. 344.
[62] Fee, *God's Empowering Presence*, p. 722.
[63] Fee observes the leading role the Spirit plays in both ethics and worship, and decries the modern artificial bifurcation between gifts and fruit of the Spirit. To him they are inextricably linked (*Paul, the Spirit, and the People of God*, pp. 99, 153) .
[64] See Harvey Cox, *Fire From Heaven: The Rise of Pentecostal Spirituality and the Reshaping of Religion in the Twenty-First Century* (New York: Addison-Wesley, 1995); Vinson Synan, *The Century of the Holy Spirit: 100 Years of Pentecostal and Charismatic Renewal* (Nashville: Thomas Nelson, 2001).
[65] Larry Hart, *Truth Aflame* (Nashville: Thomas Nelson, 1999), pp. 343-56.

There are convincing points of connection between Acts and Ephesians, not the least of which are linguistic and literary, none more
compelling than Acts 20.17-38. Is it by sheer coincidence that Luke
(Acts 13.52) and Paul (Eph. 5.18) use the same word (πληρόω) for the
Spirit-filled life? What conclusion should one draw from the glossolalic
praise of the Pentecost crowd ('we hear them declaring the wonders of
God in our own tongues', Acts 2.11) and Paul's exhortation (Eph.
5.19) 'Speak to one another with psalms, hymns, and spiritual songs'? Is
Luke's 'filled with joy' (Acts 13.52) equivalent to Paul's 'make music in
your heart to the Lord'? And is this spontaneous singing the glossolalic
praise or singing in tongues (singing with the spirit) Paul adumbrates in
1 Cor. 14.15?[66] Their verbal and literary parallels notwithstanding, it is
reasonable to conclude that Luke and Paul do highlight different yet
complementary aspects of the Spirit's work. With his evangelistic and
empowerment emphasis, Luke is event-oriented. The Spirit's purpose
is mission-driven. Much stress is therefore placed upon power and
evangelism. Paul, dealing with life issues in the community of faith,
while not reducing the importance of missions and enduement, has an
ethical intent. The people of God are called to a lifestyle ('always be
filled with the Spirit') with concomitant, distinctive and corresponding
fruit of the Spirit (Eph. 5.18-21). To be filled with the Spirit for Paul
is the same as to live/walk in the Spirit (Gal. 5.16-26). One should not
equate the infilling of the Holy Spirit and manifestation of the gifts of
the Spirit *per se* with proof of the Spirit-filled life. As tragically evidenced in the Corinthian church, it is possible to possess the Holy
Spirit and demonstrate his gifts and yet fail to live the Spirit-filled life
(1 Cor. 1.5-7; 3.1-4).

Whereas drunkenness results in debauchery and imprudent conduct,
the Spirit-filled life is one of joyful celebration that both glorifies God
and builds up the Christian community (cf. Col. 3.16). Verses 19-21
portray through five participles behaviors that are distinctive of the
Spirit-filled life: 'speaking to one another in psalms and hymns and
spiritual songs, singing and making melody in your heart to the Lord,
giving thanks always ... submitting to one another ...' (NKJV).[67] Although praise and worship are the function of these actions, their di-
dactic, edificatory, and exhortatory goal should not be overlooked.
The first clause ('speaking to one another in psalms and hymns and
spiritual songs') addresses what the believers do corporately in wor-

---

[66] While he does not make a connection between Luke and Acts at this juncture,
James Dunn, unlike Lincoln, does allow for spontaneous singing in tongues in 1 Cor.
14.15 and Eph. 5.19/Col. 3.16.

[67] The NIV translates the participles as commands. In this way, these actions are not
viewed as characteristics of the Spirit-filled life.

ship[68] and other social settings, the second (singing and making melody) probably a description of the same activity from a different viewpoint.[69] All of these musical modes collectively (not only song) may be described as 'spiritual', the emphasis being placed not on spontaneity[70] but on the inspiration of the Spirit. One should not confine these musical forms to the three compositional types identified in the OT Psalter under their Hebrew titles: *mizmorim, tehillim, and shirim*;[71] allowance must be made for overlap, expansion, and adaptation.

'Psalms' may allude to the OT Psalter which was incorporated into Christian worship (1 Cor. 14.26; Eph. 5.19; Col. 3.16) and probably sung with a stringed instrument.[72] The origin of 'hymns' is uncertain. Occurring only here and in Col. 3.16 in the NT,[73] the word may denote any joyful song of praise. 'Songs' translates the Greek word (ᾠδή) from which the English word 'ode' derives. Though used of a dirge in Greek tragedy, it more frequently refers to festive or joyful songs – sometimes accompanied by music (1 Chron. 16.42) or dancing (2 Sam. 6.5) – or just singing. In Revelation it describes a new song of praise and rejoicing to the Lamb (5.9; 14.3) and for God's marvelous deeds (15.3). 'Hymns' may be 'Christian canticles' and 'spiritual songs' 'unpremeditated words sung "in the Spirit", voicing holy aspirations'.[74] As an examination of the uses of these terms and their cognates in Scripture will reveal, making hard and fast distinctions and classification among these three musical modes may not be possible. All that Paul probably intends to convey by the categorization is the rich variety of sacred songs present in the early church.

'Singing and making melody', now directed to the Lord, refers to one activity, the two participles being joined by 'and'. 'Singing' (ᾄδω) is the verbal cognate of the noun ᾠδή and is used in Rev. 5.9 and 14.3

---

[68] In *Epistulae* 10.96.7 Pliny the Younger, procurator of Bithynia in a letter addressed to Emperor Trajan, c. 112 CE, mentions Christians meeting before dawn to recite antiphonal hymns to Christ as God. Similarly, in describing a Christian love feast Tertullian notes, 'after water for the hands and lights have been brought in, each is invited to sing to God in the presence of the others from what he knows of the holy scriptures or from his own heart' (*Apology* 39.18).

[69] O'Brien, *Ephesians*, p. 394.

[70] James Dunn says to the contrary, 'Paul does not forbid all spontaneous singing, but urges a spontaneity that comes from the impulse of the Spirit and not from the stimulus of drink' (*Jesus and the Spirit*, p. 238).

[71] Bruce, *Colossians*, pp. 158-59 n. 155

[72] The Greek ψαλμός originally referred to the plucking of strings, stringed instruments, and later the Psalms. The word appears in Lk. 20.42; 24.44; Acts 1.20; 13.33.

[73] Its cognates appear in Mt. 26.30; Mk. 14.26; Acts 16.25; Eph. 5.19; Col. 3.16; Heb. 2.12). See Bruce's examination of Christian canticles which were likely reproduced in the NT; *Colossians*, p. 159 n. 156.

[74] Bruce, *Colossians* (Grand Rapids: Eerdmans, 1984), pp. 158-59. See nn. 155-56 on the same pages.

of the new song offered to the Lamb. ψάλλω is the verb form of the noun ψαλμός, rendered 'psalm' earlier in this chapter, and here means 'psalming' or making music by singing (cf. Rom. 15.9; 1 Cor. 14.15; Jas 5.13). 'In your heart' may indicate the place the singing and making melody occurs (NIV, NEB, KJV), but this does not take into account outward expressions of joy. It appears, rather, that Paul is stating how such cheerfulness should be expressed – from the heart, 'outward expression of a joy that is rooted in the innermost depths of [one's] being'[75] – 'with your heart' (NASB, ASB), 'with all your heart' (RSV). Heartfelt joy is accompanied by an attitude of thankfulness – 'always giving thanks ... for everything' (v. 20). The Spirit-filled life not only makes music to Christ, but constantly offers gratitude to God the Father in Jesus' name[76] 'for everything'. Everything cannot mean patent evil and 'the most appalling calamities of life', which God abominates. Thanksgiving should be offered for his 'loving providence' which can make evil bring about good, and for everything which is 'consistent with the loving Fatherhood of God and the self-revelation he has given us in Jesus Christ'.[77]

Reflection and Response (Part 5)

Reflection

In the section that immediately precedes this one, the apostle focused on vices that disrupted the harmony of the community. At the beginning of this chapter, he admonishes the Gentile believers to be imitators of God and to exercise the self-sacrificial love exemplified by Christ (vv. 1-2). He prohibits any participation in the self-indulgent sensuality that characterized their pagan past – a lifestyle totally incongruous with the divine model set before them in God and Christ (vv. 4-5).

Without muting his call for the unity and purity of the community trumpeted earlier, in ch. 5 Paul now shifts from demanding appropriate Christian behavior to motivations for such conduct. In 5.5-7 he appeals for purity of life in view of the coming kingdom and certain judgment, issuing a warning of the serious consequences to those who practice unrighteousness, namely, exclusion from the eschatological kingdom and experience of God's wrath. The gravity and certainty of the caveat is highlighted by two emphatic phrases: 'of this you can be

---

[75] Leon Morris, *Expository Reflections*, p. 178.

[76] See Rom. 1.8 and Col. 3.17, where thanksgiving is offered 'through' Christ. His name represents all he stands for and has accomplished (O'Brien, *Ephesians*, p. 398; see H. Bietenhard, *TDNT* V, 270-281).

[77] Stott, *The Message of Ephesians*, p. 207.

sure' (v. 5) and 'Let no one deceive you' (v. 6). God's kingdom is a righteous kingdom, and only the righteous can enter there.

To the certainty of the coming judgment as an inducement for righteous living Paul adds an existential one – the stark positive difference between the present life in Christ and the past pagan life in sin (vv. 8-14). The contrast is presented under the ethical symbolism of darkness and light. (Paul heightens the contrast in v. 14, comparing conversion to awakening out of sleep and a resurrection from the dead.) The Ephesian believers were once darkness, but now they are light in the Lord. Darkness represents moral blindness, ignorance, evil, unrighteousness, bondage to sin, hopelessness, falsehood, secrecy, decadence, moral death – all of which are inspired by Satan. Light represents the exact opposite and finds its source in God. Paul's point here is that Christians have been radically transformed. To live in darkness is inconsistent with who they are. As children of light (v. 8) they must, therefore, emit the light that they are and live as people of the light.

Paul's third incentive for living holy rather than debauched lives is based upon the notion that Christians are wise (vv. 15-17). This kind of practical wisdom instructs one how to conduct oneself, disallowing worldly and sinful pagan practices, but embracing a life worthy of God's call. Wise people that they are, Christians take seriously how they navigate life, being careful to live 'like sensible men, not like simpletons' (NEB, v. 15), taking the fullest advantage of every God-given opportunity for doing good, and discerning the will of the Lord.

The final motivation Paul gives for godly living is the Spirit-filled life (vv. 18-21). This positive admonition is preceded, however, by the prohibition, 'Do not be drunk' (v. 18a), probably a warning against such conduct ever gaining a foothold in the lives of the people of God. The reason for the prohibition is the negative consequence of the behavior it discourages: drunkenness 'leads to debauchery', a casting-off of restraints, lack of self-control, dissipation, and sexual excesses – behaviors that result in personal and communal ruin. Paul, then, lifts up Spirit-filled living as worthy and wise living. In his command that believers be filled with the Spirit (v. 18), he makes the requirement obligatory to all, not optional to a few. The daily Spirit-filled life is one of joyful celebration that both magnifies God and builds up the Christian community.

To provoke further reflection on motivations for holy living the following questions are submitted. Does the ethical condition among Christians today warrant the need for such incentives? Can you call to mind a few churches that take Paul's ethical incentives for holy living seriously? How well do Christians respond to such 'rewards'? What do your Christian friends give as the foremost reasons for maintaining pure lives? How do incentives for holy living differ from works righteousness, which Scripture teaches can never bring about salvation or commend one to God? How may one reconcile this approach to Christian living with grace?

In an effort to make the reflection more personal the following questions are raised. What goads you to live a pure life before God and the world? How do the motivations stated by Paul in the passage consciously or unconsciously help you to live a holy life? What role, if any, do future 'rewards' play in how you live for God? If there were no future 'rewards' would you still live a holy life? What practical benefits to you see in living a life of purity?

Response

How may one respond to the notion of incentives to live the Christian life discussed in the earlier section? The following points are submitted for your consideration.

1. Carefully examine your theology and practice to determine why you live the Christian life. Making a list for further consideration may be helpful.

2. Determine whether your personal relationship with Christ is a greater or lesser incentive in living for him than the future 'rewards'.

3. In a Bible class explore and discuss with your colleagues the role of grace and incentives in living the Christian life.

4. Discern in the testimonies of others aspects of the Christian life that promote holiness and sanctification of life.

4. Living in mutual submission (5.21–6.9)

Verse 21 serves as a pivot, providing the last of five elements of the Spirit-filled life (vv. 18–21), namely submission, and concurrently introducing it as a new topic which will be developed throughout the household code governing domestic relationships (5.22–6.9), especially in 5.22-33. Some interpreters argue that v. 21 does not begin a new section but rather concludes the admonition to wise living begun in v. 17 and more specifically Spirit-filling in v. 18. To substantiate this notion, they further urge that Paul's last of five participles (ὑποτασσόμενοι) describing the Spirit-filled life cannot begin a new sentence or be translated as an imperative as some translations do, but must be rendered in a way to express result.[1] Other scholars, without arguing against the nature and function of the participle, maintain that whereas the first four of the participles are used in the context of corporate worship, the last one, 'submitting' (ὑποτασσόμενοι), has to do with household conduct – a new major section Paul is about to take up.[2] While submission in household relationships is subsequently dealt with, the reciprocal deference Paul urges in general terms in v. 21 should not be limited solely to the domestic context. 'Submitting' to one another most likely relates to Christian conduct within or without the church.

In the lengthy section that follows (5.22–6.9), like its parallel[3] Col. 3.18–4.1, three sets of relationships are addressed: wives–husbands (5.22-33), children–parents (6.1-4), and slaves–masters (6.5-9). Rules established in Greco-Roman society to govern these relationships and attendant responsibilities were probably adopted by Christian households. Such rules are called 'station codes' because they address each paired member in relation to his or her role and position, duties and responsibilities, and 'household codes' or *Haustafeln* (household rules, Luther), because they regulate and stabilize behavior in the Christian household and maintain unity and harmony among its members.[4]

---

[1] Hoehner, *Ephesians*, p. 716.
[2] Thielman, *Ephesians*, p. 365.
[3] Similar parallels are 1 Tim. 2.8-15; 6.1-10; Tit. 2.1-10; 1 Pet. 2.18-3.7.
[4] For further study, see Hoehner, *Ephesians*, pp. 720-29 and his exhaustive list of sources; Lincoln, pp. 357-65; O'Brien, *Ephesians*, pp. 405-409. As regards the origin, source, and true purpose of the New Testament household codes, theories abound. In any given society specific rules are established to govern and stabilize life. Might this have been true for the early Christian communities? Some early 20th-century scholars viewed the *Haustafel* as a Christianized version of Stoic moral ethic. Later studies jetti-

What was the purpose of the household codes? This is another area of debate. It has been proposed that Paul was battling social unrest of slaves inspired by his Corinthian teaching regarding their manumission (1 Cor. 7.21). However, no evidence exists that Paul had such a problem in the Ephesian church. Nor can the view that they were an apologetic to smother slander by unbelievers against the Christian faith (cf. 1 Pet. 2.11-15; 3.15-16) be substantiated in the Ephesian context. It is far more reasonable to see the station codes as supportive of the theme of unity that threads through the Epistle (2.11–3.13; 4.1-16) and an expression of the wise and Spirit-filled lives believers were encouraged to live (5.15-21), Paul here wedding his eschatological and ethical vision in relation to God's objective of uniting all things in Christ (1.9, 10). The spin-off of this for the secular state is that the church becomes the model for social order. To the first of the paired relationships – wives-husbands – Paul devotes 5.22-33, beginning with the wife's responsibility to the husband (vv. 22-24) and followed by the husband's responsibility to the wife (vv. 25-33).

'Submit to one another', Paul exhorts in v. 21. Contra the NIV imperative translation of the participle ὑποτασσόμενοι, it seems better to translate it to indicate the consequence and evidence of Spirit-fullness (v. 18).[5] Appearing 23 times in Paul's writings and used of a wide range of relationships,[6] the term 'submit', ὑποτάσσω, literally means to 'arrange under' or 'order oneself under', and often denotes subordination to persons deemed worthy of respect either because of their position, age, or admirable qualities. Of its 40 or so NT uses, the verb intones authority and subjection/submission.[7] Paul calls on certain groups. to exercise such an attitude – believers to the state (Rom. 13. 1, 5; Tit. 3.1), women (1 Cor. 14.34; Col. 3.18; 1 Tim. 2.11; Tit. 2.5), children

---

soned this approach in favor of seeing them as a syncretistic fusion of Greek ethical codes and Jewish moral injunctions mediated through Hellenistic Judaism during the course of the church's Gentile missionary outreach. Stoicism's ethical mandate addressed individual, not social classes as represented in the New Testament. More recent scholarship ties the household rules to the Greco-Roman world, which regarded the household as the foundation of the state and household management as having vital political and social function. For an excellent discussion of the social and political relationship between the state and the household, see Thielman, *Ephesians*, pp. 366-69. Undoubtedly, Aristotle's household management concepts were the ancestral fount for the Greek, Roman, and Jewish household codes through the first century CE, represented in the likes of the Peripatetics, Dio Chrysostom, Seneca, Philo, and Josephus. It is reasonable to conclude that, notwithstanding the similarities with other household rules, the Christian codes contain a distinctive content and are based on no single model. See Lincoln, *Ephesians*, p. 360.

[5] Wallace, *Greek Grammar beyond the Basics*, pp. 651, 659 (n. 6).

[6] For example Rom. 8.20; 13.1; 1 Cor. 15.24-28; Eph. 1.21, 22; Phil. 3.21; Col. 3.18; Heb. 2.8; 1 Pet. 3.21.

[7] O'Brien, *Ephesians*, p. 399.

(1 Tim. 3.4), and slaves (Tit. 2.9). But only here (v. 21) does he urge reciprocal deference among believers without consideration of status, although within a coexisting hierarchy of household roles.

Exactly what mutual submission means and how it relates to the household table (5.22–6.9) are issues of much debate. Put simply, does mutual submission rule out hierarchical distinctions, introducing horizontal modes of interaction among peers regardless of rank, function, gender, or status? Or does it mean submission to appropriate authorities within distinct hierarchical structures and relationships? The first view appeals to the example of Christ who humbled himself, becoming a servant (Phil. 2.3), and Paul's call to reciprocal servanthood in the Galatian letter (5.13).[8] The latter view interprets submission in light of the hierarchical structures endemic to the Greco-Roman world of which the church and Christian family were a microcosm.[9] It is quite apparent in his letters that Paul did not dismantle the hierarchical structures and roles that existed in the church communities. What he made clear, however, was that those roles should not negatively affect the mutual and fraternal relationships that existed among the people of God. Love and humility inspired by Christ's selfless life and sacrificial death should govern all relationships (Phil. 2.1-11), but also here 'out of reverence for Christ' (5.21). 'Reverence for Christ' renders the Greek 'fear of Christ' (φόβῳ Χριστοῦ). While 'reverence' or 'respect' correctly translates the term φόβος on many occasions in Scripture, here in an eschatological context the more common term 'fear' is a more appropriate rendition, better capturing 'the sense of awe in the presence of one who is Lord and coming Judge'.[10] Concluding and summarizing the proof of Spirit-filling with the participle 'submitting', Paul uses the same word to commence a new section in which that characteristic is developed and applied practically in different relationships.

a. The wife's responsibility to the husband (5.21-24)

While Paul commences the household codes with an appeal for reciprocal submission (5.21), the subordination commanded in the code itself is not reciprocal. Much like in its counterpart code in Col. 3.18–4.1, wives are here enjoined to submit to their husbands, children to

---

[8] G. Bilezikian, *Beyond Sex Roles* (Grand Rapids: Baker, 1985), p. 154; Ben Witherington, *Women in the Earliest Churches* (Cambridge: University Press, 1988), p. 56; and G.W. Dawes, *The Body in Question: Metaphor and Meaning in the Interpretation of Ephesians 5:21-33* (Leiden: Brill, 1998), p. 216, advocate this position.

[9] This is the approach taken by O'Brien, *Ephesians*, pp. 401-405; Wayne Grudem, *Recovering Biblical Manhood and Womanhood: A Response to Evangelical Feminism*, ed. John. Piper and Wayne Grudem (Wheaton: Crossway, 1991), pp. 493-94.

[10] O'Brien, *Ephesians*, p. 404.

parents, and slave to their masters, but the submissiveness is not recip-
rocated in kind. Instead, husbands are exhorted to love their wives,
parents to rear their children wisely, and masters to treat their slaves
compassionately.

In 5.22 wives are instructed to 'submit to your husbands'. Although
the imperative 'submit' is absent in the Greek, it is implied from the
sense of the participle in v. 21. While 'wives' and 'husbands' can be
translated 'women' and 'men', respectively, it is clear from the context
that Paul is not urging women to submit to men, but wives to their
husbands. Contrary to the custom of first-century society, submission
of wife to husband here implies neither a demeaning inferiority or
docile servility on the part of the wife nor tyranny and exploitation on
the part of the husband. Paul consistently interprets the household rules
in light of the new humanity which Ephesians stresses. Fundamental to
this is the dignity, equality, and unity of persons, though roles may
differ.[11] Subsequently, Paul will lift up the selfless, sacrificial, and servant life of Christ as the model that should govern the relationship of a
husband to his wife. As the wife's motivation for voluntary submission
is 'as to the Lord' (ὡς τῷ κυρίῳ) – 'as fitting in the Lord', Col. 3.18 –
(which does not mean giving the husband the same deference as she
gives the Lord, but is rather another way of serving Christ and showing
obedience to him; cf. 3.23, said of servants), so the husband's authority
is modulated by the example of Christ and the principle of love. In the
household code (5.22; 6.1, 5, 7), those who are asked to submit/obey
are admonished to do so as an expression of their commitment to
Christ, not merely because of the authority (*patria potestas*) invested in
the male as head of the family (*pater familias*).

In v. 23 Paul states the reason for the wife's submission. 'For the
husband is the head of the wife as Christ is the head of the church'.
On two earlier occasions the term 'head' (κεφαλή) was used with regard to Christ (1.22; 4.15). Here for the first time it is used of the husband's headship and presented as the basis for the wife's subordination.
But for Paul, 'Christ's headship over the church is the pattern in which
husbands and wives are to understand their relationship to each other'.[12] As the 'appropriate order is for wives to have a relationship with
their husbands similar to the relationship the church has with Christ',
so 'Paul instructs husbands to love their wives as Christ loves the
church'.[13] There are two fundamentally different interpretations of

---

[11] Stott, *The Message of Ephesians*, pp. 216-18.

[12] Kimberly E. Alexander and R. Hollis Gause, *Women in Leadership: A Pentecostal Perspective* (Pentecostal Leadership Series; Cleveland, TN: Center for Pentecostal Leadership
and Care, 2006), p. 88.

[13] Alexander and Gause, *Women in Leadership*, p. 89.

'headship', each attracting its own ardent advocates. Traditionalists[14] view it as a symbol of authority, rulership, and supremacy. The more modern approach[15] understands it as denoting source or origin.

'Head' as a metaphor for leader or person in authority is rare in ancient Greek. It does occur in the LXX with that implication, however (Judg. 11.11; 2 Sam. 22.44). The juxtaposition of the terms 'head', 'submission', and 'body' in 5.22 heavily weights the interpretation of 'head' in the direction of authority or rulership, and is strengthened by Paul's instruction that the wife must 'respect' (φοβῆται) her husband (v. 33). A factor crucial to the discussion is the 'cultural expectation' the language activates. How would the Ephesian believers, accustomed to the Greco-Roman *patria potestas* governance of the family, understand the male-female relationship in marriage? It is reasonable to conclude from the context, but more precisely from what immediately follows (5.23-33), that Paul, without attempting to dismantle the hierarchical structure[16] of the household, presents Christ and the church as the model and hermeneutical key to the wife-husband relationship. In this way, the Christian husband's authority must be patterned after Christ's servant leadership, 'which expresses care rather than control, responsibility rather than rule'.[17] However one construes headship, when the husband exemplifies Christ's headship, far from devaluing the wife's womanhood, he positively enhances and enriches it.[18] Only in the position of authority is a comparison drawn between the husband and Christ, for Christ alone is savior of the church, his body (5.23b) which he rescued from eternal condemnation at the price of his own life (2.1-10, 14-18).

Paul's injunction in v. 22 that wives should submit to their husbands is reiterated and reinforced in v. 24, with the church's subordination to

---

[14] Proponents of this view are Wayne Grudem, 'Does *Kephale* ('head') Mean 'Source' or 'Authority Over' in Greek Literature? A Survey of 2,336 Examples', *Trinity Journal* 6 (1985), pp. 38-59; G.W. Dawes, *The Body in Question*, pp. 122-149; H. Hoehner, *Ephesians*, pp. 738-41; J.A. Fitzmyer, '*Kephale* in 1 Corinthians 11:3', *Interpretation* 47 (1993), pp. 52-59; cf. David M. Park, 'The Structure of Authority in Marriage: An Evaluation of *Hupotasso* and *Kephale* in Eph 5:22-33', *Evangelical Quarterly* 59 (April 1987), p. 120.

[15] Advocates of the 'source'/'origin' position are S. Bedale, 'The Meaning of κεφαλη, in the Pauline Epistles', *Journal of Theological Studies* 5 (1954), pp. 211-15; Berkley and Alvera Mickelsen, 'The "Head" of the Epistles', pp. 20-23; Gordon Fee, *The First Epistle to the Corinthians* (Grand Rapids: Eerdmans, 1987), pp. 502-3 n. 42; C.C. Kroeger, 'The Classical Concept of Head as "Source"', in: *Equal to Serve*, ed. G.G. Hull (London: Scripture Union, 1987), pp. 267-83. Biblical context is the best arbiter in the oscillation between the literal and metaphorical senses present in the NT.

[16] Paul's approach in dealing with the wife in a hierarchical system endemic to the Greco-Roman world is analogous to how he deals with the issue of slavery: allowing the 'leaven effect' of the gospel to bring about the desired transformation over time.

[17] Stott, *The Message of Ephesians*, p. 225.

[18] Stott, *The Message of Ephesians*, p. 226.

Christ lifted up as a model of the wife's voluntary submission to her husband and the addition of the words 'in everything'. In the household rules in Colossians 'in everything' is used of the obedience of children to parents (3.20) and slaves to masters (3.22; cf. Tit. 3.9). Since 'everything' cannot include anything that contravenes the law of God (cf. Acts 5.29), applied to the wife's subjection, it likely suggests total surrender in all legally justifiable aspects of life. If, as is the case, the husband must pattern his life and behavior on Christ, that fact alone governs how the husband relates to his wife.

b. The husband's responsibility to the wife (5.25-33)

The ancient world was a man's world, a world in which a wife had obligations to her husband, but not the converse. Scorn and oppression of women was nearly universal. In no place was this attitude more acutely mirrored than in the home. Without legal rights, a Jewish woman was regarded not as a person, but a thing. Her Greek counterpart's role was to bear and rear children, and the home her domain. Fidelity in the marriage bonds was only a distant wish, the husband pursuing pleasure and companionship with paramours. Treated as a mere chattel, in the Roman Empire the wife was completely under the tyrannical control of her husband. In this section Paul offers a nobler way, presenting the Christological model as the template that should govern and sustain marital, ecclesiastical, and social relationships.

Verse 25. 'Husbands, love your wives, just as Christ loved the church.'

That a wife should submit to her husband was a common expectation in Greco-Roman society. But to command and expect a husband to love his wife selflessly and sacrificially was a uniquely Christian and revolutionary approach in marriage, a practice not found in the OT, rabbinic literature, or household rules of the Greco-Roman period,[19] raising the virtue of marriage and placing it on a firmer foundation as a domestic ideal. Repeatedly Paul urges husbands not to rule over (cf. Col. 3.19), but to love their wives with a distinctively Christian form of love (ἀγάπη)[20] (vv. 25, 28, 33) patterned after the selfless, self-sacrificing love Christ has for the church – here depicted as a virgin for

---

[19] Hoehner, *Ephesians*, p. 748. This fact is not overruled by Plutarch's entreaty that 'The husband should rule over his wife not as a despot over a thing, but rather as the soul over the body, empathizing and permeated with affection' (*Praecepta Conjugalia* 33).

[20] Stott has observed that Paul's Stoic contemporaries instructed husbands to love their wives, but they used the weaker verb for love – φιλέω (*The Message of Ephesians*, p. 226); cf. *Pseudo-Phocylides* 195-97; *b. Yebamot* 62b.

whom he voluntarily lays down his life to make her his bride[21] (Rom. 4.25; 8.32; Gal. 1.4).

If Christ's love for the church harks back to his eternal pre-existence and his giving himself on the cross,[22] the present and future goal of his self-sacrificing love is spelled out in three purpose clauses in vv. 26 and 27: 'to make her holy' (v. 26), 'to present her to himself as a radiant church' (v. 27a), and to facilitate her becoming 'holy and blameless' (v. 27c). Paul's allusion to the customary bridal bath ('washing with water', v. 26) that occurred before Jewish and Greek weddings is almost certainly borrowed from the imagery in Ezek. 16.1-14 of Yahweh's covenantal marriage[23] to Jerusalem (symbolically designating Judah or all Israel), depicted first as an abandoned infant who later becomes his child-bride and queen. Christ's first and present aim in dying for the church is to make her holy, i.e. to sanctify her, which implies separation from what is evil or unclean[24] and consecration to the will and purpose of God (cf. 1 Cor. 1.2; 6.11; 1 Tim. 4.5).

Christ not only sanctifies the church; he also cleanses it (v. 26). Does this cleansing precede the sanctification, or is it simultaneous with it? Some translators view the action of the participle καθαρίσας as antecedent to the principal verb, and render it 'having cleansed it' (NASB, NRSV, RV, RSV); others see it as concurrent, and translate it 'cleansing it/her' (AV, NIV, NEB, NJB). As represented in the NRSV, the participle is best taken to indicate the means or manner by which the action of the main verb is achieved: Christ died on behalf of the church to make her holy 'by cleansing her'. Sanctification focuses on consecration to God, cleansing centers on the removal of sin or evil.

What Paul means by 'the washing with water through the word' (v. 26) has been a matter of strenuous debate. Does he picture the washing as a nuptial bath that purifies the church (cf. Ezek. 16.8-14)? And what does the washing signify? Scholarly support for the Jewish concept of a bridal bath lying behind the metaphor here is widespread. There is far less agreement, however, as to whether washing refers to baptism or

---

[21] Marriage is often portrayed in the OT as the covenantal relationship between God and his people (Isa. 54.5-8; Jer. 2.1-3; 31.31-32; Ezek. 23; Hos. 1–3). In Mk 2.18-20 (cf. Jn 3.29), Jesus refers to himself as bridegroom, and Paul's goal was to present the church as a pure virgin to one husband, Christ (2 Cor. 11.2). For further study, see R.C. Ortlund, *Whoredom: God's Unfaithful Wife in Biblical Theology* (Leicester: Apollos, 1996).

[22] Stott, *The Message of Ephesians*, p. 227.

[23] The rabbis used Hos. 2.16; Isa. 54.4-5; 62.4-5 and Ezek. 16.7-8 to extol the covenant between Yahweh and Israel at Sinai in terms of a marriage treaty (cf. *Philo, de Cherubim* 13). Where Moses acted as mediator of that covenant, Paul sees his role as that of presenting the bride (church) to Christ as a pure virgin (2 Cor. 11.2).

[24] O'Brien does not regard sanctification here as an ongoing moral renewal, but the bringing of the church into a dedicated relationship with God (*Ephesians*, p. 421).

spiritual cleansing.[25] The majority of interpreters opt for the former. The baptismal view is implicit in the imagery of nuptial bath and the death of Jesus for the church.[26] Furthermore, the teaching of the early church depicts baptism as a moral washing (Jn 13.10; Acts 2.38; 22.16; 1 Cor. 6.11; Tit. 3.5; Heb. 10.22; 1 Pet. 3.20, 21). In the NT the close association of baptism with a spoken word is inescapable. In this context the word may refer to some kind of gospel utterance, confession from the candidate, a prebaptismal word of instruction, or a baptismal formula (Acts 2.38; 8.16; 19.5; 22.16; 1 Cor. 6.11; Mt. 28.19). 'The new, or perhaps unusual, idea of Ephesians at this point is that the entire church receives this bath.'[27]

Another view deems the washing as a spiritual cleansing accomplished by Christ. Only at 4.5 does such a motif appear in the entire Epistle; nowhere else in the NT is the church corporately baptized.[28] Washing, therefore, is synonymous with 'the washing of rebirth' in which the bestowal of the Holy Spirit was a part (Tit. 3.5). It is not a mere external and physical act, but a present inward and spiritual reality (Acts 22.16; 1 Pet. 3.21). The qualifying phrase 'through/by the word'[29] suggests it does not denote a mechanical or magical view of the sacrament whereby baptismal regeneration is experienced *ex opere operato* (from the work done).

Christ's ultimate aim in giving himself for the church (v. 25), and for sanctifying and purifying her (v. 26), is that he might present her to himself[30] 'as a radiant church' (v. 27), a bride adorned in unsullied splendor for her husband (2 Cor. 11.2; Rev. 21.2; cf. Ezek. 16.9-14; Ps. 45.13). Exactly when this wedding takes place is an issue of debate among scholars. The minority view[31] is that Christ's presentation of the church occurs during this present age. For not only does the one flesh union (v. 32) apply to the present relationship between Christ and the church, but Ephesians' realized eschatology treats glory and holiness as existing attributes Christ bestows upon the church. Hence, the church

[25] At Qumran sanctification and purification were associated with ritual washing (cf. 1QH 11.10-12; 1QS 3.4.8-10.
[26] Arthur G. Patzia, *Ephesians, Colossians, Philemon*, pp. 270-71.
[27] Patzia, *Ephesians, Colossians, Philemon*, p. 271.
[28] O'Brien, *Ephesians*, p. 422.
[29] The differing views of 'the word' mentioned here include the gospel that accomplishes cleansing (Jn 15.3; 17.7), a baptismal formula (Mt. 28.19; Acts 2.38; 8.16; 19.5), some pre-baptismal words of instruction to the baptizand, or the baptizand's confession of the name of Jesus (Acts 22.16; 1 Pet. 3.21).
[30] Here the normal custom of a friend (παρανυμφίος) giving away the bride (Jn 3.29) is disposed of and Christ presents the bride to himself.
[31] Represented by Lincoln, *Ephesians*; Snodgrass, *Ephesians*; Schnackenburg, *Ephesians*. The opposing perspective is championed by Stott, *Ephesians*; Hoehner, *Ephesians*; Morris, *Expository Reflections*.

is already the fullness of Christ (cf. 4.1-16).[32] The overwhelming majority position, however, is that this eschatological event will occur at the *parousia*. What Paul means by 'radiant church' is further explained in the rest of v. 27. It is said of this radiant church/bride, 'No ugly spots or lines of age disfigure [its] appearance.' It becomes what God purposed it to be – 'holy and blameless' (Eph. 1.4)[33] – purged of 'all disfigurements and deformities'.[34]

At pains that no one should miss the point, Paul reprises in v. 28 the analogy he made in vv. 25-27, namely, that Christ's love for the church is both model and motivation for husbands' love for their wives. But, probably with Gen. 2.24 in mind, now he adds that because of the uniquely intimate relationship they share, when a husband loves his wife he loves his own body. As it is natural for a person to love his or her body, the husband cannot after all hate his wife who is his own flesh;[35] rather, he will feed and cherish[36] her. So Christ all the more acts toward the church (v. 29) of which each Christian is a member (v. 30).

Verse 31 is clearly a quotation from Gen. 2.24. Appearing also in Mt. 19.5 and Mk 10.7-8, it sets forth God's plan for marriage and the exclusive one-flesh union,[37] which constitutes an arrangement in which the husband 'leaves behind' his parents and 'cleaves to' (κολλάω means to glue/cement together) his wife. The parent-child relationship for all its closeness and distinctiveness is surpassed by that of the husband and wife. Paul sees far more than the literal in the one-flesh union of husband and wife. Marriage is but a human illustration drawn from the loving spiritual and paradigmatic relationship between Christ and the church – a relationship Paul calls 'a profound mystery'[38] (v. 32). Prefigured in Adam and Eve (Gen. 2.24) and exemplified in God's relationship with his covenant people, Israel (Isa. 54.5-8; Jer. 2.1-3), marriage

---

[32] Lincoln, *Ephesians*, p. 377.

[33] Wood, *Ephesians*, p. 77.

[34] C.L. Mitton, *Ephesians* (New Century Bible; Greenwood: Attic Press, 1976), p. 204.

[35] It is obvious that 'body' (σῶμα, v. 28a) and 'flesh' (σάρξ, v. 29a) are used interchangeably, the latter anticipating the quotation in v. 31.

[36] Paul culls the words 'feed' and 'cherish' from nursery language infused with affection, the former meaning to rear from childhood or to nourish/feed (ἐκτρέφω) and the latter to heat or nurse/care for.

[37] Sexual union is here intimated in this becoming 'one flesh' (cf. 1 Cor. 6.16). Paradoxically, rabbinical *halakhah* understands Gen. 2.24 as providing the proviso for divorce.

[38] A careful examination of the context and Paul's use of 'mystery' in Ephesians (divinely revealed truth) eliminates the idea that it refers to human marriage relationship. A part of the mystery certainly is that God's intention from the very inception of this institution was to portray the profound and loving relationship between Christ and the church.

is a miniature reflection of Christ's deep love for the church, a picture that both testifies to what is meant by two becoming one and is a demonstration of the mystery of the gospel.

At v. 33 Paul wraps up the hortatory section with two concluding appeals that briefly restate the duties and responsibilities of husbands and wives and the need that they clearly understand the implications the relationship of Christ and the church has for their marriage. Beginning with a collective admonition to husbands, he switches to an individual appeal: 'let each one of you so love his wife as himself' (more literally translated) – an echo of the second great commandment (Lev. 19.8) – making the exhortation direct and personal. The wife is also addressed individually, and her responsibility is to respect or fear her husband. Some scholars believe the construction 'that she fears/respects' (ἵνα φοβῆται) implies that such esteem comes as a direct result of the husband loving her, but it is more probably a command[39] to do so inspired by the fear of Christ (v. 21).

c. Parents and Children (6.1-4)

Paul's instructions of reciprocal duties between wives and husbands (5.22-33) are now followed by similar exhortations to parents and children (6.1-4) and slaves to masters (6.5-9), completing the list of ethical behaviors which characterize the lives of believers who live wisely in properly discerning God's will and are filled with the Spirit (5.15-18). The list of ethical duties in 6.1-9 finds a close parallel in Col. 3.20–4:1, and maintains Paul's pattern of first addressing the subordinate group: children, obey (6.1); slaves, obey (6.5).

In addressing the family, Paul first speaks to the children (v. 4). While the term 'children' may refer to growing children, it probably encompasses the broader adult filial relation.[40] In the ancient world, children of all ages owed their parents, especially fathers, respect and honor[41] (see Exod. 20.12; Deut. 15.16). The unlimited obedience Paul demands of children in Col. 3.20 – 'in everything' (κατὰ πάντα) – is certainly expected here, though he omits such a qualification. Aptly stated, 'obedience is the duty; honour is the disposition of which the

---

[39] Four such uses of the Greek construction occur in the NT (Mk 5.23; 2 Cor. 8.7; Gal. 2.10; Eph. 5.33).

[40] Peter O'Brien, *Ephesians*, p. 440.

[41] In addition to honor, love for parents, caring for their needs in old age, burying them, and esteeming them after death were at the heart of ancient Roman *pietas* – love for family and country. The Mosaic law prescribes death for any child who strikes or curses a parent (Exod. 21.15, 17). See Lincoln, *Ephesians*, pp. 398-402 for a thorough discussion of the authority of parents, especially fathers, over their children in the ancient world. Caring for aging parents was the duty of adult children who had left home (Lincoln, *Ephesians*, p. 405).

obedience is born'.[42] Paul viewed disobedience as a mark of Gentile dissoluteness (Rom. 1.30) and a sign of the end-time (2 Tim. 3.2). Though only fathers are mentioned in 6.4, children, now responsible members of the local assembly, are urged to obey (ὑπακούετε) both parents at all times (present imperative) – a command that carries a similar force and meaning to subjecting oneself (ὑποτάσσω), used of Sarah's attitude toward her husband Abraham (1 Pet. 3.5).[43] Such obedience is done 'in the Lord'[44] (6.1), i.e. as an expression of one's submission to Christ and part of Christian discipleship,[45] and 'is right' (δίκαιος) – which may allude to the justness of God's commandment,[46] or more probably to the appropriateness of such obedience.[47] Paul adds in Col. 3.20 that such deference 'pleases the Lord'. In Jewish religion and culture, 'children's attitude to their parents was often set alongside and seen as part of their relationship to God'.[48]

Paul conscripts the LXX's version of the fifth commandment in Exod. 20.12[49] in support of his injunction to children to obey their parents (vv. 2-3), and adds 'which is the first commandment with a promise' attached to it[50] (v. 2). In what sense can this commandment be deemed the first when the second commandment in vv. 4-6 also seems to include one – that of God's enduring love for those who love him? Some interpreters suggest that it is the first commandment in the purported second table dealing with relationships. The commandments were, however, divided into two groups of five. Others understand it to mean the first commandment to be learned by children, but the text does not say so; it says it is the first with a promise. Equally unconvincing is the argument that 'first' means primacy of importance rather than numerical sequence. To view it as the first promise in the Decalogue,

---

[42] S.D.F. Salmond, *The Epistle to the Ephesians* (The Expositor's Greek Testament; Grand Rapids: Eerdmans, n.d.), p. 375.

[43] The two terms are used interchangeably in 1 Pet. 3.5-6 of Sarah's attitude toward her husband.

[44] Though 'in the Lord' is missing from several Alexandrian and Western manuscripts, their inclusion in most translations rests upon compelling arguments.

[45] While the prepositional phrase 'in the Lord' speaks of incorporation into Christ (2.21; 4.1; 4.17; 5.8), obedience to Christian parents alone can hardly be the intent here.

[46] John Calvin, *Ephesians* (Calvin's Commentaries; trans. Parker; Edinburgh: Oliver & Boyd, 1965), p. 212; J. Robinson, *Ephesians*, p. 127. The word conveys the idea of 'fairness'/'propriety' in Mt. 20.4; Lk. 12.57; Phil. 4.8.

[47] T. Moritz believes the two ideas of social propriety and legal mandate must be kept together. *A Profound Mystery*, p. 171.

[48] Lincoln, *Ephesians*, p. 402.

[49] The reading of Eph. 6.2, 3 is closer to the LXX version of Exod. 20.12 than to Deut. 5.16.

[50] Of the seven instances that this commandment appears in the NT (Mt. 15.4; 19.19; Mk 7.10; 10.19; Lk. 18.20; Eph. 6.2, 3) only in the Pauline text is the attached promise also quoted.

which functions as an introductory summary of the whole law, has high currency among scholars. It may, however, simply mean that it is the first commandment with a promise attached to it.[51]

The Promised Land referred to in Exod. 20.12 represents God's promised gift to ancient Israel. In applying the promise to believers, Paul maintains the ideas of prosperity and longevity but replaces 'so that you may live long in the land' with 'on the earth', and generalizes and universalizes the promise to all children who esteem their parents. Evenhanded exegesis in applying Paul's words will avoid three interpretive extremes: spiritualizing the promise and equating 'long life' with immortality; adopting a rigid application that ignores the harsh contradictory realities of life; and interpreting it in view of some idealized community where children care for their aging parents. Paul does not here lay down a law, but states a principle. The promise is 'a revelation of a general purpose of God, and makes known what will be the usual course of his providence'.[52] As a general rule, children who are obedient are prosperous and happy. The general promise is, however, individually realized in so far as it redounds to God's glory and the good of individuals.[53]

In 6.4 Paul turns to the responsibility of parents to their children. The change from 'parents' (6.1) to 'fathers' (6.4) may be significant and strategic. Although fathers can denote parents (see Heb. 11. 23), the use of both in such close proximity argues against that possibility. In a society where fathers wielded unlimited and absolute power over their children, and were responsible for their education, Paul's summons to a Christian exercise of paternal influence is revolutionary.

Negatively, Paul exhorts fathers not to 'provoke' or 'exasperate' (παροργίζετε) their children, i.e. not to bring them to deep-seated anger. Not only would this have negative consequences on the Christian community, but treating children unfairly and harshly and placing unreasonable demands and unwarranted restrictions on them could breed discouragement (Col. 3.21), goad them into resentment and rebellion, and deaden their affections toward their parents and, ultimately, God. Positively, fathers must 'bring them up in the training and instruction of the Lord.' The term 'bring up' (ἐκτρέφετε), employed in 5.29 of Christ's nourishing the church, is often used of the bringing up of children to maturity, providing for their physical and

---

[51] Noting that the quotation is taken from Deut. 5.16 rather than Exod. 20.12, Bruce adds that the promise accompanying this commandment is 'the promise of prosperity and long life; no such promise is attached to any of the four preceding commandments'. See *Ephesians*, p. 398.

[52] Hodge, *A Commentary on the Epistle to the Ephesians* (Thornapple Commentaries; Grand Rapids: Baker, 1980), p. 359.

[53] Hodge, *Epistle to the Ephesians*, p. 359.

emotional needs. Such care is given through training (παιδεία) and instruction (νουθεσία).

'Training' (παιδεία) sometimes denotes education or guidance in a comprehensive way (see Acts 7.22; 22.3; 2 Tim. 3.16) or in the restricted sense of discipline or correction (1 Cor. 11.32; 2 Cor. 6.9; Heb. 12.5, 7, 8, 11), which better serves this context (see Prov. 3.11). The distinction between training and instruction fuels much scholarly debate. Some interpreters see a clear distinction, advocating that the former refers to training by disciplinary action and the latter verbal instruction.[54] Others believe they are interchangeable, conjointly working to inculcate 'patterns of behaviour worthy of a Christian and also verbal instruction about the contents of the faith'.[55] This training and instruction is neither teacher-centered as in Greek pedagogy nor law-centered as in rabbinic teaching; it is, rather, Christ-centered and sallies from him and is to be exercised in a Christian way and following the example of Christ (2 Cor. 10.1).

d. Slaves and Masters (6.5-9)

The relationship between slaves and masters constitutes the third pairing in the household code which is intended to display wise and Spirit-filled living and exemplify mutual submission within the family of God (5.15-18, 21). Colossians 3.22–4.1 includes similar household rules and admonitions; the household tables in 1 Pet. 2.18–3.7 have no correlative exhortations to masters (cf. 1 Tim. 6.1-2; Tit. 2.9-10). The prevalence of these passages in the New Testament bears eloquent testimony to the impact of the gospel on an inhumane institution that held at least one-third of the population of the Greco-Roman world in its iron grip.

Greco-Roman civilization was fashioned on and fueled by the sweat and blood of slaves. Evil though the system may seem to the modern reader, the institution of slavery was an accepted fact and indispensable for the economic and social life of society.[56] No ancient government sought to abolish it, and though the Stoics, represented by Seneca,[57]

---

[54] F. Foulkes, *The Epistle of Paul to the Ephesians* (Grand Rapids: Eerdmans, 1963), p. 166; Richard C. Trench, *Synonyms of the New Testament* (Grand Rapids: Eerdmans, 1958), p. 113; Stott, *The Message of Ephesians*, p. 248.

[55] C.L. Mitton, *Ephesians* (New Century Bible; Greenwood: Attic Press, 1976), p. 213.

[56] For extensive discussions on slavery, see W.L. Westermann, *The Slave Systems of Greek and Roman Antiquity* (Philadelphia: American Philosophical Society, 1964); T. Wiedemann, *Greek and Roman Slavery* (London: Croon Helm, 1981); S.S. Bartchy, ΜΑΛΛΟΝ ΧΡΗΣΑΙ: *First-Century Slavery and the Interpretation of 1 Corinthians 7:21* (Missoula, MT: Scholars, 1973).

[57] Seneca, *Epistulae Morales* 47 (cf. Epictetus *Dissertationes* 4).

took a philosophical stand against it, nothing was done practically to change it, let alone bring it to an end. Paul's aim in Ephesians, as elsewhere, is neither to embrace the prevailing establishment nor to offer a social critique of it. He seeks rather to address from the Christian perspective the glaring antinomy between the freedom Christian slaves enjoyed in Christ and the harsh reality of slavery under earthly masters. This he does by appealing to slaves to obey their 'earthly' (literally 'fleshly', κατὰ σάρκα) masters and perform their duties with diligence out of allegiance to Christ (vv. 5-7) and in view of the coming eschatological judgment and its rewards (v. 8). He reminds Christian masters that they should treat their slaves fairly and kindly because both slave and master are equally accountable to a higher and impartial Master in heaven (v. 9).

Paul's direct appeal to slaves (v. 5) is revolutionary, unprecedented, and ennobling – treating persons who were regarded as nothing more than 'living tools'[58] and chattels as 'ethically responsible persons who are as fully members of the Christian community as their masters'.[59] The service slaves render must be done with respect (φόβος),[60] timidity (τρόμος),[61] sincerity, i.e. without duplicity (ἁπλότης, singleness, simplicity), and wholehearted zeal (v. 7). The reason for such service is both Christological and eschatological: slaves should carry out their obligations enthusiastically, not merely because it is expected and demanded by their earthly masters but because it is rendered to Christ (v. 7; see also Col. 3.17), who cannot be deceived and will duly reward each one at the final judgment (v. 8; see also Col. 3.24-25; Rom. 2.6-10; Mt. 16.27).

Consonant with the pattern in the *Haustafel*, after speaking to the subordinate group, Paul turns to addressing the group in authority (v. 9). In what might be viewed as a radical and outrageous idea, Paul reminds slave-owners of their responsibility to their slaves, dismissing any 'privileged superiority'[62] to which they may lay claim and submitting them to the Golden Rule: they are to treat their slaves the way they expect to be treated (literally, 'do the same things to them'), i.e.

---

[58] Aristotle, *Ethica Nicomachea* 5.6.8, 1134b.

[59] Lincoln, *Ephesians*, p. 424.

[60] Though the verb form of this word is used in 5.33 to describe the respect a wife must give her husband, the noun used here is better rendered 'dread' since this was the way masters controlled their slaves.

[61] The term literally means 'trembling,' 'quivering,' or 'shaking,' and with *phobos* graphically describes the manner slaves generally related to their masters who believed that controlling slaves this way resulted in greater loyalty. See K.R. Bradley, *Slaves and Masters in the Roman Empire: A Study in Social Control* (Oxford: University Press, 1987), pp. 113-37.

[62] Stott, *Ephesians*, p. 254.

'with Christian consideration,'[63] because[64] they both serve and are accountable to the same Master in heaven who does not give preferential treatment (προσωπολημψία, literally, 'raising the face' – partiality). Browbeating and intimidating slaves with warning of dire reprisals in an attempt to coerce loyalty and diligent service, then, should not occur. All threat of violence (ἀπειλή, v. 9) against them to compel compliance must cease.

Reflection and Response (Part 6)

Reflection

Paul, it would appear, has made a quantum leap from the broad and wide-ranging admonitions on ethical life and corporate worship to narrow and specific directives concerning household relationships. Continuity remains, however, Paul consistently interpreting the household rules in light of the new humanity, and now placing how the Christian family relates at home within the broader sweep of Spirit-filled living. The theme of submission runs through 5.21–6.9, v. 21 with its call to mutual submission 'out of reverence for Christ' serving as its pivot and fulcrum around which all the subsequent relationships revolve. On the one hand, those who are exhorted to submit/obey are told to deem that humble act as part of their loyal and loving service to Christ. On the other hand, the ones to whom submission/obedience is given do not possess the authority of Christ. Patterning themselves after Christ, husbands are admonished to use their authority for the profit of their wives; fathers are instructed to use their positions of authority lovingly for the good of their children; and masters are charged to get rid of the threat of violence against their slaves.

The reflection that follows centers upon the prominent theme of submission in 5.21–6.9. The questions below are aimed at extending and deepening reflection on the topic. Paul launches into his discussion of submission in the household with a general exhortation to the submission of each believer to the other. How is this being done in the churches? What forms does it take? In a general way, what is the nature of the relationships among Christians you know? How seriously do marital relationships, parent–children relationships, and employer–employee relationships among believers you know reflect the ideal of

---

[63] Bruce, *Ephesians*, p. 401.

[64] In both v. 8 and v. 9 Paul uses the perfect participle εἰδότες to indicate the reason both slaves and slave masters must behave toward one another in an appropriate manner. Slaves must work wholeheartedly 'because they know' they will be rewarded by the Lord (v. 8), and masters must treat their slaves with goodwill because they, like their slaves, are subject to an impartial Lord who is their Master (who will also reward them).

reciprocal submission Paul presents in the text? What similarities and/or differences have you observed among such relationships and the authoritarian ones Paul addresses? How extensive are the similarities and differences? What are the signs that indicate similarity? What are the signs that indicate difference? How are the churches you know trying to assist their members to exemplify Paul's admonition of mutual submission? Are there ways in which submission may be expressed in our culture that does not carry the baggage of the first-century Greco-Roman culture?

The reflection would be inadequate without making it personal to you. It is to facilitate personal reflection that the following questions are asked. How do you understand Paul's injunction that Christians ought to submit to each other? What forms would you expect such submission to take when done to you? How do you apply this practically in your life toward others? How do you deal with fellow Christians and structures that are authoritarian?

Response

What kind of personal response should be given to such critical questions raised earlier in the reflection?

1. Reflect on your own understanding of what is entailed in submission, noting whether your home and church tended to embrace the more traditional authoritarian model or the Pauline one.

2. Make a list of influences that model of submission has had on your life and relationships and what you would change.

3. Get into a discussion group or Bible study where serious and deep thought is given to the implications and implementation of Paul's admonition in the passage.

4. Prayerfully ask God to help you to cultivate a submissive spirit and to show you how and when to submit to others.

Ephesians 6.10-24

F. The Church: A Community at War (6.10-20)

This final section both concludes Paul's admonitory material begun in 4.1 and brings the letter to an end. In it Paul uses military word pictures and makes a parting appeal to the Ephesian believers to appropriate God's mighty power (6.10), fully arm and protect themselves, and stand firm in a present and ongoing cosmic spiritual battle against an array of cunning, cruel, and superhuman forces (6.11-19). The primacy of prayer in this conflict is indicated in v. 18. Far from being a parenthesis, the passage brings to a steady crescendo Paul's plan for the Epistle.[1] There is no evidence to support the theory that the intent of Eph. 6.10-20 is simply to 'arouse the audience's emotions'.[2] Paradoxically, the terrible conflict described in 6.10-20 almost seems anticlimactic in light of the triumphant note that resounds throughout chs. 1–3.

In enjoining the Ephesian readers to implement the doctrines he set forth in chs. 1–3, five times Paul summons them to a distinctive Christian lifestyle with the verb περιπατέω – 'walk' or 'live' – (4.1, 17; 5.2, 8, 15). Paul's final command – 'to walk wisely' (5.15) – is closely followed by the concluding practical directive of the Epistle which illustrates wise and Spirit-filled living (5.21–6.9). In 6.10-20, Paul drafts into service imagery of military warfare to recapitulate and reinforce earlier admonitions, to provoke a sense of urgency and intensity as he appeals to his readers to take a firm and courageous stand against spiritual wickedness. Attempts to connect this pericope with baptism,[3] notwithstanding its presence in Ignatius's letter to Polycarp in this respect,[4] have been unconvincing. The most that can be concluded is that the final exhortation is erected upon 'traditional imagery of the Christian warrior and early catechetical material on steadfastness and watchfulness in the Christian life'.[5]

A rousing summons to arms, the section is divided into three parts: (a) Verses 10-11 encourage believers to be strong. Such strength for the

---

[1] Gordon Fee, *God's Empowering Presence*, p. 723.

[2] Lincoln, *Ephesians*, p. 432. *Peroratio* and *epilogos* are equivalent terms that denote a rhetorical technique to bring a speech or writing to an effective close by making a strong emotional appeal for action based upon the facts presented.

[3] E.g. P. Carrington, *The Primitive Christian Catechism* (Cambridge: Cambridge University Press, 1940), pp. 31-57.

[4] 'Let your baptism be your arms; your faith, your helmet; your love, your spear; your endurance, your armor', says Ignatius (6.2).

[5] Arthur G. Patzia, *Ephesians, Colossians, Philemon*, p. 284.

conflict comes from the Lord and the protection his armor provides. (b) Verse 12 reveals the source of the conflict and the reason why the Lord's power and protection are necessary: to repel powerful evil spiritual and cosmic forces under Satan's leadership. (c) The strategy for conquest is indicated in vv. 13-20, where Paul twice exhorts the reader to 'stand your ground' (v. 13) and 'stand firm' (v. 14). This is achieved by appropriating the divine resources for battle, which include a life of moral integrity, dependence on God's word, and Spirit-inspired prayers.

1. Strength for the conflict (6.10-11)

With 'finally' (v. 10) Paul transitions from the household table to the last in his series of exhortations which brings the Epistle to a close.[6] Although the first imperative, ἐνδυναμοῦσθε, could be taken as middle voice, 'strengthen yourselves',[7] it is best understood as a passive, 'be strong',[8] or more literally, 'be strengthened' (as in Acts 9.22; Rom. 4.10; 2 Tim. 2.1) and recalls God's command to Joshua (Josh. 1.6, 7, 9) and Paul's to the Corinthians (1 Cor. 16.13) and to Timothy (2 Tim. 2.1). The victory, though secure, must be won through conflict against mighty supernatural and stygian forces. Christians are engaged in a spiritual battle of titanic proportions and face a formidable enemy who seeks their eternal destruction. To overcome this foe they need greater resources than any human person can muster. Thankfully, all the Christian warrior needs to achieve final triumph is 'in the Lord' and in 'his mighty power' – literally, 'the power of his might' (v. 10) – a power that raised Christ from the dead (Eph. 1.19-20), brought believers to life (2.1), is available to the children of God, and for which Paul prayed they would appropriate (3.16). Our ability to fight successfully the evil supernatural spiritual forces arrayed against us lies in our being strengthened by God's power.

---

[6] 'Finally' renders τοῦ λοιποῦ here and its substitute τὸ λοιπόν, both of which sometimes have a temporal force – 'from now on, in the future' (Gal. 6.17; 1 Cor. 7.29; Heb. 10.13). Although their struggle will become more intense in the future, the Ephesians need strength for a battle in which they are presently engaged, hence necessitating the adoption of the preferred contextual translation of 'finally'. Thielman argues against the traditional rendition 'finally', urging that τοῦ λοιποῦ means 'from now on', 'in the time that remains'. He adopts the natural 'natural reading' of the term, believing it serves as an 'introduction to an admonition that outlines what Paul wants his readers to do' from this point forward. It is a reveille rousing the believers to leave discouragement or encumbering elements of their past lives behind and from now on 'actively resist the onslaught of the devil and his minions with the gifts of "armor" that God has given his people' (*Ephesians*, p. 417).

[7] F.F. Bruce, *Ephesians*, p. 403, adopts this translation and finds support for its use in David's life (1 Sam. 30.6).

[8] So most translations. The present tense indicates an ongoing or continual state.

In v. 11a, which explains how the earlier entreaty, 'Be strong in the Lord' (v. 10), is to be fulfilled, with a directive similar to that in 1 Thess. 5.8, Paul appeals to his readers to 'put on the full armor of God' (literally, be clothed in – ἐνδύσασθε), and quickly explains why: 'so that you can take your stand against the devil's schemes' (v. 11b), and because of our struggle against an array of formidable superhuman forces (v. 12). The spiritual armor[9] (πανοπλία) Christian soldiers are urged to put on is provided by God[10] and is patterned on what he himself wears as he wages war in order to vindicate his people (Isa. 11.5; 52.7; 59.17).[11] Roman soldiers were omnipresent in the world in which Paul lived. Meticulously armored and assiduously disciplined, they proved to be an almost indomitable force, affording the supreme model for the Christian soldier. Military weaponry recruited and applied as metaphors in the Christian's life and spiritual struggle against diabolical forces are common in the NT (Rom. 13.1-12; 2 Cor. 6.7; 10.4; 1 Thess. 5.8).

A fully armed Roman foot soldier or hoplite was clad from head to foot with all the necessary accoutrements for defensive or offensive warfare. Paul's listing of instruments in the panoply is not intended to be exhaustive,[12] but to show how important it is for Christians to be protected and how serious is the danger they face in this spiritual conflict.[13] Underestimating these malevolent powers comes at a very high price, for they are powerful, wicked, and cunning,[14] but they are not invincible.

The object of putting on the divine armor is so that the readers might be able to 'stand against the devil's schemes'. A key term in the section, 'stand' occurs four times in three verses (11, 13, 14). The first meaning is to defend at all costs or to hold on to one's position. The obdurate hostility of the enemy, who is a master strategist and inventor

---

[9] The Gk πανοπλία designates the full or total armor of an infantryman.

[10] The genitive 'of God' that describes the armor to be put on is one of source or origin – it comes from and is provided by God. If taken as a possessive genitive it means the armament God himself wears (cf. Isa. 59.17), and would speak of divine traits believers should emulate (5.1).

[11] While Roman soldiers were universal in the Greco-Roman world with which Paul was very familiar, scriptural depictions of God as warrior and not the Roman soldier was likely the source of Paul's battle and military imagery. The presence of similar imagery in Qumran and Stoic literature and the mystery cults is discussed by Lincoln in *Ephesians*, pp. 437-38.

[12] Polybius mentions, in addition, two javelins and greaves (6.23.2).

[13] O'Brien, *Ephesians*, p. 462; Lincoln, *Ephesians*, p. 442.

[14] Stott, *Ephesians*, pp. 263-64.

of deceptive schemes[15] (μεθοδείας; cf. 4.14), is intimated in the use of
the fourfold 'against' in v. 12.[16] Followers of Christ need not be intimi-
dated by the evil one, for Paul says, 'The weapons we fight with are
not the weapons of the world. On the contrary, they have divine power to demolish strongholds' (2 Cor. 10.4). The decisive victory having
been won by Christ, believers are not called upon to win, but to stand,
i.e. 'to preserve and maintain what has been won'.[17]

2. Source of the conflict (6.12)

Verse 12 describes the source of the conflict and the nature of the enemy.[18] Powerful, spiritual cosmic powers – not puny and frail human
beings (literally, blood and flesh; cf. Heb. 2.14) – are the cause of the
present struggle (hence the need to don the entire armor of God; cf. 2
Cor. 10.4), which Paul calls a *palē* (πάλη). Nothing but the totality of
the divine armament can protect the believer and defeat the hordes of
demonic spiritual intelligences.

Common in the world of sports in the first century but found only
here in the Scripture, the term *palē* was used of wrestling, a popular
event in western Asia Minor and Greece. Its choice over other synonyms[19] may hold special significance, wrestling depicting close-quarter
tussle. Hand–to–hand combat may be in view, though the athletic imagery could be transposed to military settings or to struggle in general.[20]

Paul states negatively whom the Christian combat is not against:
'flesh and blood' (αἷμα καὶ σάρκα, literally, 'blood and flesh').
Whether appearing in this more common form 'flesh and blood' (σάρξ
καὶ αἷμα), or the less frequent 'blood and flesh' (αἷμα καὶ σάρξ), the

---

[15] Paul earlier used μεθοδείας to describe persons who tried to weaken the unity of the
church. It can simply refer to 'technique' or 'tactic', but 'schemes', 'wiles', or 'stratagems'
best translates the word in this context.

[16] Wood, *Ephesians*, p. 86.

[17] Lincoln, *Ephesians*, p. 443.

[18] Wesley Carr contends that the spiritual characterization portrayed here does not
represent the worldview of the first century CE, and therefore is a second-century Gnostic
interpolation. See his work, *Angels and Principalities* (Cambridge: University Press, 1981),
pp. 104-10 and Clinton Arnold's scorching critique in 'The "Exorcism" of Ephesians
6:12 in Recent Research: A Critique of Wesley Carr's View of the Role of Evil Powers
in First-Century AD Belief', *JSNT* 30 (June 1987), pp. 71-87. Not only is it consistent
with, pagan, Jewish, and NT thought of the first century, there is no manuscript support
for its omission.

[19] Other more common terms Paul uses to describe struggle, warfare and general conflict are ἀγών (Phil. 1.30; Col. 2.1), μάχη (2 Cor. 7.5; 2 Tim. 2.23; Tit. 3.9), and
στρατεία (2 Cor. 10.4; 1 Tim. 1.18).

[20] Euripides *Heraclidae* 159; Heinrich Greeven, "πάλη", *TDNT* V (1968), p. 721. Michael Gudorf's claim that the fully clad soldier was a seasoned wrestler is unsubstantiated.
'The Use of πάλη in Ephesians 6:12', *JBL* 117 (Summer 1998), pp. 332-34.

meaning is the same and speaks of feeble humanity or humankind in frailty, weakness, and dependence. If the enemy were flesh and blood he could be engaged with human resources. But he is spiritual, super-natural, and sinister. Four terms, all in themselves morally neutral but here in 6.12 conveying a sinister and inimical character, are employed to designate the hierarchy of invisible and insidious spiritual powers against which Christians wage an ongoing and relentless war: 'rulers' (ἀρχαί), 'authorities' (ἐξουσίαι), 'powers' (κοσμοκράτορες), and 'spiritu-al forces of evil' (τὰ πνευματικὰ τῆς πονηρίας). Though the language intones Jewish apocalyptic thought, it seems unlikely that Paul has in mind a stratified order of four classes of demonic forces. Each term describes the same reality in a distinctive way. In fact, Paul uses various combinations of terms in his lists of spiritual powers (e.g. Eph. 1.21; 6.12; Col. 1.16). It is important to note that they do not act autono-mously; nor are their objectives and strategies for destroying believers any different from those of the devil.[21]

'Rulers', also translated 'cosmic powers' (NEB), 'principalities' (NKJV), or 'cosmic or celestial potentates' (Matthew Black) refers to their primacy of rank (leaders) and the power they wield. 'Authorities' signifies their enduement with freedom to act.[22] Paul indicated earlier that Christ presently exercises lordship over these rulers and authorities (1.21) and that through the church God's manifold wisdom would be revealed to them (3.10). In Col. 2.15 Paul says that Christ has con-quered, disarmed, and disgraced them. 'Powers' (of this dark world) is better translated 'cosmocrats', 'world-rulers' or 'cosmic potentates'[23] (cf. 1 Cor. 2.6, 8). A designation found only here in the NT, it depicts their control over a world in rebellion against God (2 Cor. 4.4). It was used of Roman emperors, pagan monarchs, the planets which were believed to control the destiny of humankind, mythic and magical deities, and evil spirits that ostensibly ruled the world.[24]

'Spiritual forces of evil' ('spiritual hosts of wickedness', ASV) pictures an organized supernatural and cosmic army that forms a united front. Fundamentally characterized by evil, it is on a nefarious mission in its rule of 'this dark world'. The opposite of light in which God dwells (1

[21] O' Brien, *Ephesians*, p. 468.
[22] Hoehner, *Ephesians*, p. 826.
[23] Hoehner states that the title was not used before the NT period. 'World-rulers of the darkness' – the identical terminology found in 6.12 – appears in the 2nd-century Jewish work *Testament of Solomon* 8.2; 18.2, and may have been borrowed from Paul. Salmond remarks that it was used in the Orphic Hymns (III, 3, of Satan), in inscriptions with reference to the emperor, in Gnostic writings of the devil, and in rabbinic literature of the angel of death (*Ephesians*, p. 383).
[24] Leon Morris, *Expository Reflections*, p. 203; Stott, *Ephesians*, p. 264; O'Brien, *Ephe-sians*, p. 467; Hoehner, *Ephesians*, p. 827.

Jn 1.4), dark is an ethical concept that characterizes all that is evil and a
dominion from which God has rescued the saints (5.8, 16; Col. 1.13).
'This dark world' (τοῦ σκότους τούτου, literally 'this darkness') limits
the dominion and theater of operation of these spiritual hosts to this
sphere of spiritual darkness. Described here are diabolical powers and a
world system alienated from God and opposed to everything he stands
for. To interpret these powers in terms of social, economic, institution-
al, legal, natural, cultural, or political forces which believers struggle
against is to import into the text a theological inventiveness and historical anachronism alien to Paul's intention.[25] While it must be acknowledged that Satan may exploit these agencies to accomplish his fiendish
ends, all three references of Paul to rulers and authorities in Ephesians
are qualified by 'in the heavenly realms' (1.20-21; 3.10; 6.12), which
calls into question any interpretation that discounts its governing significance. The only adequate conclusion that does justice to the NT characterization of these evil agencies is that they are supernatural, personal
and demonic.

The locale of these malign superterrestrial spirits is 'the heavenly
realms', a phrase that appears five times in the NT and only in Ephesians (1.3, 20; 2.6; 3.10; 6.12), and refers to the supermundane spiritual
realm of conquest and conflict. On the one hand, 'the heavenly realms'
are the abode of the risen and victorious Lord (1.20-21) and of believers who are in him (2.6). On the other hand, it is the locale of minions
of hostile supernatural powers (3.10; 6.12). Some interpreters regard
this spiritual realm as having 'a succession of levels, with the throne of
God on the highest of these and the hostile forces occupying the lowest'.[26] The lowest level may be identical to 'the kingdom of the air'
presently governed by the spirit now at work in the disobedient (2:2).
Whatever else it may be perceived to be, it is certainly 'the sphere of
invisible reality'.[27] It is the domain where the resurrected Christ sits
exalted and enthroned (1.20-21), where believers are made beneficiar-
ies of his spiritual blessings (1.3), and are seated with him (2.6).

From this scene of triumph, the language changes to one of conflict.
In 3.10 Paul says that to these scrutinizing spiritual powers in the heavenly realms God's manifold wisdom is being revealed through the
church on earth. And God's people are locked in a deadly war with
these forces in the heavenly realms – which suggests that this combat is
not taking place in heaven. Since believers live in this evil age (5.16)

---

[25] Ernest Gordon Rupp, *Principalities and Powers: Studies in the Christian conflict in history*
(London: Epworth, 1952), p. 83; Markus Barth, *The Broken Wall: A Study of the Epistle to
the Ephesians* (Chicago: Judson Press, 1959), pp. 82-3.

[26] Bruce, *Ephesians*, p. 406.

[27] Stott, *Ephesians*, p. 264.

and in the heavenly realms (2.6), the battle is being fought on earth and in the heavenly realms to which Satan's authority extends (2 Cor. 4.4). While God's people share the victory of Christ over all evil powers, in reality that victory is only partial. The current struggle with the devil and his minions will culminate at the second coming of Christ (Eph. 1.10, 21; cf. 1 Cor. 15.24-28).

3. Strategy for conquest (6.13-20)

Because of the terrifying cosmic malevolent and superhuman powers arrayed against believers (v. 12), Paul authorizes them to put on the full armor of God so that they can hold their ground against the devil's schemes (v. 11). Verse 13 repeats the command of v. 11 ('Put on the full armor of God')[28] with a different verb (ἀναλάβετε(literally, 'take up'), the reason being that 'you may be able to withstand/resist'[29] (ἀντιστῆναι) and 'to stand' (στῆναι).[30] With the divine panoply on, the Christian warrior is prepared to withstand the onslaught 'when the day of evil comes' (v. 13). A phrase fraught with end-time apocalyptic overtones and occurring three times in the Old Testament (Jer. 17.17, 18; Obad. 13; cf. Dan. 12.1), 'the day of evil'[31] is used in the NT only by Paul and betrays his two-age eschatological motif (see 1.21) – the present age (עולם הזה) and the age to come (עולם הבא). The former is evil and is under the control of Satan and his demonic operatives; the latter is the age of all goodness, the time of salvation when all God's blessings are fully realized in his people.

'The day of evil' is variously understood by interpreters. Some view the phrase as depicting the last vicious, climactic satanic outbreak just prior to the second advent of Christ[32] – during this present period

---

[28] The armor is described as 'full', not because it is complete or exhaustive of all the 'weapons' with which the heavily-armed Roman soldier was equipped (cf. Polybius, *History* 6.24), but the picture portrays preparedness for fierce conflict, no vital part of the soldier left unprotected. The armor is the one that God wears and provides for Christians. Unlike Archilles whose armor, though fashioned by the gods (*Illiad* 18.478-616), betrayed a place of vulnerability, God's armor leaves no vital part of the body unguarded.

[29] In military settings the word means 'to resist' or 'oppose' (BAGD, 67). It maintains a similar connotation in the various contexts in which it is used in the NT (e.g. Mt. 5.39; Lk. 21.15; Acts 6.10; Gal. 2.11; 2 Tim. 3.8; 1 Pet. 5.9).

[30] Paul uses two cognate infinitives in v. 13 to describe the soldier's posture in warfare in the evil day – ἀντιστῆναι, 'to withstand'/'resist' and στῆναι, 'to stand', the first describing the 'ability to withstand when the fight is on'; the latter the 'holding one's position when the conflict is at the end, – neither dislodged nor felled, but *standing* victorious at one's post'. Salmond, *Ephesians*, p. 385.

[31] Gal. 1.4 and Eph. 5.16 refer to 'the present evil age' and 'the days are evil,' respectively, both having a meaning similar to 'the day of evil' (Eph. 6.13).

[32] H. Meyer, *Ephesians and Philemon* (Edinburgh: T. & T. Clark, 1880), p. 331; Caird, *Paul's Letters from Prison*, p. 92. The War Scrolls of Qumran similarly associate the time of

termed in Jewish eschatology 'end times' or 'latter days' (אחרית הימים) when this evil age (עולם הזה) is drawing to an end and the perfect age (עולם הבה) is about to begin. Others explain it as critical times in the lives of believers 'when the devil and his underlings will assault you most vehemently,'[33] 'when things are at their worst' (NEB). Then, it is sometimes taken as a synonym for the entire present age and seen as identical with the cognate expression in 5.16.[34] Contextually, it is clear that Paul is dealing with a present ongoing conflict. His use of the definite article with 'day' further suggests that he has a particularly critical day in mind.[35] Therefore, an interpretation that accommodates the present age with all its daily devilish woes and a time of critical emergency when the battle is fiercest – 'a time of special pressure,'[36] or 'times of heightened and unexpected spiritual battles'[37] – seems to do justice to the term. Because of the present conflict and intensified assault to come, believers can at no time lay the armor down.

Paul's use of the word 'stand' indicates that Christian soldiers are not a marching army invading enemy territory, but are an opposing and repelling force that protects the castle. Securing the results of Christ's victory, not the conquest of new territory, is the believer's task. Unyielding steadfastness in the heat of battle was a hallmark of the Roman centurion. Paul expects nothing less of the Christian soldier engaged in spiritual warfare. His admonition is: 'and after you have done everything, to stand' (ἅπαντα κατεργασάμενοι στῆναι). While the Greek participle translated 'have done' (κατεργασάμενοι) derives from a verb that most commonly means 'to do' or 'to accomplish' (κατεργάζεσ-θαι), on rare occasions the infinitive verb signifies 'to overpower' or 'to overcome'. The imagery here is one of triumph, depicting the victor who has vanquished the foe,[38] and the *Complete Jewish Bible* renders the clause, 'and when the battle is won, you will still be standing'. There is much that argues against this view, however. The rendition

---

the end with battle (1QM 1.10-13), some exegetes then taking 'the day of evil' to mean the final battle of Armageddon (Rev. 16.12-16; 20.7, 8) or some future eschatological denouement (Mk 13; 2 Thess. 2.8-10).

[33] William Hendriksen, *Galatians and Ephesians* (NTC; Grand Rapids: Baker, 1979), p. 273.

[34] Arnold, *Ephesians,* p. 114.

[35] S.D.F. Salmond, *Ephesians* (The Expositor's Greek Testament, 3; London: Hodder and Stroughton, 1903), p. 384; Günther Harder, *TDNT* VI (1968), p.554.

[36] Bruce, *Ephesians*, p. 275.

[37] Hoehner, *Ephesians*, p. 834.

[38] Meyer, *Ephesians* and *Philemon* , pp. 331-32. See also T.Y. Neufeld, *Put On the Armour of God: The Divine Warrior from Isaiah to Ephesians* (Sheffield, UK: Sheffield Academic Press, 1997), pp.128-31. The notion of the soldier left standing after final triumph is challenged by Thielman who maintains that the soldier fully prepared for battle has contextual support (*Ephesians*, p. 423).

'to accomplish' or 'to achieve' is consistent with the twenty-one uses in the NT, and aptly fits the context. Further, no soldier would be charged to get fully equipped after a telling victory, as Paul is here doing to believers. To the contrary, believers are able to stand only with the help of the spiritual equipment afforded them (vv. 14-17). Finally, the command to stand in v. 14 is puzzling if victory is already secured. The stance of the soldier here depicted is best understood as confronting the attacking enemy rather having conquered them.[39] It is possible to combine both perspectives, viewing 'the spiritual warrior who has kept his position victorious and stood above his conquered foe in one "evil day"' but is now exhorted to take a stand 'again ready to face another such critical day, should it come'.[40] Having made all essential preparations by putting on God's armor, Christians are expected to make a firm defensive stand against the assaults of the evil powers who seek to rob them of the victory already won by Christ.

To endure Satan's dastardly and deadly tactics and assaults, both the individual Christian and the church need to procure total resources God has placed at their disposal. Victory depends on doing it. Human resources are vastly inadequate for the challenge we face.

In vv. 14-18 Paul details six pieces of the armor,[41] each piece corresponding to some divine virtue, demonstrating by them what it means to put on the full armor of God and to be fully prepared for battle. With four participles (ASV) – 'having girded' (v. 14), 'having put on' (v. 14), 'having shod' (v. 15), 'having taken up' (v. 16) – each modifying the imperative 'stand', he explains the antecedent actions to have been taken if the believer is to stand victorious at the end of the fray. Not the literal pieces of armament but the spiritual truth each illustrates is Paul's aim in putting them into service.

The *'belt of truth'* is the first piece of the defensive armor presented. According to Tacitus, as a sign of readiness the Roman soldier on parade (*miles accinctus*) had his belt (*cingulum*) securely fastened in place.[42] However, this belt is more probably the leather apron or girdle worn under the armor like breeches to protect the thighs (*cingulum militare* or *balteus*), gather the tunic together, and hold the sword securely, rather than the metal-studded protective belt worn over the armor or the sword-belt.[43] An imagery commonplace in Oriental culture, it depicts both readiness and freedom for action.

[39] Cf. Twentieth Century New Testament, 'having fought to the end.'

[40] Salmond, *Ephesians,* p. 385.

[41] Wis 5.18-22 contains similar pieces of armory, but the spiritual signification of some is sometimes different.

[42] *Annals* 11.18.

[43] Lincoln, *Ephesians,* p. 447; Hoehner, *Ephesians,* p. 839; see also A. Oepke, 'ζω,νη', *TDNT* V, pp. 303, 307; Stott, *Ephesians,* p. 277. Étan Levine argues that references to

The notion of securely girding one's clothes reflects a culture in which long, loose-fitting garments were worn. To facilitate quick, unimpeded action or vigorous activity, clothes were tied securely around the waist (Lk. 12.35, 37; 17.8). In exhorting the suffering believers in Asia Minor to correct and clear thinking, Peter makes an appeal similar to Paul's in Eph. 6.14. 'Therefore gird up the loins of your mind' (1 Pet. 1.13, NKJV), 'Therefore, prepare your minds for action' (NIV). By way of application, in Ephesians (6.14) Paul is urging Christians to be armed in a fashion that shows preparedness for spiritual warfare.

Paul identifies the belt that supports the Christian ready for action as truth. Commentators understand the truth, a prominent idea in Ephesians, to be held securely in two ways: objective truth or subjective truth. The former speaks of the Christian faith as revealed in Christ and Scripture or the gospel, and is the only means of counteracting the devil's deceptions and setting captive people free (Jn 8.31-36, 43-45; Eph. 1.13; 4.15, 21, 24). Other commentators argue that the Old Testament context of the whole imagery in which it is said of Messiah, 'Righteousness will be his belt and righteousness the sash around his waist', and the absence of the article with 'truth' lead compellingly to the conclusion that sincerity, truthfulness, trustworthiness, virtue, or personal integrity (cf. 4.25-29) are in view. A combination of the two perspectives is possible here. Defection becomes an attractive option for some soldiers in the heat of battle. Similarly, the temptation to abandon objective truth and embrace false teaching is very real in spiritual warfare (4.14). Likewise, personal integrity and truthfulness can become a casualty when the battle gets fierce. Without truth God's people will be unable to stand in intense spiritual conflict.

'*The breastplate of righteousness*' (v. 14) is another vital part of the Christian's equipment, protecting the vital organs against blows and arrows from the evil powers. 'Of righteousness' (δικαιοσύνης) is a genitive of apposition or identity, defining righteousness as the breastplate. It is significant that the imperatival participle (ἐνδυσάμενοι) translated 'put on' is connected to the main verb 'stand', strongly implying that one cannot stand without righteousness.

The language and imagery employed here is borrowed from the Old Testament, and depicts God as coming to deliver his people clothed with 'righteousness as his breastplate, and the helmet of salvation on his head' (Isa. 59.17; cf. 11.5; Wis. 5.18). (Elsewhere, Paul portrays faith

---

belt or girdle derive from an ancient Near Eastern belt-wrestling custom and here symbolizes a spiritual wrestling belt of virtue – an interpretation without sufficient and reliable scholarly support. See 'The Wrestling-Belt Legacy in the New Testament', NTS 28 (October, 1982), p. 562.

and love as the breastplate of believers, 1 Thess. 5.8.) It is this very righteousness (δικαιοσύνη) surrounding God that Paul calls upon believers to display. Protecting the chest and vital organs against blows and arrows from the evil powers as a breastplate (θώραξ), righteousness is here regarded as either justification (forensic righteousness) whereby one is brought into right relationship with Christ (Rom. 3.21-22; 4.3, 5), or sanctification – moral righteousness (1 Cor. 1.30; 2 Cor. 6.7; Eph. 4.24; 5.9). A bifurcation is unnecessary. The two – forensic righteousness and ethical righteousness – are inseparably interwoven and complementary and reflected in the Christian's 'righteousness of character and conduct'.[44] God requires that his children imitate him in practicing righteousness and justice. Armed this way, the Christian can resist the assault of the devil.

Thirdly, much like the Roman infantryman who frequently wore the heavy low half-boot (Latin *caligula*) with its sole made of layers of leather and studded with hobnails for long marches and firm traction, so the Christian warrior's feet must be 'fitted with *the readiness that comes from the gospel of peace*' (v. 15). Quoted also in Rom. 10.15, the language and imagery are clearly borrowed from Isaiah 52.7. 'How beautiful on the mountains are the feet of those who bring good news, who proclaim peace, who bring good tidings, who proclaim salvation'. The *crux interpretum* is determining whether the term translated readiness (ἑτοιμασία) – omitted in Isa. 52.7 but occurring only here[45] in the NT – means equipment, preparedness to proclaim the gospel, preparedness for warfare, or steadfastness derived from firm grounding in the gospel of peace. Further, how does 'readiness' relate to the 'gospel of peace'? Does the gospel produce readiness, or is readiness to share the gospel a natural and necessary duty of those who have received it?

The Greek term literally means 'preparation' or 'readiness', but some interpreters adopt the translation 'firm footing' (connecting it with the admonition to stand, v. 14) or 'solid foundation' based on the fact that the term and its cognates often bear these meanings in the LXX.[46] The NEB reflects this understanding. 'Let the shoes on your feet be the gospel of peace, to give you a firm footing', but the GNB renders the phrase 'readiness to announce the Good News of peace'. Undeniably, the gospel gives believers both peace and a solid footing from which to wage spiritual warfare against the enemy. Those who have experienced its transforming and reconciling power (2.11-22) can hardly refrain from taking this good news even into enemy territory.

---

[44] Stott, 'Ephesians', p. 279.

[45] Paul does use the cognate verb three times (1 Cor. 2.9; 2 Tim. 2.21; Phlm. 22).

[46] Its twelve occurrences in the LXX bear such connotations, e. g., Ps. 89.14; Ezra 2.68; 3.3; Zech. 5.11, but these do not exhaust the meaning of the term.

Conversely, soldiers of the cross should always be ready to declare Christ as God's peacemaker (2.14-15).

Some interpret and apply the verse to the existential reality of the community of faith. Locked in a vicious spiritual struggle, the church is bound to sustain casualties and experience discord in its ranks. Paul's admonition is that the Christians remain firm in their faith and preserve unity and harmony through the bond of peace (4.3), which will make its peacemaking message believable. This readiness to announce the peace-producing gospel is clearly illustrated in the messenger of Isa. 52.7, who declares the good news of peace to Jerusalem, a good news demonstrated by Christ through his apostles (2.17). Such is what Paul further emphasizes in the parallel passage. 'Be wise in the way you act toward outsiders; make the most of every opportunity. Let your conversation be always full of grace, seasoned with salt' (Col. 4.5, 6).

Faith,[47] which the believer is admonished to take up in addition to the weapons already mentioned (v. 16), Paul likens to the larger (4 x 2½ ft) long rectangular double-layered door-shaped shield (Lat. *scutum*, Gk θυρεός, from θύρα, door) that protected the whole person and was carried on the left arm of the heavily armed Roman soldier. Bound together with iron above and below, its wooden base was covered with flame-resistant hide designed to extinguish any incendiary missile (βέλος), such as flaming arrows,[48] and also to prevent penetration. An image of God himself as protector of his people who take refuge in him (Gen. 15.1; Pss. 5.12; 18.2, 30, 35; Prov. 30.5), the metaphor represents him as the only sure refuge in which believers can hide and the only one on whom they must rely for protection and victory over the evil one and his frightful and diabolical assaults. None of Satan's deadliest weapons (insidious wiles, v. 11) can harm those who appropriate the promises of God, put their full trust in his mighty power (v. 10), and stand firm in faith (1 Pet. 5.9).

Paul uses faith here not only in the passive sense of being a shield which protects from assaults, but also in an active sense of being an extinguisher of Satan's 'fire-tipped' (πεπτυρωμένα), determined, and deadly intentions to deceive, discourage, create doubt, and cause defection. Trust in God (cf. 3.12, 17) is that to which Paul appeals. This is not the trust (faith) that saves, but that which sustains through the relentless onslaught of battle. The battle is lost without it.

The '*helmet of salvation* and the sword of the Spirit, which is the word of God' are the next pieces of equipment mentioned. Made of bronze or tough leather and having cheek pieces to protect the head,

---

[47] The Greek construction (τῆς πίστεως) is a genitive of apposition or identity which depicts the shield as faith or consisting of faith.

[48] At Actium Octavius used flaming darts against Anthony's fleet.

the helmet was the Roman soldier's most important weapon. Borrowed from Isa. 59.17 where Yahweh is described as a victorious warrior wearing a helmet of salvation, the imagery here might well be termed the helmet of victory since God's victory is the salvation he provides his people[49] (see 1 Thess. 5.8). Since Ephesians stresses the salvation of believers as a present reality,[50] Paul's admonition that they 'take up'[51] the helmet of salvation cannot be taken as a summons to receive salvation but as a challenge to a constant awareness, appropriation and actualization of the reality of salvation and living confidently in light of the victory and power believers share with Christ (2.5, 6). Confidence in the reality of one's salvation and certainty of the outcome of the conflict can help guard and fortify the Christian soldier when the battle rages.

'*The sword of the Spirit*'[52] is the only piece of offensive weaponry in the believer's panoply. Identified as the word of God, it was a short sword or dagger[53] carried by the heavily armed Roman legionary and used in close combat. The writer of Hebrews describes God's word[54] (λόγος) as 'living and active and 'sharper than any double-edged sword' (4.12). Paul in 6.17 uses a non-military term (ῥῆμα) to designate the sword. *Rhēma* (word) is sometimes used in the NT for the proclaimed word or an inspired utterance the Spirit gives inwardly (Rom. 10.8, 17; Eph. 5.26; 1 Pet. 1.25). Scholarly discussion on what exactly this 'word' is has centered upon the proclaimed gospel[55] or the written word.[56] Paul 'never uses the language to refer to Scripture',[57] but to

---

[49] Bruce, *Ephesians*, p. 409. The phrase 'helmet of salvation' means 'helmet which is salvation', Paul employing the genitive of apposition/identity here.

[50] As with 1 Thess. 5.8 where Paul speaks of the hope of salvation to be realized at the *parousia*, Ephesians also speaks of the future consummation of salvation (1.10) as well as the anticipated 'day of redemption' (4.30).

[51] Paul's switch to the aorist imperative here may be merely stylistic.

[52] The genitive here is not one of apposition but source or possession. Fee understands the Spirit's giving of the sword as his making it effective (*God's Empowering Presence*, p. 728 n. 208). See also Thielman, *Ephesians*, p. 429.

[53] The μάχαιρα, termed *gladius* in Latin, unlike the large Thracian ῥομφαι,α (e.g., Lk. 2.35; Rev. 1.16; 2.12, 16), was a short double-edged cut-and-thrust sword used in close combat. Stott opines that it was used for both offensive and defensive purposes (*Ephesians*, p. 282).

[54] Paul uses ῥῆμα here. Though interchangeable with λόγος, it tends at times to emphasize divine utterance or spoken word at a point in time whereas λόγος focuses on the content of the message. 'The word of God' more frequently translates the Greek ὁ λόγος τοῦ θεοῦ (Lk. 8.11; Jn 10.35; Acts 6.7; 12.24; Rom. 9.6; 1 Cor. 14.36; 2 Tim. 2.9).

[55] This is the way Paul usually uses the phrase, e. g. 1 Cor. 14.36; 2 Cor. 2.17; 4.2; Col. 1.25; 1 Thess. 1.8; 2 Thess. 3.1

[56] Hoehner understands the 'sword of the Spirit' as both 'God's spoken word to put his enemies to flight' and the believer's utterance to God in prayer in the power of the Holy Spirit to aid in the struggle against the evil powers' (*Ephesians*, p. 857).

[57] Fee, *God's Empowering Presence*, p. 728 n. 211.

proclamation based upon it. While primacy must be given to canonical revelation, the Spirit's work in and through the early Christian community apart from the written word warns against too narrow a definition. Full of the Spirit, Jesus demonstrated the effectiveness of the sword of the Spirit – the word of God – in the temptation narrative, on each of the three occasions, defeating the devil with the *rhēma* that 'proceeds from the mouth of God' (Mt. 4.4; cf. Deut. 8.3). The context of vv. 18-20 lends support to the conclusion that the word of God, which is the Spirit's sword, is 'the faithful speaking forth of the gospel in the arena of darkness, so that men and women might hear and be delivered from Satan's grasp'.[58] Just as Christ used the sword of the Spirit to overcome the devil's onslaught, Christians need it to combat him to achieve a similar victory.

Setting aside the military language and highlighting the necessity of constant and prevailing prayer in view of the fearsome nature of the demonic struggle, in v. 18 Paul exhorts the church to 'pray in the Spirit on all occasions with all kinds of prayers and requests'. The importance and centrality of this activity in the conflict is underscored by the disproportionate attention Paul gives to it. The tedium in getting a handle on this verse lies in determining how the participle 'praying'[59] (imperative 'pray', NIV) relates to v. 17 and ultimately to vv. 14-16, the purpose of the language 'praying in/by the Spirit', and the connection of this phrase to what immediately follows. Some scholars[60] relate 'praying' back to 'stand firm' in v. 14. Those who perceive the attack as imminent, the enemy's schemes as cunning, thus needing God's power and insight, understand it as expressing the attitude with which the helmet of salvation and the sword of the Spirit (v. 17) must be taken up.[61] When related to the verb 'receive' (δέξασθε) in v. 17 and the military metaphor of the Christian soldier 'being on the alert with all perseverance and prayer', praying and preaching become another weapon in the warfare, proclaiming the word of God being 'speech directed toward people' and prayer being 'speech directed toward God'.[62]

Both Paul (6.18) and Jude (v. 20) exhort their church communities to pray in the Spirit. The exactitude of language (Paul uses 'Spirit', Jude 'Holy Spirit') seems to suggest that both writers have the same

---

[58] Fee, *God's Empowering Presence*, p. 729. See also Salmond, *Ephesians*, p. 388.

[59] There are actually two participles, but the second, 'watching /being alert', is less tedious. Both must modify the same verb. It is debatable whether the participle 'praying' can be rendered with the imperative 'pray', as seen in some translations, e.g. NIV. Appearing in the present tense, the participles indicate continuous activity.

[60] E.g. O'Brien, *Ephesians*, p. 483; Lincoln, *Ephesians*, p. 451.

[61] E.g. Hoehner, *Ephesians*, pp. 855, 857.

[62] Fee, *God's Empowering Presence*, p. 730.

experience in mind. There is no scholarly unanimity, however, as to what 'praying in/by the Spirit' means. Allowing the Spirit to be the 'atmosphere' in which one prays, praying 'in the power of the Spirit' (NEB), praying the Spirit's desires, or 'praying under the Spirit's influence and with his assistance'[63] are common Evangelical understandings. It is observed that in this context 'Prayer is "militarized" and drawn into the struggle with the powers'.[64] Any worthy interpretation will consider the parallel passage in 1 Cor. 14.14-15 (cf. Rom. 8.26-27), where it refers 'specifically to that form of prayer in which the Spirit assumes a special role in the praying, especially, though probably not exclusively, praying in tongues'.[65] Spirit-empowered proclamation and Spirit-inspired praying clearly demonstrate the Spirit's vital role in the ongoing spiritual warfare in which believers are engaged. Paul admonishes that Spirit-inspired praying be done 'on all occasions' (NIV), 'at all times' (NAS), and 'with all kinds of prayers and requests' (NIV).

The fourfold use of 'all' in v. 18 of the Greek text alerts us to the importance, intensity, variety, constancy, and universal scope of prayer. Christians are encouraged to pray at 'all times' ('on all occasions', NIV, cf. 1 Thess. 5.17). Since the struggle with the evil powers is unceasing, prayers must be unceasing. The temptation to reserve prayer for situations of crisis or special occasions is very real. That will not do! It is not enough to pray in the crisis of battle. The success of this crucial battle depends on persistence and constancy. Further, in protracted and intense warfare it is easy to become battle-weary and lose heart. To do that is to hoist the white flag of surrender to the enemy. Praying with all prayer and supplication ('all kinds of prayers and requests') may indicate that as the devil's tactics and schemes are multifarious, so must be the prayers of God's people in their effort to counteract them. No form, no avenue of praying, should go unexplored. Believers should pray with all perseverance, with steadfastness – never giving up. Supplication for all the saints ('keep on praying for all the saints') is Paul's final entreaty. Uncertainty and scarcity that accompany war can lead to a narcissistic self-absorption with oneself and one's needs. Selfishness and self-preservation are Siamese twins that war creates. Since, however, all believers are involved in spiritual warfare, there is no place for insular individualism. Christians form a common army and share a common cause. Concern for all must be expressed in prayer for all. 'No soldier entering battle prays for himself alone, but for all his fel-

---

[63] Bruce, *Ephesians*, p. 410.

[64] Thomas R. Yoder Neufeld, *Ephesians* (Believers Church Bible Commentary; Scottdale, PA: Herald Press, 2002), p. 305.

[65] Fee, *God's Empowering Presence*, pp. 730-31; cf. Robert Jamieson, A.R. Fausset, David Brown, *Commentary on the Whole Bible* (London: Oliphants/ Grand Rapids: Zondervan, 1964), p. 1299.

low-soldiers also. They form one army, and the success of one is the success of all'.[66]

Too much should not be made of the types of petitions offered – prayers (προσευχή) and requests (δέησις). While the former is often used of general prayer and the latter of a special form of prayer (e.g. petition, intercession), they are at times used synonymously. The Greek rendition for the frequency of praying – 'every occasion', 'every season' (παντὶ καιρῷ) – is reminiscent of Paul's admonition in 5.16 to buy up 'every opportunity' (τὸ καιρόν) because the days are evil. Always vulnerable to surprise attacks by the enemy, believers must be alert and vigilant (see Mk 13.33; 14.38; Lk. 21.36). The ardent devotion to prayer to which Paul summons the believers is worthy of attention. Translated 'perseverance' (NASB), 'perfect devotion' (NT, by Charles Wms.), 'never give up' (Good News), προσκαρτέρησις means 'to persist obstinately in',[67] and prior to Ephesians appeared only twice, once in the second and first centuries BCE, respectively. It was used in the context of one giving in to 'painstaking detail' or 'particular devotion' to a profession. By using the word, Paul 'urges believers to give themselves over to prayer with the kind of enthusiasm and zeal normally associated with the committed practice of a craft or trade'.[68] Only with such devotion could victory over Satan and his diabolical hordes be achieved.

Despite his apostolic vocation and authority, Paul, recognizing his own dependence on the prayers of the people of God, shadows his exhortation to 'pray for all the saints' with a characteristically personal request. 'Pray also for me, that whenever I open my mouth, words may be given me' (v. 19; cf. Rom. 15.30-32; 2 Cor. 1.11; Phil. 1.19; Col. 4.3-4; 1 Thess. 5.25). Here as elsewhere in his Epistles, the apostle to the Gentiles makes the advance of the gospel central focus of spiritual warfare (cf. 1 Cor. 16.9; Col. 4.3). Imprisoned in Rome (v. 20) and anticipating an appearance before Caesar's imperial tribunal, instead of requesting prayer that he be released, Paul may well be asking that through prayer God may grant him the precise words,[69] the clarity and boldness to present a worthy apology for Christianity and also for suc-

---

[66] C. Hodge, *A Commentary on the Epistle to the Ephesians* (Grand Rapids: Eerdmans, n.d.), 392

[67] Hoehner, *Ephesians*, p. 858, quoting Polybius I.55.4; Diodorus Siculus 14.87.5; Josephus *Bell.* 6.1.3.

[68] Thielman, *Ephesians*, p. 434.

[69] O'Brien notes: 'The expression "to open the mouth" appears in contexts of solemnity where a grave or important utterance from God is about to be made' (*Ephesians*, p. 487). This finds support in Mt. 5.2.

cess in his evangelistic ministry[70] in Caesar's palace and throughout the Roman empire. Paul's desire is to leave nothing and no one in doubt concerning the implications of the gospel, and he wants to do so 'fearlessly' (literally, courageously or confidently) – probably meaning with uninhibited candor and unfettered openness of speech.

Verse 20 highlights the paradoxical – even oxymoronic – nature of Paul's circumstances. He is an ambassador (πρεσβεύω) responsible for unveiling God's mystery to the Gentiles (cf. 3.1-13). Now a prisoner because of doing so he is without diplomatic immunity. Instead of wearing a gold chain that befits the office, he sports a ball and chain that shackles him to a Roman soldier and will appear before Caesar's court as a prisoner. Paul is Christ's ambassador nonetheless, and his physical chains are credentials of his apostleship and loyalty to Christ. Not his plight but the potential it affords for the proclamation of the gospel is what receives attention. For this reason he is depending on the prayers of the saints. Through them he will be able to represent the gospel of Christ with confidence, candor, and clarity before Caesar in Rome.

G. Closing Greetings (6.21-24)

Paul's instructions to Tychicus, which reflect a near verbatim parallel[71] in Col. 4.7-8, is partly to affirm his *protégé* who appears to be Paul's representative to the churches in Asia and carrier of both the Ephesian (6.21) and Colossian (4.7) Epistles and likely the one to Philemon. Little is known of Tychicus. An Asian (Acts 20.4) whom Paul sent to Ephesus (2 Tim. 4.12) and a messenger to Titus in Crete (Tit. 3.12), he is commended for his faithfulness, reliability, and loyalty to Paul.

There is only so much one can say in a letter. Paul's purpose for sending Tychicus is to provide the churches around Ephesus information about Paul's circumstances in prison. This would be a source of encouragement to the believers – 'put fresh heart into' them (NEB) after any discouragement they may have experienced because of Paul's sufferings for their sake (3.13). News of Paul's freedom to preach to his visitors (Acts 28.17-31) and the Roman sentinels who guard him would certainly lift their spirits.

---

[70] Paul's use of μυστήριον here to describe the gospel (v. 19) is consistent with his earlier uses of it in 3.3-4, 9 to refer to the proclamation of the message of salvation. At the time of Paul's writing, Christianity was proscribed and regarded as a heretical sect of the Jews. In his request for prayer, Paul probably anticipates an appearance before the Roman tribunal, where he hopes to make clear the nature of Christianity and how it differs from Judaism.

[71] What some regard as the clear fingerprints of a pseudepigraphist seems to reveal Paul's hand most clearly. An imitator of the apostle would tend to avoid plagiarism and the specificity reflected in vv. 21, 22.

The closing 'syncopated'[72] apostolic benediction (vv. 23, 24), which is liturgical in nature, contains Paul's 'prayer-wish' for the saints. Its form is inconsistent with the form of benedictions in others of Paul's writings. It is written in the more impersonal third, rather than the second, person and has two parts instead of one. The addressees are called simply 'all who love our Lord Jesus Christ', a point that some see as irrefragable proof for the circular theory of the letter. In the benediction Paul recapitulates four of the major themes of the Epistle begun in 1.13-14 – peace, love, faith, and grace – all of which are gifts reflective of the character of God. The first three receive attention in the first part of the benediction, and serve less as a farewell greeting and more as a prayer for Jewish and Gentile believers to live in harmony as the family of God. Grace, the recurrent theme and hallmark of the Epistle, fittingly concludes the letter (and benediction) just as it introduced it (1:2).

In Greek Paul's two final words (ἐν ἀφθαρσίᾳ, cf. Rom. 2.7; 1 Cor. 15.42, 50, 53-54; 2 Tim. 1.10) seem to be somewhat of a conundrum. They mean literally 'in incorruption', incorruptibility, or 'in immortality'. At issue is what word they qualify. Most commentators connect the phrase with people's 'love' for Christ (RSV, GNB, NEB, NIV). The NIV and NRSV translate it 'undying love', the NASB 'incorruptible love', and the NEB 'love undying'. These translations reflect both a temporal and moral sense, the prayer here being that believers' love for the Lord be enduring and eternal, or pure, untainted by impure motives or furtive disloyalties. Others see them as modifying 'grace', the benediction entreating that imperishable grace be with the believers (in 2.7 grace is said to extend into eternity). Reflecting the REB ('in immortality') a few scholars think it simply means 'forever', Paul's prayer-wish being that all who love the Lord Jesus may experience God's grace forever. Feeling that this makes a gratuitous bifurcation between eternal and transitory love, some connect it with grace rather than human love. The NKJV rendition 'in sincerity' appears to be a paraphrase of the term. Amid the struggle to determine Paul's exact meaning, of this we can be sure: God's love for his children is as immeasurable as it is incorruptible, his grace as enduring as it is amazing.

---

[72] E.K. Simpson, *Ephesians* (NIC; Grand Rapids: Eerdmans, 1979), p. 157.

Reflection and Response (Part 7)

Reflection

It appears paradoxical that the first half of the Epistle emphasizes the peace the gospel brings about but concludes with cosmic conflict. A picture that began with non-believers being held under the sway of the prince of the power of the air, at the end of the Epistle gives way to believers being viciously assaulted by powerful, superhuman, supernatural, and super-terrestrial insidious forces in the heavenly realms. That which began in conquest for the people of God concludes with conflict against them.

Demonic powers are real and active in the world today as in biblical times. Christians are engaged in a spiritual battle of titanic proportions and face formidable supernatural and superhuman diabolical forces that seek their eternal destruction. Though powerful, they are not, however, omnipotent; though invisible, they are not invincible. Yet to overcome them God's people need greater resources than any human person can muster. Paul assures us, however, that all the Christian warrior needs in order to achieve final triumph is in the Lord and in his mighty power.

Paul's imagery of the Christian in 6.10-20 is that of a fully-clad Roman infantryman armed for battle. The oft-repeated call to 'stand/withstand' implies that the aim of the conflict is not to win, because victory has already been achieved through Christ. Rather, the battle is a mop-up operation and the holding of territory already won. But as with every conflict, care must be taken against a wily enemy – hence Paul's reveille to 'be strong in the Lord', to 'put on the full armor of God,' and to watch in prayer. At once the imagery communicates the challenge and urgency of the task before us, and calls for alertness, prayer and perseverance. But it also conveys the idea of safety and security the Lord provides. God provides the strength to withstand every demonic assault, but his power is not automatic; there must be a willing obedience on our part to cooperate by appropriating the resources he supplies. Each piece of equipment in the panoply symbolizes some spiritual quality necessary for protection.

Though prayer is not physically represented in the armor, its supreme significance is highlighted by the attention it receives. Paul admonishes the saints to pray 'with all prayer and supplication praying at all seasons in the Spirit, and watching thereunto in all perseverance and supplication for all the saints' (v. 18, ASV, 1901 ed.). Paul's fourfold use of 'all' alerts us to the importance, intensity, variety, constancy, and universal scope of prayer. This kind of praying is necessary because the conflict is inexorable, craftily waged, and the enemy's tactics multiform. No soldier fights alone. All believers fight a common foe. Concern for all, therefore, should be expressed in prayer for all.

The Christian in spiritual warfare is the subject of reflection in this section. The questions that follow are given to broaden and facilitate further reflection on the text. Some Christians believe Paul's idea of the spiritual world is primitive and outmoded. What is the perspective of Christians you know on the issue of spiritual warfare today? How can Christians know they are in spiritual warfare? What signs should they look for to substantiate this fact? How may Christians reconcile the fact that the cross and resurrection of Christ announce Satan's defeat yet they are still engaged in warfare against him? What are some of the ways the devil attacks the people of God? How may a Christian know when he or she is being assailed by the devil since God uses difficult situations to develop character in his children? Can Christians give Satan inroads into their lives? If yes, what are some ways we may open the door of our lives to the devil?

On a more personal level, how do you know you are engaged in spiritual warfare? Have you ever sensed that you were being attacked by hostile spiritual forces? In what ways did the attacks occur? What did they feel like? How did you achieve victory? What comes to mind of something you did or some decision you made that may have opened a door to demonic attack?

Response
The issues the text presents and the questions raised warrant an appropriate response of which the following is submitted.

1. First, pinpoint occasions or events in your life that you are absolutely sure were diabolically inspired.

2. In light of the teaching of Scripture evaluate the nature and effects of those incidents in your life.

3. Permit other spiritually mature members of the community to assess your experiences, comparing them with similar ones they may have had and in light of Scripture.

4. Commit yourself to a life of prayer that will access the divine strength and protection available for spiritual attacks you may encounter.

Bibliography

Alexander, Kimberly E., and R. Hollis Gause. *Women in Leadership: A Pentecostal Perspective*, Pentecostal Leadership Series. Cleveland, TN: Center for Pentecostal Leadership and Care, 2006

Arnold, Clinton, 'Letter to the Ephesians'. *Dictionary of Paul and His Letters*. Ed. G.F. Hawthorne, R.P. Martin and D.G. Reid. Downers Grove: IL and Leicester; UK: InterVarsity, 1993

Barclay, William. 'The Letters to the Galatians and Ephesians'. *Daily Study Bible*. Philadelphia: Westminster, 1976

Bartchy, S.S. MALLON CRHSAI: *First-Century Slavery and the Interpretation of 1 Corinthians 7:21*. Missoula, MT: Scholars, 1973

Barth, Markus. *Ephesians*. The Anchor Bible, 34. Garden City, NY: Doubleday & Co., 1974

Beare, F.W. *The Epistle to the Ephesians*. The Interpreter's Bible Commentary, 10. Nashville: Abingdon, 1953

Bedale, S. 'The Meaning of *kefale* in the Pauline Epistles'. *Journal of Theological Studies* 5 (1954): 211-215

Bilezikian, G. *Beyond Sex Roles*. Grand Rapids: Baker, 1985

Bruce, F.F. *Ephesians*. The New International Commentary on the New Testament. Grand Rapids: Eerdmans, 1984

Calvin, John. *The Epistles of Paul and the Apostles to the Galatians, Ephesians, Philippians and Colossians*. Trans. T.H.L. Parker. Grand Rapids: Eerdmans, 1974

Carson, D.A. et al. *An Introduction to the New Testament*. Grand Rapids: Zondervan, 1992

Dawes, G.W. *The Body in Question: Metaphor and Meaning in the Interpretation of Ephesians 5:21-33*. Leiden: Brill, 1998

Dodd, C.H. *Ephesians*. The Abingdon Bible Commentary. Ed. F.C. Eiselen et al. Nashville: Abingdon, 1957

—— 'The Message of the Epistles: Ephesians'. *Expository Times* 45 (November 1933): 60-66

Douglas, J.D., ed. 'Ephesus'. *The New Bible Dictionary*. London: InterVarsity, 1967

Dunn, James D.G. *Jesus and the Spirit*. London: SCM, 1975

Dunnam, Maxie D. 'Galatians, Ephesians, Philippians, Colossians, Philemon'. *The Communicator's Commentary*. Waco, TX: Word Books, 1982

Eadie, John. *Commentary on the Epistle of Paul to the Ephesians.* Grand Rapids: Zondervan, 1979

Edwards, Jonathan. *The Works of Jonathan Edwards.* Vol. I. Ed. Edward Hickman. Edinburgh: Banner of Truth Trust, 1974

Farrar, F.W. *The Life and Work of St. Paul.* London, Paris & New York: Cassell & Co, 1884

Fee, Gordon. *God's Empowering Presence.* Peabody. MA: Hendrickson, 1994

—— *The First Epistle to the Corinthians.* Grand Rapids: Eerdmans, 1987

—— *Paul, the Spirit, and the People of God.* Peabody, MA: Hendrickson, 1997

Findlay, George G. *The Epistle to the Ephesians.* The Expositor's Bible. Reprint edition, 6. Grand Rapids: Eerdmans, 1950

Fitzmyer, J.A. 'Kephale in 1 Corinthians 11:3'. *Interpretation* 47 (1993): 52-59

Foulkes, F. *The Epistle of Paul to the Ephesians.* Grand Rapids: Eerdmans, 1963

Gaebelein, Frank E., Gen. ed. "Isaiah – Ezekiel." The Expositor's Bible Commentary, 6. Grand Rapids: Zondervan, 1986

Goodspeed, E.J. *The Meaning of Ephesians.* Chicago: University Press, 1933.

Grudem, Wayne. *Recovering Biblical Manhood and Womanhood: A Response to Evangelical Feminism.* Ed. John Piper and Wayne Grudem. Wheaton: Crossway, 1991

—— 'Does *Kephale,* "Head', Mean "Source" or "Authority Over" in Greek Literature? A Survey of 2,336 Examples'. *Trinity Journal* 6 (1985): 38-55.

Guthrie, Donald. *New Testament Introduction.* Downer's Grove: InterVarsity, 1976

Harris, Murray. *Raised Immortal: Resurrection and Immortality in the New Testament.* London: Marshall, Morgan & Scott, 1983

Hart, Larry D. *Truth Aflame.* Nashville: Thomas Nelson, 1999

Hendriksen, William. *Exposition of Ephesians.* Grand Rapids: Baker, 1967

Hiebert, Edmond. *An Introduction to the Pauline Epistles.* Chicago: Moody, 1954

Hodge, Charles. *A Commentary on the Epistle to the Ephesians.* Thornapple Commentaries. Grand Rapids: Baker, 1980

—— *An Exposition of Ephesians.* Wilmington, DE: Sovereign Grace, 1972

Houlden, J.H. *Paul's Letters from Prison.* Westminster Pelican Commentaries. Philadelphia: Westminster, 1977

Klein, William W. *Ephesians.* The Expositor's Bible Commentary, 12. Gen. eds., Tremper Longman III and David E. Garland. Grand Rapids: Zondervan, 2006

Kroeger, C.C. 'The Classical Concept of *Head* as "Source"'. *Equal to Serve.* Ed. G.G. Hull. London: Scripture Union, 1987

Kümmel, Georg. *Introduction to the New Testament.* Trans. Howard Clark Key. Nashville: Abingdon, 1975

Lincoln, Andrew. *Ephesians.* Word Bible Commentary, 42. Dallas: Word, 1990.

Lloyd-Jones, D. Martyn. *God's Way of Reconciliation: Studies in Ephesians Chapter 2.* Grand Rapids: Baker, 1972

MacDonald, Margaret. 'Colossians and Ephesians'. *Sacra Pagina Series* (Collegeville, MN: Liturgical Press, 2000)

Mackay, John. *God's Order: The Ephesian Letter and this Present Time.* New York: Macmillan, 1964

Martin, Ralph. *Ephesians, Colossians and Philemon.* Interpretation. Atlanta: John Knox, 1991

Metzger, Bruce. *Textual Commentary on the Greek New Testament.* Stuttgart: Deutsche Bibelgesellschaft, 1994

Mickelsen, Berkley and Alvera Mickelsen. 'The "Head" of the Epistles'. *Christianity Today* 20. February 1981, 20-23

Mitton, C.L. *The Epistle to the Ephesians.* Oxford: Clarendon, 1951

—— *Ephesians.* New Century Bible. Greenwood, SC: Attic Press, 1976

Moritz, J. *A Profound Mystery: The Use of the Old Testament in Ephesians.* Leiden: Brill, 1966

Morris, Leon. *Expository Reflections on the Letter to the Ephesians.* Grand Rapids: Baker Books, 1994

Moule, H.C.G. *Ephesians Studies.* New York: Fleming H. Revell, n.d.

Murphy-O'Connor, Jerome. "Who Wrote Ephesians?" *The Bible Today* 18 (April 1965)

Nicoll, W. Robertson ed., *The Expositor's Greek Testament.* Vol. III. Grand Rapids: Eerdmans, 1974

O'Brien, Peter. *The Letter to the Ephesians.* Pillar New Testament Commentary. Grand Rapids: Eerdmans; Cambridge, UK: Apollos, 1999

Patzia, Arthur G. *Ephesians, Colossians, Philemon.* NIBC. Peabody: Hendrickson, 1990

Paxon, Ruth, *The Wealth, Walk and Warfare of the Christian.* Westwood, NJ: Revell, 1939

Robinson, J. Armitage. *Commentary on Ephesians.* Grand Rapids: Kregel, 1979

Rogers, Cleon and Rogers. *Linguistic and Exegetical Greek New Testament.* Grand Rapids: Zondervan, 1998

Schnackenburg, Rudolf. *Ephesians.* Trans. Helen Heron. Edinburgh: T & T Clark, 1991

Scott, E.F. 'Ephesians'. *The Moffatt New Testament Commentary.* London: Hodder and Stroughton, 1930

Scroggie, Graham. *Paul's Prison Prayers.* London: Pickering and Inglis, n.d.

Snodgrass, Klyne. *Ephesians.* New Application Commentary. Grand Rapids: Zondervan, 1996

Stifler, J.M. *An Introduction to the Study of the Acts of the Apostles.* New York: Fleming & Revell, 1892.

Stott, John. 'The Message of Romans'. *The Bible Speaks Today.* Downers Grove. IL: InterVarsity, 1994

Thayer, Joseph H. *A Greek-English Lexicon of the New Testament* (Grand Rapids: Zondervan, 1974

Thielman, Frank. *Ephesians.* Baker Exegetical Commentary on the New Testament. Grand Rapids: Baker, 2010

Trench, Richard C. *Synonyms of the New Testament.* Grand Rapids: Eerdmans, 1958

van Roon, A. *The Authenticity of Ephesians.* NovT Supplement, 39. Leiden: Brill, 1974

Vaughan, Curtis. *Ephesians.* Bible Study Commentary. Grand Rapids: Zondervan. 1977

Wallace, Daniel. *Greek Grammar beyond the Basics: An Exegetical Syntax of the New Testament*. Grand Rapids: Zondervan, 1996

Walvoord, J.F. and R.B. Zuck, eds. *The Bible Knowledge Commentary*. 2nd edition. Colorado Springs: Victor, 2000

Westcott, Brooke Foss, *Saint Paul's Epistle to the Ephesians*. Minneapolis: Klock & Klock, 1978

Westermann, W.L. *The Slave Systems of Greek and Roman Antiquity*. Philadelphia: American Philosophical Society, 1964

Wiedemann, T. *Greek and Roman Slavery*. London: Croon Helm, 1981

Wiersbe, Warren W. *The Bible Exposition Commentary*. Vol. II. Wheaton, IL: Victor Books, 1989

Witherington, Ben. *The Letters to Philemon, the Colossians, and the Ephesians: A Socio-Rhetorical Commentary on the Captivity Epistles*. Grand Rapids: Eerdmans, 2007

Wood, Skevington. *The Expositor's Bible Commentary*. Vol. II. Ed. Frank E. Gaebelein. Grand Rapids: Zondervan, 1978

Index of Names